'OWER DAWNING'

BY

Atlas D'four.

Authors Note & Warning!

Dear Reader.

The following narrative evolved from a series of accounts written in the 1970s and then hidden away in a drawer for over thirty years. The original manuscripts were penned in a burning desire to be brutally honest with oneself and with a desire to encapsulate the memories before time began its insidious pastime of erasing the majority of them and decorating those remaining with a 'rose tinted hue'.

There are many forms of 'truth', i.e. that which the conscious mind accepts and then that which the sub-conscious knows to be the case and buries deep down because of its supposedly unpalatable nature. However. If we as individuals are ever to be our true selves, the first requirement is to accept who and what we are, regardless of the end product.

We are told, we are each one of us, a product of our genes and our upbringing. A prisoner of our own experiences and memories.
What we delighted in or suffered under, has made us what we have become today, a fact, which because of our youthful vulnerability, we were then powerless to control.
We are what our fellow man has made us – Which *should* be a *warning* to us all.

It is incumbent upon me as the author to issue the following
Reader's Health Warning:-
Persons of tender sensibilities or of a delicate nature should *NOT* read the following narrative.
Parents with children under the age of *ten* should avoid this material coming into possession of their offspring, as it may confuse an otherwise stable upbringing.
Parts of the material include 'warnings' in the narrative, thus allowing the reader to avoid those paragraphs that might cause distress.

Finally. I commend this narrative to all who may have forgotten that children are not possessions in which to attempt to mould our own imperfect images. They are gifts from nature. Gifts we should nurture with the utmost care until such times, as they are ready to 'fly' from the bosom of our presumed 'safe keeping'. 'Ower Dawning' has nothing added and nothing taken away and takes no cognisance of 'political correctness' of the present day. It is, the way it was.

Kindest regards, **Atlas D'four.** 2003.

'Ower Kid' series. Book 2.

'As things 'stood' in the 1950's'

There was once a time when everyone knew what they were and who they were in the greater scope of things and another time when everyone thought they knew what they were and who they were. Well this wasn't one of those times.

This was a time when to think was allowed providing you didn't tell anyone that you were doing it. Dangerous said the 'great and the good'. Seditious said the 'high and the mighty'. Oooo. It's fun but it hurts said the ' low and the humble'. There's no gain without the pain said the 'wise and decrepit'.

And so it was and would come to pass that the 'low' did attempt to rise high and came to be sore afraid. For it was a long way down and precarious.

(Target the 'spire'. Move west. Ower school lies amidst the dark square of buildings therein. Spooky!)

It is the 1950's - The 'war' to end all 'wars' - didn't - so we had another one to see if it might work a second time and deprivation began its slow tortuous crawl towards the tantalising vision of 'fairness and justice'. That didn't happen either.

'What do yer want'? A bloody fairy-story -? Sorry.

I might have just turned fourteen years of age and entered the 'twilight' world of the teenager. That didn't make me totally stupid. I could see when a 'sadist' was enjoying himself, no matter how hard he might try and hide it. - Swine!

1958.

'Slim Fielding' was having a beefer. New boys. 'Oh what a 'perfic' day', said the sardonic grin above the alpine slope of his chin, 'New innocents to terrorise. Happy days, happy days. Someone up there must love me.' Slim turned his face from the heavens and pointedly in my direction as if daring me to comment on his feeling euphoric, albeit only momentarily.

' Go on then boy. Push yer luck', said his eyes as they narrowed before darting away to focus in on his first victim of the day.

We were at the start of a new school term. The holidays were over – and a fantastic experience it had been, for a change. Not that I didn't always enjoy any time away from the claustrophobic incarcerations ower school engendered, but this last holiday had been somewhat special. I had become one of the grown-ups, well, not quite a grown-up more sort of getting there if you know what I mean. Not a kid any more. One of the budding 'blokes'. Oh fer Christ's sake. I wasn't firing blanks any more. You know what I mean? Virile. Dangerous – well perhaps not dangerous. More like a bit dodgy. Got to be more careful like in future. If you know what I mean? Yea. That was me. 'Atlas' was what they called me. Well maybe not much body but I certainly had plenty of balls. And they were both working beautifully thank-you.

"STAND STILL - - - ." Slim Fielding's nasal trumpet blasted out across the cobbled quadrangle and funnelled a path towards the heavens between the everlastingly tall redbrick buildings.

"Do not but move one inch -," he glared casting a gaze over his vari-focals looking for that one who never listened. There was always one. In twenty years he had never failed to find one when he wanted one, a victim that is.

"You boy -." he shrieked, snaking a long spindle of an arm and an even longer spindle of an index finger in the direction of one unfortunate short pants who paled the colour of vanilla ice cream in the same instant. "Come here, wretch."

The boy shrank back towards what he thought might be the safety of the brick wall. Hesitantly the trembling figure raised a hand.

"Please sir." the boy spluttered. "It's, it's Pritchard sir – He's Rich sir." said the lad pointing to another short pants drooping alongside. Fielding drew in his chin. Excellent. Stupid as well! What joy? What ecstasy!

"Well that's interesting isn't it? Hoping to buy his way out is he-?" leered the Science Master beginning to enjoy himself.

Young Prichard looked confused. It wasn't fair he should be asked questions which he couldn't understand. Not on his first day. And who was this man with the long pointed nose anyway?

"Do as he says. Go on." I chunnered from the corner of my mouth. The youth looked up at me without the merest modicum of trust in his doleful eyes.

"HE DOESN'T NEED YOUR HELP BIG MOUTH -." Fielding screamed angrily, as both sides of his grey unshaven cheeks turned a dull crimson red. "IF HE LISTENS TO THE RUBBISH YOU HAVE TO SAY BOY HE WON'T SURVIVE TO THE SECOND TERM -." The quadrangle went completely silent. There must have been at least two hundred boys milling around – and you could have heard a pin drop – providing it was the size of a dustbin lid, not one of them small things- Anyway. It went quiet. The Science Master was furious. With us older boys around we cramped his style. He knew left to his own devices he could do whatever was his wont with these 'new' boys. It would be a while before they wised up sufficiently to 'survive' his 'bullying'. Right now he didn't want yours truly or any of the rest of us getting in his way.

"All you older boys – inside NOW," he shrieked. I put on one of my infamous smirks. At least he hadn't had it all his own way – then again, the day was still young, a lot could happen before it was over. And it usually did!

But I suppose I had first better introduce myself. Give you an insight so to speak:-

My name is 'Atlas'.
My frame belies it.
They say from the North I come.
My game is truth.
My fame, forsooth, "Will be known 'fore all is done."
"Illiterate yob. Lazy slob. Short of a full shilling that boy."
"Foul-mouthed bugger." "Well I blame his mother!" What's more he isn't much joy!"

"He'll come to no good. Thick as wood. Needs a good thrashing I say." "He'll end up in 'Clink'! Well that's what I think. Come the end of the day." *(It was nice to know people cared about me.* It's fifty years on. The past has all gone. With little to show that was worthy. For the days when we 'struggled' in a young life 'befuddled' in a world that was all topsy-turvy.

'The Second World War' is well and truly over and my sceptred isle (that bit I know about) has begun to show some promise at last.

We still have two or three other wars going on somewhere. Well you've got to keep the troops entertained somehow otherwise they get rowdy and obstreperous. Rationing went out last year. The last thing to come 'off' was chocolate or so the old woman (ower mother) says. Not that we could afford to buy it anyway. My days as a 'child' are over. Nine-year-old and it's time to become a youth. I've been a youth now for nearly five years and I've progressed from totally illiterate to semi-illiterate or so my school report says – that and a number of other things that will shortly become apparent. The short pants went out last year, which in some respects was a godsend. It's a lot easier to keep things in place with long trousers. (You fella's will know what I mean). It might have been psychological. But that apart I felt a dam sight better for it. Anyway
– I'll move on with the story. For those discerning ones amongst you who haven't yet read 'Ower Darkling' (my previous ramblings) we will pick up all the rest of the other bits and pieces of my past excuse for a life later. For now it's back to 'school' (And I use the word loosely) -.

'Ower School'. Just before demolition in 1985. Not before time if yer ask me. – But who will?
 Yes. I know it's hazy. The whole bloody place was – inside and out.

'Shopping'.
Only it seems this 1st year boy is using 'real' money.
He'll learn - soon enough!

"Technical's. Padlocks & Pussies'.

I viewed the proceedings from the sanctuary of the 'Assembly Hall' doors. 'Slim' had his 'troops' on the march.

"Straighten up that line." he bellowed. The young boys fell over each other in a haste to do his bidding.

"Cretins! Insignificant cretins!"

Ower illustrious Science Master was beginning to lose it. He always reverted to insults before throwing a complete wobbler. "On the left only - - That's your blasted right you idiots. Left. Left. Left. Cr-hrist! Imbeciles."

The 'new' boys scrambled for position hoping rather than knowing they had understood the 'frothing at the mouth' man's orders.

"Halt! - - Those boys with surnames beginning 'A' to 'H' will form a line by taking one pace forward – Go!" Total chaos ensued.

"AS YOU WERE. AS YOU WERE. FOR PETE'S SAKE -!" It was pointless. By now the whole lot were terrified out of their wits. The man turned on one tall unsuspecting pimply-faced youth whose uniform appeared two sizes too big for his willow-like pubic frame.

"You! You boy. If your name was Alexander Marcus Fotheringay your surname would begin with -?" The boy stared at him.

"Fotheringay? Alexander Marcus? Your surname would begin with -?" asked the Science Master again.

"Errrrr -." For a moment the boy seemed to have it. Unfortunately it was a moment too long as 'Slims' thin taloned fingers grabbed itchingly for the boy's innocently exposed throat." F.F. YOU STUPID MORON. F.F.F." The boy's pained twisted features began to turn a bright blue as the teacher's bony grip fastened even tighter. "F. F. YOU STUPID BOY." With a snort of disgust he released his grip and turned away. The boy fell back and slid down the glazed brickwork into a gangling heap on the floor. The Science Master couldn't have cared less. The fun was just beginning. The start of a new year. Oh happy days. Happy, happy days. - For some!

Towards the end of the summer break and a little before it was time to re-enter those portals of gloom, school, my good friend Turnip and I had scored a minor victory of sorts in the form of a new 'continental' contact. 'Big Molly' the plump Italian Expresso Coffee Queen. The description only bore reference to her extremely large bosom not her build. Mollie stood four foot six inches short in her alligator calf length riding boots and was old enough to have been ower grandmother. But she owned the new coffee bar on the main road adjacent the school and had a need for oodles of 'hot' milk. As much as we could supply. The temptation was just too much for the both of us. Turnip set the price and did the bargaining. Yours truly organised the 'removals'.

Every day the school received masses of fresh milk in the form of half-pint bottles, twenty-four to the crate. The 'Boy's' school complement, when full, was 560 pupils. But not everyone drank their milk or even liked the watered down rubbish. After morning break the 'used' and 'none used' crates were stacked for collection by the school's side entrance. Next to the side entrance was an oil tank housing with a low wall. Perfect for a few crates to disappear behind. The price was 1d per bottle, two shillings per crate. Cigarettes and money for the snooker tables was assured for the rest of the year providing we didn't overdo it. We didn't. It was our 'Mollie' whose nerve was the first to crack. She panicked following a raid by the 'fuzz' (police) on her coffee bar.

They were looking for 'purple hearts' (pep pills/barbiturates). Mollie, whose knowledge of the English language was limited to 'hello good looking' and 'you gotta da money', thought she'd been collared for 'receiving' 'hot' school milk. I told her. I said, "No momma, it's not that sort of 'white stuff' they's after." (Not that we would have been aware of the 'real' stuff either.) She wasn't convinced. After that little debacle we had to think up something else to supplement ower meagre earnings. But it had been fun while it lasted.

"Naw. Sorry. That's a new one on me."

"What? Aw bugger. I need to get my books. We've got old 'Sagar' (reputedly a Maths teacher) for the next double period. There's no way I can con it for two hours without my books. Are you sure you can't do owt?" Now it behoves me to say it but 'a friend with money in need', how could I not try and be helpful. I scrutinised the broken key stub with a well-practised eye and tapped it gently on the desk. I had recognised it instantly of course, but to admit such would have reduced my bargaining power considerably.

"I suppose I could give it a whirl. Where are yer?" The boy's eyes lit up. He looked upon me now in a completely new light. His saviour cometh. Well practically. If I could open the lock on his desk without him having to smash the woodwork apart -?

"B6. Can yer do it now?" I blew on the end of the broken key stub and rubbed it gingerly on the lapel of my jacket.

"Lead on Macduff -." I grinned cockily. "Lead on."

The lock was a cheap Woolworth's single lever. It didn't need a genius to open it. In fact, one well-aimed swipe with the side of a flick-knife and the thing would capitulate immediately. Not that I was going to show this second year swot (he was from 2a – the 'A' stream were supposed to be the brainy ones) all my hard-earned secrets. I took out my trusty compass and using the steel point extracted the remainder of the broken key and flicked the hidden lock lever asunder all in one deft movement. The lock, followed closely with the boy's amazed pupils, popped out from their respective apertures.

"Bugger me rigid!" came a surprised squeak. I gave him a stare.

"Not just now if you don't mind -," I replied, "I dare say the Maths teacher will oblige yer if you ask him nicely – they usually do. One way or another."

"Eh?"

It's no good. Brainy they might have been. Quick witted – Never!

"That'll be a tanner (sixpence). Nine pence if you want I should give you a new key -?"

"Eh! Oh. Yea. Right. Done," he replied. It was and he had been. Not that he had the 'nounce' to realise it.

There were any number of ways to make a quid or two from the daily goings-on. Flogging milk or picking locks just two of ower ancillary occupations. It was necessary for the number of extra-curricular activities in which we were only too pleased to immerse ourselves in an effort to survive what was otherwise a truly boring, painful existence.

The ringing of the bell signalled the end of the morning's lessons. Time now for one of the most important activities of the day, a trip to the local 'chippy' for some snap (food) and into the local billiard hall for a couple of games of snooker, which I have to say we were hopeless at. Not that we thought so at the time. But with not one of us any good at trigonometry, calculating the correct angles and ball positioning was never going to be one of ower forte's. The only balls we had any modicum of control over were not the ones rolling about a green beige tabletop, (and that might also have been wistful thinking come to think of it).

'Pussy for a wooing and we should ride hey hey', hey hey.

'Pussy for a wooing and we should ride hey hey'

'Pussy for a wooing and we should ride, Keep them 'bints' safe by ower side hey hey.

To the tune of 'Froggy going a-wooing' from a popular ditty based on a song from the school musical of 'Toad of Toad Hall', an off-shoot of 'Wind in the Willows'. (*For those not conversant with this classic of a bygone age – shame on yer!*)

'Pussy' was all we ever wanted. If you are a parent and have a teenage son who has begun to act like some throw-back from the Neanderthal age, who growls and grunts continuously and crawls around on all fours with his chin almost on the floor, the only thing that is wrong with him is he isn't getting any 'pussy'. He hasn't suddenly lost his mind. Nor has his befuddled brain suddenly decided it hates you or your pet cat personally. In truth his grey-matter has begun to over-produce testosterone. By the bucket full. And his body can't handle it. What do you do about it? I could proffer any number of suggestions, none of which any self-respecting mother would accept for a moment (I prefer the pre-battle 'Spartan' method myself). My main advice. Keep out of his way – and pray it will pass quickly (which it won't). It's your only hope!

'God she was ugly.' I'm not sure what it is about uniforms that had a tendency to turn my head but in this instance I must have been looking somewhere other than at her face when we had first met the previous night.
Quite often I went to the 'pictures' (cinema) on my own. I liked the films and would sometimes go as often as I could. The town had nine picture-places. Five others had closed in the past few years.
Television had come 'North' and it's insidious hold on a more than willing population was beginning to produce a dwindling of 'picture' going audiences. We had one, a television that is, with three channels, black and white or murky grey depending on the weather outside, which was about as exciting as having a tooth extracted apart from Wednesday night at eight-o-clock when 'Dragnet' was on. Not that I will bore you with the details – but I liked Joe Friday the hard-bitten Yankee cop and his dynamic exploits.

My only excuse, which didn't impress Wozzle who had agreed to go on the blind date I had arranged for him, was that it was dark and in the light from her ice cream tray, the 'tart with the cart' looked a bit of alright.
"Yea. But what's with this mate of hers?" Wozzle asked.
God she was ugly.
"How do I know? I haven't seen her," I replied truthfully -.

God was she ugly. I know I shouldn't go on about the unfortunate girl's features. After all neither Wozzle nor yours truly were anything to write home about. But heavens above, she really was excruciatingly ugly.

"I want to go home -." said Wozzle, under his breath, as the two females advanced towards ower prescribed meeting place.

"Don't be a pillock. We can't go home. They's seen us," I replied turning away and hoping that when I turned back the ugly one might have had a head transplant.

"Well I'm bloody going home whether you like it or not. Don't bother telling me which is mine. Let me guess. The one wi' the eye in the middle of her forehead -?"

It has to be said. I must have been under the influence of a testosterone blast when I made the date the previous night. Mine was passable. In other words with a bit of luck one might pass her on to somebody else. I certainly didn't want her. Not in the daylight.

But beggars can't be choosers. And like the wise man says, 'Whose non gazing at the mantelpiece when one's stoking up the fire." But Wozzle had his limits and this was one of those times he wasn't going to compromise. We left on the excuse that we had exams come the morning and had to get back home to do some swotting. Ha. Bloody liars. I was sick. There might have been a chance for a bit of 'hanky-panky' with mine. She seemed up for it to me. Wozzle was just sick and pursued my 'taste' in prospective one-night stands with venom for the next two weeks or more. But he was right. She really was very ugly indeed. Poor girl.

'Butchers, Bandits, Boozers &
Welcome to the 'Man'Club.

Talk about domineering women. God knows why he ever allowed it. God that is. There was nothing that 'man' could have done about it. God knows I tried my best.

Ken Taylor was a first class butcher. As a human being he fared less well. It wasn't his fault. Derbyshire bred. Not that there's much wrong with being born in Derbyshire. But if one had a preference one shouldn't pick granite outcrops and witches enclaves as a first choice. Personally I blame his choice in females for his lack of 'male' attributes. Ruby, his heptathlon built missus, obscured whatever God had given him when sending him forth. He couldn't have come in twenty-fourth with so many obstacles she constantly put in his path. One is reminded of a particular sit-com that went by the name 'The Last of the Summer Wine', although that takes place in West Yorkshire, that's just where the similarity begins.

Ken weighed in at around a neat nine stone his wife at about twelve to thirteen. She also had a voice to match. And with a swingeing right hook that would have floored Cassias Clay (Mohammed Ali) at a good ten paces. What the good Lord had giveth, Ruby Taylor would invariably grab away. Self respect being first in line.

Yours truly got on very well with her. Mainly because I was used to strong willed women and I knew how to avoid trouble. Ower old woman was a good teacher in that respect. More to the point I had to spend a great deal of my time working under her instructions and it didn't do to get on the wrong side of her. Just like the old woman. Strange as it may seem to those not conversant with ower Northern ways the Northern man was brought up to have a great deal of respect for the fairer sex, although it was a rather mixed up affair. For example, swearing in the presence of females was strictly forbidden. I have seen grown men 'floored' on the spot by other men when this golden rule was broken. Yet on many occasions it was forbidden for females to enter upon certain premises that had been designated as all male preserves, tap-rooms in Public Houses and certain area's in the Working Men's Clubs and so on to name but some.

It was difficult to understand why when we males held the females in such high esteem we often refused to allow them to socialise with us? Extraordinary!

But to return to the 'Family Butchers' and ower Ruby and Kenny, her beau!

The shop was in an area of town reputed to be middle-class. That is some of the houses had indoor loos and occasionally the odd bathroom. I suppose a better description might have been upper lower class as opposed to lower upper class. I was never one for 'classes' (as my school record showed). As far as I was concerned they were all the same to me. I think they are called 'people'. Some good, some bad, some fair to middling. But all OK in one respect or another. They never tried it on, if you know what I mean. Not that they would have stood a chance against ower Ruby. Sharp she was. Not the last out of the knife box by any stretch of the imagination.

I can only remember the one occasion when Kenny had been bold enough to stand up to her. Either that or he suffered some sudden attack of lunacy that day. To go up against Ower Ruby took some guts I can tell you.

"Where's the bloody order for 10 Moorside -," came Ruby's dulcet tones from inside the cold room. Ken who a moment before had been proffering a leg of Welsh lamb to a prospective customer smiled one of his 'excuse me madam' smiles and stepped aside.

"On the top shelf my precious," he replied and quickly moved back again for the sell. "Shall I weigh it for you madam," he asked turning the leg of lamb around in his hands to catch the light like some precious Ming vase at a Sotheby's auction.

"Where on't top bloody shelf?" came the retort. Ken widened his smile even more then mumbling an apology he gave the customer a slight bow and edged his way to the half open door.

"On the left hand side petal. Top shelf next to the fan unit," He returned to his customer lifting the leg forth like a waiter offering up a bottle of vintage wine.

"It's Welsh lamb madam, from ower suppliers in Cheshire. Beautiful quality. Well worth the extra. Don't you think?"

"It's bloody not," came the sharp retort from inside the cold room. The customer blinked both eyes sharply in surprise and thrust a hand to her mouth in confusion. Ken stumbled back a step holding his best Saturday morning smile pressed tightly across his lips.

"Would madam excuse me for a moment please," he mumbled making for the cold room door. Lifting the leg of lamb onto his shoulder he stepped inside. There was a barely audible 'thump' followed by a less distinguishable 'grunt' and he reappeared the leg of lamb now dangling freely between his fingertips. He approached the counter scales, set the lamb down and spun the dial.

"That would be just twenty one shillings and five pence madam," he beamed turning the lamb shank over and kneading out a large indentation with his bony knuckles.

"There's no charge for the tenderising or the interesting back-room conversations. At this emporium we aim to please – madam."

Ken was of a thin wiry build and walked with a permanent stoop. He had a shock of mousy grey hair covering his chiselled out features. When not in the sales area he could invariably be seen with the remains of a half smoked cigarette sprouting from between his bloodless lips the long wilting grey ash always on the point of falling into whatever meat he happened to be handling at the time. He was a chain-smoker. Capstan Full Strength. One thousand packets and you get a free iron lung thrown in. Terrible things. It wasn't necessary to smoke oneself. All one needed to do was stand within ten yards of a 'Capstan' smoker and breath in deeply. The wooden workbenches bore the evidence of his passing. Hundreds of scorch marks littered the surfaces. It was one of my tasks to try and remove these with soda crystals and scouring powder every Saturday evening before closing time.

I suppose the reason I stayed at this establishment for all the years that I did was for the genuine respect I had for the man's talents. As far as butchering went he was indeed one of the masters and one of the most conscientious at his trade I ever met. His skill with preparation and presentation was beyond reproach. As too his insistence on selling only the best quality meats and produce. Ruby, for all her feminine traits, also maintained a keen eye for anything not 'up to scratch'. 'Waste nowt an' want fer nowt', was a Derbyshire way of saying 'pay attention to what you're doing as, mistakes cost money'.

You were allowed one mistake only in Ruby's book, after that you paid dearly for making them. It was a cock-sure way of getting things done properly though! There must have been something about the place. I had been a 'butchers boy' since being ten years old and had progressed to this new employer after a bout of 'whacking off' school for which I received six of the best on both hands and the loss of my previous part-time job. The butcher was 'miffed' I used his butcher's bicycle for my daily 'wanderings'. Not that I cared a great deal about the job. The three weeks off school had been worth it. I was soon to find another job. I thoroughly enjoyed the work and would eventually become one of Ken's managers during the six years in which he was to teach me the trade. Can't have been all bad – as they say 'up North'. The work did however take up a very large part of my free time. I had to get my 'kicks' when and where I could find them -.

From the position I was crouching I could see the top of 'Tim Bobbins' grave, or at least the sharp metal points of the wrought iron railings that surrounded it. The grave rested amongst a multitude of others in the carefully tended area around the town's parish church. And who was 'Tim Bobbin' then? Why this fact should strike me as important at that particular moment I have no idea other than I hadn't the faintest idea what the hell I was supposed to do with my 'willie' throbbing away in a frenzy of ignorant anticipation between my quivering thighs. Oh, you might ask? Yes. I reply. 'It' was there and 'it' was more than ready, I was ready. She was ready - and if it was up to me, not a lot else was about to happen. Why? Because I'd never got this far before and I'd forgotten to do my homework properly – as usual! - Idiot!

It all came about right out of the blue, unexpectedly and as a result of a 'ragging' that became a de-bagging, much to the delight of the 'Spud' Gang.

As in all animal groupings, and we of the school's 'C' stream were most definitely of that ilk, there's a 'pecking order'. My group, that was 'those four' as we were known to the teaching fraternity, came second in the line.

The first were the 'Spud' gang. Cock of the class 'Spud' Wood, 'Blondie' Howarth his gofer and 'Big' Kenny 'Spuds' second cousin and strong-arm lieutenant. More often than not they left us alone. Together, the four of us could be more than a handful. Which was why it was a mistake to have been on my own when 'Spuds' lot came through the town hall gardens that day and decided to have some 'fun'.

Vanessa, not her real name (I believe a young lady's reputation should remain intact, especially after the favour she did for me), and her friends, came across my somewhat battered prostrate body, minus all of its clothing, in amongst the rhododendron bushes. I was fastened (with my own school tie) to a large tree at the time and was having difficulty releasing myself from the large knot 'Spud' had 'grannyed' around the trunk of the tree on purpose. I was also about to suffer a seizure at the acute embarrassment of being discovered by a bevy of Technical School girls, those whom we 'boys' were duty bound to avoid under pain of a thrashing, garbed only in my birthing suit. What was I supposed to do? Another ten minutes and I would have been late for school. I could hardly tell her to go away. Not even when one of her friends went into a dead feint at the sight of my naked lean body. (I like to think she just swooned at my dashing good looks – but I don't really think that was the case at all). The upshot was I was released and in my gratitude I invited her for coffee at 'Molly's' that evening after school. To my absolute astonishment she agreed. And now here we are. Me with my big ukulele in my hand (well expansive) and she with her neat guitar case awaiting. What the hell do I do now – mother! (On second thoughts forget that. She would not have approved at all.)

My luck was in. Vanessa wanted sex as much as did I. Wanted! I would have given my right arm for it.

Or so I thought at the time anyway. With a lot of fumbling and missing the point of entry, until she herself took over the guidance system, I finally got into position. It was over in seconds and messy to say the least. All ower teachings had told us not to do 'it' without a 'french letter' but I didn't have one to spare. Nor was I going to pass up the chance of sexual intercourse by wandering off looking for one. This was supposed to be one of those 'golden' moments in a boy's life. The moment when he is no longer a 'youth' but enters into that mysterious world of 'manhood'. It was all utter tosh of course, but that's what we believed.

As immature, unprofessional and unsatisfactory as it was I had at last made it into the ranks of men. Fourteen years of age. Not before time. But in truth it was! Much too early. And down right 'bloody' stupid. Not to mention idiotic, unintelligent and down right bloody dangerous. Not that I was thinking that at the time or even 'thinking' at the time. It was to Vanessa's credit she ensured in the final mind-bending moments that my frenzied northern seed didn't pollute her delicate feminine enclave. A swift nip on my scrotum with her 'Dracula' like fingernails and ower thighs sprang apart like a snapped brassiere strap. Something like the 'agony' and the 'ecstasy' springs to mind as I sprayed the grassy hollow with what felt like a gallon of powerful seeds. To say it was a heady experience is an understatement. It was definitely lots of head and masses and masses of body I can tell you and I'm not talking about the rest of me, just that bit waving a victorious salute from below my midriff. It was wonderful and I would never, ever, forget it. To say it was an introduction to the world of true love or a coming of manhood. Well lads. Not quite. The 'real' thing (thankfully) was still yet to come and when it did there would be no earthly comparison, believe me. But for now – I was 'King of the Castle' and boy did I feel 'GREAT', apart that was for the trembling which I was having the greatest of difficulty controlling and the sweat trickling in rivulets from under both armpits and the apparent lack of oxygen as my chest heaved in and out like a pair of worn out bellows. I put it all down to too many 'fags' and not as it was, totally freaked out, shagged out and seedless. But hey – boy - it was worth it. But of course I got away with it, and again, I was 'lucky' that day. So beware. - **You might not be -!**

To the right of the 'wooden stocks' lies the grave of 'Tim Bobbin'. A 'hallowed' spot for yours truly. Yea.

It was also about this time we started trying ower hand at the 'boozing'. More often than not it was possible to buy bottled beer at one of the back-street 'off-licences', corner shops that were allowed to sell beer providing it wasn't drunk on the premises, having convinced the 'greedy' shop owner we had passed the age of eighteen. But this was too easy and less than satisfactory. What we wanted was the thrill of the 'chase'. We wanted to buy ower booze in the town's pubs and consume it like the rest of the 'guys'. And stand the chance of getting nabbed by the 'fuzz' for under-aged drinking. Quite a serious offence in ower days. Apart from which the 'pub' had a much larger choice and a number of other 'attractions' on offer.

"How's about a game of 'brag' -." Brag. A card game. Poor man's 'poker'. Played with a dealt hand of three cards and guaranteed to relieve you of all your money in one foul swoop – and I do mean 'foul'. But first it was necessary to get 'accepted'.

"A black velvet an' a pint er bitter please." I said in my best deep throated growl. The landlord looked at me then at Wozzle who was trying to appear as if he wasn't the least bit interested in the proceedings and hadn't a care in the world.

"Would that be wi' champagne er cider then." The man growled back. Oops. I wasn't ready for that one.

"Champagne." "Cider." We sang back in unison. The landlord smirked an evil grin.

"Would that be champagne cider or cider champagne? Wi got both," he replied. We were obviously out of ower depth. The man pointed at the door.

"Thall get some black and blue if tha doesn't get thi arses out of here sharpish. Now piss orf." And that was the end of that particular foray.

It wasn't long before we got the hang of it. A word or two from the right direction pointed us to those establishments whose liberal interpretation of the law allowed for illegal libations. We were soon frequenting a number of the 'right' public houses on a regular basis. And getting fleeced from the 'brag' merchants. If Wozzle had a weakness it was for card playing. He soon became quite a dab hand at nine card stud and cribbage and 'blind' betting but also thought himself impervious to the odd 'hustler' or two we sometimes came up against. Much to his dismay. For myself, I hated losing. It wasn't the money, although that could be quite unpleasant, it was the thought I had been outfoxed or more often than not 'conned' by a cardsharp. There's no better cure for gambling than to get fleeced a few times whilst you're still young. It's the best time to learn.

What made matters worse was Ower Kid. He'd been done for under-age drinking and the old woman was none too pleased.

"Ower name will be all over the damn newspaper." she retorted angrily when Ower Kid asked her what all the fuss was about.

"Eee. Will we be famous then?" I asked brightly. 'CRACK'.

"And you can shut up bugger." 'Ouch'. Whoa. Hang on a minute. It's not me who's been stupid enough to get 'nabbed'. What am I getting a slugging for?

"I'm not having it. D'yer hear. I'm not having it," she roared angrily. I was tempted to say. 'Well don't get onto us, have a word with mi dad.' But I thought that would most definitely get me 'grounded' considering the circumstances.

Ower Kid had a tendency to 'overdo' the 'boozing' and would sometimes come home later than curfew, stagger into bed, which was the same room as yours truly, and regurgitate the nights consumption all over the linoleum. Not too much of a problem as regards cleaning the following morning but it had a tendency to run across the sloping floor in the direction of my bed. Getting out of bed in a morning in a pool of stagnant vomit is no joke. Especially when it's not yours. But then Ower Kid was sixteen. Regardless of the law, most people considered sixteen to be the cut-off point. The 'no longer the child time to grow up' point and as such, certain 'things' were tolerated. Like breaking curfew and spewing ones entrails all over my bedroom floor. It was the quickest way to learn – so the grown-ups said. I think I begged to differ. And come to think of it would have had to beg a hell of a lot just to get a word in edgeways at that point in time. But that was the way of things. It wasn't the same when I set fire to the bed by falling asleep with a fag in my hand. There wasn't too much 'understanding' going on then if I recall. Mind you I wasn't sixteen at the time either!

This is the first Co-Op established in 1866.(With derelict cotton-mill in the background). Renovated in the 1970s and prior to part of ower cobbled 'bogey' run. Some of the cobbled street can still be seen beyond the barriers. *(See: Ower Darkling.)*

'Barmy Rules & Barmier Rulers'.

It is often said that the 1960s were the time when the youth of ower fair country threw off its shackles of conformity and launched the 'freedom' revolution. It was. But not until the very late sixties and not without a great deal of pain and bloodshed, albeit not yours truly, if I could help it.

The wind of change was blowing. But most of it was passing over the top of ower valley. Only the occasional light breeze wafted in ower direction. And then with the utmost reticence if the facts are to be believed.

True it was still the late 'fifties', but I had expected at least some 'change' to come over the town now the war was won and the chances of another one seemingly far distant. A war that was with a foreign foe, not one of the home-grown variety. But there was another 'war' smouldering silently away amongst the throwbacks from ower Victorian past and ower lust for a 'bright New World'. The forces of 'darkness' versus the 'torch-bearers of change'. I was one of the latter. Surprising, considering my angelic features, lush blonde hair (that had rapidly turned a muddy brown with the onset of hormone production) and my innocent appealing smile. (Well that's my story and I'm sticking to it and bugger the rest of them.)

It's probably obvious I didn't much care for 'rules'. Not being 'thick', as was the opinion of the majority of my peers, I could see the need for them. I could also see the need to break them occasionally or if not, at least make them a bit crooked if the situation warranted. I think it was more a question of the punishment not fitting the crime that rankled me most. There seemed to be a diabolical policy of 'spirit crushing' to excess, in the strange belief that such methods were the most expedient and efficient way of removing the problem, me and a few others besides.

And it is to this I now elude.

'Don't'. The word has a very appealing attraction. There is something 'mysterious' almost tantalisingly curious about it. I was constantly being drawn towards its harsh guttural utterance as if some strange magical force was pulling me forever onwards. Sucking me in towards its compelling abruptness. 'Don't'. So easily it rolls off the speakers tongue. Like the word 'fart'. It was designed to attract immediate attention. Only in the latter people tended to melt away from the initiators rather than towards them. Understandable really!

"There will be no retaliation. I DON'T want to hear of any boy taking the law into his own hands. DON'T forget what I have said." Oh dear! I sometimes wondered if the liberal use of the word wasn't made to promote exactly the opposite reaction from ower generation. I wouldn't have put it passed any of ower persecutors – sadist's that they were. 'Don't', was akin to bashing a wet bloodstained dishcloth across a traumatised bull's nose to ower lot. The man might as well have said, 'Anything goes lads'. And that more often than not would have saved everyone a great deal of trouble.

'Don't walk on the right hand side when in school'.
'Don't attend school minus any item of the correct uniform'.
'Don't remain seated when the headmaster enters your presence'.
'Don't be seen outside school without the regulation cap set squarely atop ones cranium'.
'Don't be found outside school eating, drinking or smoking in public whilst wearing school uniform.'
'Don't act boisterously outside school whilst in school uniform.'
'Don't attend class without first attending to one's toilet.'
'Don't be late for class or attend minus that period's equipment.'
'Don't speak unless spoken to.'
'Don't ogle from the school windows during the Girl's school breaks.'
'Don't run, stop suddenly or prostrate your person anywhere on school property without prior permission.'
'Don't leave personal property unattended.'
'Don't attend classes without all relevant homework completed.'

'Don't use foul language, fisticuffs or offensive remarks
whilst in school uniform in or off school premises.'
'Don't deface school property and report all and any
offences of this nature to the appropriate authority
immediately.'
'Don't leave personal desks unsecured.'
'Don't breath or allow your presence to be realised
unless out of school uniform and in a different town.' Well
perhaps not but it wouldn't have surprised anyone had that item also
not appeared on the endless list of DON'T'S.

But it wasn't the rules themselves we had a problem with. Born of
average intelligence the need for them was apparent. It was the
'draconian' punishments that followed any lapse of 'the said rules'
that were completely beyond ower 'rational' comprehension!

The swift crack across the back of the head or the well-directed
missile wanging away from some part of ower anatomy was almost
accepted as normal procedure. The head, according to ower peers,
was quite thick in us Northerners and could stand any amount of
bashing. So that was alright with everybody. Head bashing covered
almost anything at all from tying ones shoelaces in the corridor to
looking the wrong way at the form master. Slow strangulation, or any
near variation on the theme usually came following the teacher's 'bad
time' with the wife the night before. We called it N.P.S. 'no pokey
syndrome'. To be a victim of this was a fact of life. Even ower
teachers had private lives that left a hell of a lot to be desired.
Although we rarely felt sorrow, more like pity, for them. Their wives
that is. Although you would have thought them being 'grown-ups
they' should have been able to handle their 'hang-ups' a lot better
than that. Still, that's the way it goes.

Detention. The 'stay behind after school' punishment. I often got
the worst of that particular event. I had a habit of saying to the
detention form master – "I know why the bastard put 'me' in here.
Wot are you in here for -.? With the result I rarely left the school at
the proper home time for days on end.

I once broke the form record for getting thrashed three times in the
same day. Four of the best twice and four that turned to six of the best
as a piece de la resistance.

We won't dally on the details save to say I had a 'cob' on that day. I was hoping they would 'accidentally' injure me sufficiently to require hospitalisation. That would have put the cat amongst the pigeons! I could have lived off that event for months to come, given the right 'spin'. My hands were a bit of a mess for a few days after. My 'job' didn't harden them; on the contrary they were like two slabs of sow's tit with all the cleaning fluids, grease and blood they were immersed in every day. And to add to the effect they were often covered in numerous cuts I had accidentally self-inflicted during my 'butchery' training. One of which opened up during thrashing number three. Not that 'Chinny' batted an eyelid as his cane skimmed away sideways with a splash of squishy red liquid. He had finished with that hand anyway. There was another on the other side not yet opened up so – "Right hand. FLAT BOY. HOLD IT FLAT. Idiot." SWISH-SPLAT.

"Shit -." He didn't say that. I did. And got another two whacks for using foul language, making the 'six'.

Punishments were logged in the 'Whacking Book'. But ONLY in the headmasters study. Whacking elsewhere throughout the school wasn't noted down. The result was an over-liberal use of 'corporal punishment' where no controls prevailed. The school authority took the view that each individual master had the 'common sense' to exercise class disciplines in a 'fair and judicious manner'. A grave mistake and one which sometimes had unforeseen circumstances.

The ambulance men came running down 'B' corridor like bats out of hell. "Detention". We chorused in unison as the two men flashed by heading for the rear stairwell cloakroom. Minutes later they emerged with a bundle on a stretcher and waddled back with the deputy headmaster, Chinny as we called him, in tow. Unfortunately not on the stretcher, but considerably paler than he had been an hour previously when threatening yours truly in the classroom with all kinds of doom and disaster.

"Make way. Make way you boys." Chinny screeched angrily. Both lines merged with the brickwork as the black and white uniforms trotted by in an unseemly haste.

It later transpired the boy, who's name escapes me, had tripped over his 'hush-puppies', when entering the room to receive a 'bout' of corporal punishment from ower illustrious deputy headmaster, and had inadvertently smashed his brains out on one of the coat-hanger stanchions. The truth was somewhat different. But who's going to believe a 'trouble-maker'?

The majority of minor punishments were carried out in front of the class in a bid to set examples and to instil a sense of fear and foreboding. All the rest, those requiring more than four strokes of the cane, were carried out in private. No witnesses. Not as some would have us believe to save the embarrassment or the humiliation. The teachers that is. We weren't one bit humiliated or embarrassed. But grown men knocking 'seven bells' out of small children, that I could see must have been most humiliating for men of average intelligence. Perhaps that was the problem??

"There will be no retaliation. I don't want to hear of any boy taking the law into his own hands. **'Don't'** forget what I have said."

The man's eyes wandered slowly across the sea of faces lining the terraced seating of the 'Municipal' Baths. It was the day following the 'commando' raid on ower school by pupils from the local 'Grammar' school. It was the yearly swimming gala at which every pupil had to attend, unless he had two broken legs or a more plausible excuse for not going swimming, and we had left ower school that dinner time still gaily decked out in yellow and green paint (the grammar school colours) festooned from copula to damp-course. What a mess. More to the point. What an insult!
    The culprits had come in the dead of night to the centre of ower town and tarnished ower miserable hell-hole with their snobbish corruption's. SWINE. Well. Not really. Cute and daring was the way we saw it but we could hardly admit to such thoughts openly could we?
    Yes. Of course it was me who 'retaliated' and painted Ower Kid's Grammar School in blue and red cellulose paint. Turnip and a friend of his as well, not in paint, they helped me. Try as he might ower headmaster couldn't prove it. Even when ably assisted by one of his 'high born' Prefects who had been hot on my trail.
DON'T is a word that should be used sparingly.
Unlike 'Fred's' and 'Café' the two words Turnip and yours truly

painted in bold twelve foot high letters across the main roof of the grammar school, much to the anger and frustration of the schools headmaster one <u>Fred</u>rick March. 'Oops'!

And the next object is - - - - -?   Animal, Vegetable or
　　Mineral - -?   'Thing' by 'Ower Kid'   - Artist.
Answers on a postcard to -. Fred Carno's Unusual Objects Emporium.
Nether Wallop. Bucks. Hmm -. Nearly got that right.

'Funfairs, Fractions & Fisticuffs'.

They were like never ending condoms. Sausage skins. Or to the better-educated, sheep intestines. I fiddled for a few moments slotting the slimy coil of entrails along the machine's nozzle and grasped the wooden handle. At first nothing happened, unlike what normally happened whenever I was lucky enough to get someone to grab mine, then like the onrush of a train exiting a Pennine tunnel, the sausage meat exploded from within akin to some gigantic ejaculation.

"Control it. Control it," screeched ower Ken. His final words lost in a long constricted wheeze as the smoke from his last inhale of the 'Capstan' cigarette dangling from between his lips beat seven bells of mayhem around his slowly decaying tar-filled lungs.

We were trying out the new sausage machine. It was supposed to help production and was twice the size of ower previous one. I owled at him with a look that would have killed a rabid fox.

"Where's the bloody 'Tibetan Sherpa's' then? I grunted sarcastically.

"Tha' what?"

"The Tibetan Sherpa's." I repeated. Ken scratched at his receding hairline.

"Ay I thought that's what tha said. What bloody Sherpa's?"

"The bloody Sherpa's that should have come with this dam machine to turn the bloody handle!" I snapped.
Ken was never one for seeing the funny side to things and motioned me aside with a dismissive wave of his cigarette.

"It can't be that bad laddie. Move yer arse. Here. Take the handle wi yer left hand and p–u-l-l -." he gasped, his face contorting sideways and slowly growing a bright crimson.

"Bloody hell. It – must – be stickin' – a – bit." With a supreme effort he gave the wooden handle an almighty heave. The compacted sausage meat leapt from within the cast iron container like a wire guided air to ground missile.

Ruby had just finished the 'books' and had opened the stairwell door to descend into the hallway when the 'flying sausage rope' reached her.

There was a scream followed by a loud bump and a frantic scrambling of disjointed limbs. A silence followed. Ken and I looked at each other. I could see he was looking for somewhere to run, leaving me 'holding the handle' so to speak.

"Don't you bloody dare." I growled, fully expecting him to take no notice and high-tail it for sanctuary.

"Bastard - -!" came the voice from beyond the darkness of the stairwell as with a few crashes of splintering stair tread Ruby emerged from above.

"Ee 'ello petal. I'm trying -." Ken got no further. With a snarl Ruby unhooked the flopping string of sausages from around her muscle – bound neckline and hurled them towards us.

"You're not just bloody trying Kenneth Taylor. You're bloody impossible. What were you trying – eh? To kill me – eh? Why I ever married you in the first place I'll never know. Mi' mother was right. She said it plain. Dead plain. That man's no good fer you ower Ruby. A walking accident so he is. Don't come trotting home here dead and then expect me and yer father to sort you out. I wash me hands of yer if you marry that one Ower Ruby, I wash me hands of yer I say -." Ken parried the tirade and came back fighting.

"Yower mother! Yower mother didn't like anybody she didn't. Come Christmas time even the bin-men gave her a wide berth. Some recommendation she was."

"Is." Ruby snapped angrily. " Is. She's still alive."

"Didn't look like it last time I saw her." Ken mumbled trying a sneaky smile to calm things down. Ruby was having none of it. It wasn't as if we had 'fired' the sausage rope at her on purpose. If we had I'm sure Ken would have made a far better job of it than he did. The argument went on. I left after the third round. The only 'second' to the bout I thought was a bit unfair. With no umpire in the offing things sometimes got a bit sticky. I was better off out of there.

(Dear Diary -).

"'Cause they train them to read don't they."
"What!"
Turnip's eyebrows dropped a couple of inches down his forehead.
Wozzle's face never moved. He knew me better than most.
"How?"
"How the hell do I know? What am I, the bloody Encyclopaedia
Britannica?"
"That's bollocks."
"No it isn't. How else would a blind bloke know it was a park? Look.
The bloke's walking down the street and comes to the park. The
notice on the gate say's, 'Guide dogs only'. The bloke can't see the
notice can he? He can't bloody-well read it can he? Ergo – The dog
does it and pulls him through the gates. Ergo – The dog must be able
to read the notice otherwise they'd walk straight past wouldn't they
Eh?"
Seth's brain went into overdrive. Which was unfortunate. Seth didn't
like too much thinking. Unless it was about sex. But then we were all
the same on that score.
"That's rubbish. The notice must have Braille on it somewhere. So
the bloke can feel it up." Turnip was getting bored with the
conversation. He wanted to do something more exciting or dangerous
or just downright disruptive.
"I'll feel you up in a minute if we have to stop here much longer." he
grumbled.
There was a fair on in the cattle market. We hadn't any money. Well,
not a lot anyway. A few pence and a few fags. We could always try
selling the fags to some of the 'kids' to supplement ower 'bare larder'
so to speak.
We headed off down the steep cobbled hill that led passed ower
school and the town centre. There was a municipal park opposite the
cattle market. Seth wanted to go and touch up one of the 'Guide Dogs
Only' signs. Just to see if he was right. Oh dear!

(Vicar's Field 1958.)

Rip-off merchants and excellent at the short-change trick. But then we weren't that far 'short of a shilling' to allow the young gipo's to rip us off either.

The 'Fair' came to town four times a year. Easter. Whitsun, Sow-in Eve and Christmas. Always the same company, always the same gypsy families. It wasn't cheap. Between a shilling and threepence a ride depending on the thrill and duration. But it was fun. And we were always in for picking up a good 'bonk' for the evening as the event attracted a multitude of the opposite and fairer sex. Women. By the 'truck' load. Or at least I think that was how Turnip described them. I could be wrong. It might have been something similar. Anyway -.

It might have been a good night had we not met up with Ower Kid and his mates. A mistake if ever there was one. He thought I was one and I thought he was one and it usually ended up bad – for me, but who's counting?

It's true to say me and Ower Kid rarely, if ever, saw eye to eye. Mine was usually 'black' before we got to that point. And red and swollen and marring my angelic handsome looks for days to come. I suppose it must have happened some time back at a point when the old woman began blaming him for not keeping 'things' under better control, him being the eldest and me being 'a pain in the arse'. Or even further back than that? I'm no psychologist. But he must have suffered some 'lack of attention' when in the very early days yours truly became a 'project' for medical scrutiny which was to last for almost five long years. Up until then he would have been the 'first' priority in the old woman's eyes and to lose that may well have been the cause for his present disdain. Whatever. It came to no good as the years went by.

"Fuck off."

"Yes brother dear. Do you have a suggestion brother dear."

"How's about Blackpool Tower – from the top."

"Yes brother dear. Shall I walk there or would you prefer I run."

"If yer don't fuck off now yer won't be able to crawl there. Arsehole."

"Yes brother dear. And up yours too."

'SPLAT'.

Didn't duck. Never saw it coming. Should have learned by now. Don't call your brother to his face unless you are two miles hence to begin with. He can also run quite fast.

Seth cupped his hand from the stone horse trough and splashed the icy contents all over my head.

"The bastard hit yer." he pouted in astonishment.

"Smacked you right in the eye. Crack. Guy's a bloody lunatic." I waved his hand away from my head and wiped the dripping water from around my soaking neckline.

"No. Not really. Brother's are like that. Just a friendly sparring match. Nothing to get excited about." I replied gingerly touching the extremities of my skull with the tips of both hands to make sure it was still there.

"Sparrin'! I didn't see no sparrin'. Crack, wallop was all I saw." Which to be fair was considerably more than I did, so who was arguing?

"Forget it. It's nothing." I replied.

"Nowt! Yer call that nowt? What's wrong wi the bloke?" Wozzle was not amused. Apparently, as I was to discover later, it had been Wozzle who had put his fair bulk between Ower Kid and me as I lay on the ground. Brave of him, knowing Ower Kid, who would have thought nothing at taking a fist to him also.

"He's probably not getting any. It makes some that way when they's comin' up short. Best thing is to keep out of his way. My fault. I should have known better when he's out with his mates. He likes to show off."

"Funny bloody way of showing off. Can't he find a more useful occupation?" Turnip sneered.

With Ower Kid and his mates in the neighbourhood I persuaded the others we should find somewhere else to amuse ourselves.

It was a time when the 'Teddy Boy' gangs were abroad and it didn't do to become embroiled in any 'argy bargy' with the likes of them. Ower Kid was an angel when set alongside these 'thugs', and the 'fair' had a habit of attracting their presence also as the night wore on.

The old woman had a 'thing' about her son's and their clothes. Fashion it might be. On you – forget it!

As time went by we bought ower own clothes, on the 'sly', and took to hiding them in the various cellars that made up the ground floor of ower new house, the one by the canal locks gates with the 'Drapers shop' at the front - the one that had the flush toilet set in the basement with the original door of the White Rose Pub – (which is what the house used to be way back in the old days). Anyway - fashion -. Drainpipe trousers with coloured turn-ups, winkle-picker or chisel-toed shoes, knee length jackets with roll-velvet collars, bootlace ties and a haircut to match. Mine was a 'Tony Curtis'. That was fashion -!

"THAT BOY!" Everybody froze. All except Wozzle who wasn't paying attention and skittled the next six boys in front of him who toppled like a chorus of Saturday night drunks. 'Crrrraash'. Those still standing turned in the direction of the scream.
Slim Fielding hung in the distance like a grounded vampire bat. For some reason he was wearing his cloak with the grease stained collar. All eyes transfixed the wavering apparition as it swooped angrily down the corridor towards us.

"YOU." His skeletal finger pointed in my direction.

"Who? Me sir?" I replied in mild astonishment.

"Who - me sir?" he sniggered, the sarcasm leeching its way through the tensed atmosphere. "OF COURSE YOU. YOU MINDLESS IDIOT. WHO DO YOU THINK I'M POINTING AT?"

I couldn't think what I might have done to set him off again. Various misdemeanour's shot through my agile brain as I detached myself from the line and slouched slowly towards him.
Fielding and yours truly were never good news. It was a bit like oil and water. He was 'oily' and me – well I was still a bit of a drip at that age.

All balls and an underdeveloped brain, if you get my drift. But nowhere near as stupid as he thought I was.

"WHAT, have you got, on your head boy?" Naturally my hand shot to the top of my head thinking someone had attached something thereto without my knowledge. Seth had a habit of pinning stuff to my back like – 'Arsehole for Hire. Apply below.' It amused him. We all had to find something to pass the drudgery of this place along. No. Nothing there. Not even my cap, which, we weren't allowed to wear inside school anyway. It was another of those DON'T'S we talked about.

"YOUR HAIR BOY. WHAT HAVE YOU DONE TO YOUR HAIR?" he bellowed flushing out half the dripping contents from inside his flapping jowls all over my face.

"Nothing sir." I answered meekly and then smiled.
Now Mr Fielding didn't like smiles. He had tried it once and was in dire agony for a fortnight afterwards. His fingernails slashed across my forehead in response.

"THAT! That THING adorning your forehead. What is it?" The question seemed rather pointless. It was obviously either a trick question or someone must have written something across it whilst I was asleep in 'assembly'. (I should 'qualify' that by explaining I hadn't made 'assembly' that morning and having conned my way into the room for 'Roman Catholics' I had promptly fallen asleep on one of the desks – for which I received one nights 'detention' - again.) I used the answer for which one more often than not got slugged around the ear-hole but in truth I didn't understand the situation.

"I don't know sir." CRACK. I saw stars.

"Thank you sir." I said in reply, whilst Saturn blew its rings around half the Milky Way and back.

"Don't you get smart with me boy. I'm not your mother. I don't love you."
I could have replied that she wasn't very enamoured with me these days either but I doubt it would have made much difference. Instead I continued with my usual – I don't like you mister routine – and to hell with the consequences.

"I should hope not sir. It's not allowed is it?" The Science Master raised his hand back to give me another belt around the opposite ear when - - -."Mr Fielding -."
His Master's Voice echoed down the now empty corridor. 'Loopy' Lewis, the Headmaster, approached from the gloom of the 'A' corridor stairwell.

The Science teacher redirected the swinging right hook rapidly towards a lock of hair straddling his own forehead and brushed it slowly up over his head with a innocent flourish.

"Headmaster -." he oozed in a sycophantic half smile.

"Have you a moment -." said the Headmaster giving a barely imperceptible smile in return as he glanced with an uncaring look in my direction. He blinked. Then again.

" You boy. Your hair!" he snapped in amazement. "Er- Why – er – Why is it standing out like that - - -?"

"I was just asking him the same question Headmaster." interjected the Science Master with an obsequious whine. Lewis kept his eyes transfixed to my forehead and blinked again. He was obviously quite concerned his eyes were playing tricks on him. He pouted his lips.

"We really can't have you walking around the school looking like that you know. Wrong impression. Wrong impression altogether. Dear me no. Go away and remove it. Instantly!" The Headmaster waved me aside with a whirl of his limp palm. I was obviously of no further matter or importance. Be gone inconsequential wretch. Desist from abusing my peripheral vision. Although how I was now supposed to remove the large heavily lacquered curl of hair from the centre of my forehead without the aid of a good pair of scissors and a mirror I didn't know. Not that it mattered one jot to the powers that be. That was my problem.

Having no scissors and not prepared to have 'Spud' use his flick-knife on me I went to my next lesson unimpressed by the proceedings of the last few minutes.
I got six of the best the following day, from the Headmaster, followed by a rough torturous haircut at the hands of a very angry Science Master who it seemed felt himself personally responsible for not having ripped the lock of hair out by the roots the previous day and for thus becoming the brunt of the Headmasters displeasure. Hey ho – You can't win yer know! – But I kept on trying -.
If at first 'you' can't succeed. Try getting a budgie t' do it for yer -. Or something like that.

'Tony Curtis' Actor. My 'kiss curl' was slightly larger and probably more prominent. Everybody thought it the 'bees knees' - well almost everybody -! Obviously didn't turn on the teachers or the headmaster.

'Fishing. Fracas & Flawed Fortunes.

"Fishing -. ' –Kinel. Can't yer come up with owt better than that?" Seth's face was a picture. Not a pretty one but quite viewable all the same. "D' yer mean for women?" he added suspiciously.
Wozzle owled his large eyes and motivated his huge pupils around their sockets in a slow circular motion.
"No -. I mean real fishing. Fer fish! You know. Them things that swim about in water. Glub-glub." I replied.
   "Real fish? Where the 'kinel do you think your guna find real fish around here?" Seth mooned a face, then to Wozzle. "He's flipped. Goin' barmy. Thinks there's real fish around here. It's that school. Puts daft ideas in people 'eads. Real fish. Huh. Give me a break. Only fish you'll find around 'ere are in batter in Chip Shops. Silly sod."
So that was a none starter. So we didn't. Go fishing that is.
   There was a time when I had. Gone fishing. But that was some years back and then things were less complicated. No women you see. No mind-crunching sexual thoughts rummaging around in ones tormented brain saying – If you don't get a 'bonk' today you'll die -. Or words to that effect.
Halcyon days they were called. Total crap of course. But in truth far less complicated than now.

'Froggy would a fishing and he would go Hey Hey.'

   We still lived on the 'Mount' in those days. It was a few years after the war and what we didn't have we didn't know about anyway. Consequently we didn't miss it. I was about six years old going on seven. The old woman knew I couldn't swim and encouraged me to go to the 'mill' lodge as often as she could. Well, that's not quite true. Say once a week or more.

 Anyway-.

The mill lodge was situated at the top of a long hill in a village that went by the name of Shawclough. The village was that big that if you ran too fast towards it you was on the opposite side before you knew it.. The 'lodge' or large man-made pond, was to the rear of the old mill, across some allotments that bordered the main road and in its own natural dip in the ground. The mill, a seventeenth century cotton mill, one of the very first in ower town, had closed at the turn of the century. Fifty years of inactivity had allowed the waters to clear naturally and the lodge was now sustaining a large population of roach and perch and the dreaded legendary wolf of the waters; a large humongous razor jawed pike. Or so we had been told.

On this day I had set out quite determined I was going to snare this beast of the waters and so 'tooled' myself up for the job.

Uncle Johnny's allotment provided the bamboo canes. Uncle Johnny was the old man's sister's husband. Went by the name of Johnny Parrot. I thought it was a nickname but apparently not. He was a good old 'stick' and apart from his 'roughness' was 'dead' kind to all us kids. I don't think I ever saw him clean- or with a beard. He was one of them 'designer' chinned blokes. Either that or he was just pig-idle. Anyway. Off to the midden to find the worms, the dustbin for a jam jar and the old lady's odd-bob tin for the string. For 'jaws' I needed a net. Old Grandma Kelly provided that with one of her large nylon stockings and a corset stay. Ergo, one large mouthed net for hauling the 'beastie' ashore.

For those of you who think you can't catch fish with a bent pin and a worm, think again. The trick was to bend the pin to the right shape and pinion the worm in at least three or four places, otherwise it buggered off and went swimming on its own. 'Headbanger' (otherwise known as Patrick Meeghan) always lost his. Worm that is. Quite often before it got to the water. Off it would fly like a wingless condom as he 'cast' his rod in the general direction of the pond. He scared more old ladies out of their Alzheimer reverie's than I would care to mention. Worms and hairnets don't go together. But to come back to the fishing. Today I went fishing with deadly prejudice. 'Jaws' was coming home with me tonight or I would be terminated in the attempt.

I remember it was about mid-afternoon. We had drunk all the 'Spo' (a description and manufacture of which can be found in 'Ower Darkling'.) and nibbled ower way through a half hundredweight of treacle and ginger 'Parkin' (likewise). Headbanger had gone off looking for more fish bait because he had discovered they didn't like 'Parkin' and apart from which it no sooner hit the water than it began to spread out in large oil slicks across the surface of the pond making it impossible for the fish to see my worms. I was not amused. So I asked him to depart.

"Fuck off will yer." I snapped. So very obligingly he did. Mumbling something about 'hand-grenades' and his dad's army chest he kept under the bed. (His dad was one of them Auxiliary Home Guards so it was very likely he wasn't just showing off).

I gave a long cast, heard the delicate plop of the lure entering the water and lay back on the grassy knoll closing my eyes to the brightness of the sun's rays seeping in a reddish glow through my eyelids. It was one of those Mark Twain days but without the constant hum of mosquito and the gentle snap of crocodile jaws in the distance. You know the kind of thing. It's called Summer in some places and they have those prolonged hot periods of balmy dry weather. We didn't have them. It was probably because half the people in ower town either couldn't or wouldn't pay their council tax. Reasoned - you only get what you pay for. Something like that. Anyway. It was warm and dry for a change so I took advantage because it was free and you could stop in it as long as you wanted.

The 'rod' jerked suddenly. Quick as a flash I was on to it and yanked it up smartly. Whatever was on the other end yanked back. A large smelly cloud of lodge detritus billowed to the surface.

"Oy. Headbanger!" I yelled excitedly, in the direction he had slouched away. Headbanger's face appeared from between the closely layered fronds of some rhododendron bushes nearby.

"Wot!" he grunted begrudgingly. He upset very easily for such a big lump.

"I've got it. Come 'ere I've got it."
Headbanger exited the bushes fastening up the buttons of his 'fly'.

"I know. That's why mi mum says I shouldn't play with yer." He shot back in return. (Which was no reason he should have been playing with himself in the meantime – however -.)

"O heckey peck. Come here yer soft sod and give me a lift." I puffed.

With both of us tugging and panting together we lugged the writhing black catch towards the bank and hauled it by its front gills from the water.

"It's a piggin' wellie yer twat." growled Headbanger, as the loose flaps of half an angling wader exited the water and rebounded off the stone wall showering the pair of us in a spray of evil smelling goo.

To say I was disappointed wasn't in it. Visions of totting my amazing catch through the streets of ower town and getting my picture on the front page of the 'Observer' (not that one they sell everywhere – just ower local rag) vanished in a wall of 'Parkin-mache' and a hundred years of filth. Boy was I 'hacked' off. The bloody thing had pinched my worm as well.

So why on earth was I suggesting we go fishing now? It wasn't as if I could call upon a lifetime's experience or even a couple of successful historical forays. But that's your truly. And there's no answer to that.

The old woman was busy in the 'sewing room' when I returned home in time for tea. It was a Sunday, the only day I had tea at home with the rest. Half past five and don't be late or it's not in the kitchen it's in the dog and you get nothing, other than a clout around the ear.

"I'm not a bloody café nor an 'otel'. Don't show, don't eat."
Had a 'way' with words did the old woman. They came your 'way'!
You listened, or else!

Ower Kid was picking the onions out of his short 'hotpot'* and lining them up alongside the edge of his plate like a line of dead soldiers as I entered the lounge-cum-dining room.

"She'll wang yer one if she comes in and sees that." I ventured in passing.

"She can if she wants. I couldn't care less." he muttered stuffing his mouth with a large forkful of greasy bacon and scalloped potatoes. "What's it got t' do with you anyway?"

He was so pleasant my brother. It was like having a conversation with a migrainous gorilla only ten times more hazardous. He wasn't getting any. That was abundantly clear. He had enough girlfriends in tow but as yet it appeared he hadn't persuaded one to go the whole way. I can't be sure but that's what my money was on.

What other explanation could there have been? Not that he would have discussed it with me or anyone else God forbid. Getting him just to admit I was his brother was like prising the padlock off a Jewish dustbin. And that takes some doing I can tell you.

Especially in ower town. Fort Knox was less secure.

I got my plate from under the grill. The old woman's hot pot was a 'dream'. Smooth, greasy and salty. I knew she should have par-boiled the bacon and drained it from the water before putting it in with the rest to simmer. Me being the 'butcher' and the provider of the meat as it were. But I wasn't going to venture to tell her. I was looking for some friendly heavyweight boxer to pass on such messages. It was safer that way.

"That mincemeat wus off." she said as her head appeared in the serving hatch that separated the minuscule kitchen from the lounge.

"Shouldn't have been." I countered defensively, knowing full well it had been on the turn on the Saturday but not refusing to clear the bowl in the butchers' cold-room when told to help myself to anything that was left over after the last customers had gone. It would have been all right had she cooked it immediately on the Saturday night. But who was going to tell her that? Not me. Not I. Not anyone in ower house. No way. Saturday night was 'telly' night if nothing else had been pre-booked, like one of ower famous family events, (you know the sort of thing, weddings, twenty-firsts, special birthdays, that sort of stuff). The old woman would not have taken kindly to having her 'Saturday nights' disturbed with cooking. Not at all.

So the mincemeat went off and so did the cat the following day when she tried to get him to eat it. The dog, daft as ever, wolfed the lot down and promptly regurgitated the whole heaving mess down the cellar steps, the only route to the toilet. Ahhhh! I remember it well.

"You two! Dog's been sick down the cellar steps. Needs sorting out. Get rid of it."

I looked at Ower Kid. "Got a gun anywhere?"

It wasn't very wise I have to say. She was in no mood of a Monday evening – in fact come to think of it – she was never in the mood, for 'smart Alec' remarks from gormless adolescents. It was as though the bigger we grew the more intimidating we became. Ower old woman never did like fella's. She married one but drew the line at that. The rest, them out yonder, weren't much cop as far as she was concerned. 'Thick in't arm and thick in't head and good fer only one thing – Sending out t' work. Yer can't send them out t' do owt else, otherwise they get lost.' She had such a compassionate way with her did ower old mum.

* (Short hotpot, made with bacon. Long hotpot, made with mutton-both very greasy.)

That last year and a half at ower 'reformatory' sorry 'school' became one gigantic merry-go-round of trials and tribulations. To begin with the old woman had decided to make 'economies'. That's good I thought. More stuff to sell in the shop along with the knickers, corsets and brassieres that adorned every nook and cranny of the place. I should have known better. Making an 'economy' was one of those 'intangibles' whatever one of those was and they was difficult to sell in those days. What she should have said was that she was docking my daily allowance. That I would have understood. Immediately!
From one shilling and threepence a day to nine pence halfpenny. That in percentage terms was a – er – er - a bloody lot. Too much. That's what it was. I was reduced to penury in one 'foul' swoop. Zonck! Cop fer that. Ouch!

"Thar's ninepence fer yer dinner and a halfpenny if yer need to catch the bus for any reason." said she. Wow! A full halfpenny for emergencies. I'll go t' foot of ower stairs. And here's me thinking she was tight-fisted!

"But -." And that was as far as I got. The look that shot forth as I opened my mouth put paid to any further discussion on the subject.

School dinner. Something I hadn't attempted since my first year term. I had an aversion to being slowly poisoned. So that was a non-starter. The dining 'Hall' was in effect two classrooms with the room divider removed and seated barely two hundred at most. I had broached the puzzling question to Prof. Brown one of the 'maths' teachers, (we called him 'Buzzer'), he was eccentric or to put it more succinctly, stark raving bonkers.

"What would you do sir, if everybody in the school wanted a school dinner on the same day?" He sighted me over the rims of his wire spectacles and pouted his lips in a quizzical oval shape.

"Ooooooo! Well! I suppose we would first throw out your mouth boy to make more roooooom. Then -? Hm! - Then we would send for a team of psychoanalysts to vet each pupil for the cause of the insanity epidemic. You peripatetic orb." He was spot on with most of that one. No-one in their right mind would have taken on a regular diet of ower school dinners. They were dreadful. Absolutely dreadful.

No I can't leave it at that. They were victims of some unsocial abuse. Whoever was in charge of their preparation should have been taken away and shot, or at the very least given 'life' in some foreign 'jungle' prison. I'm sure when the ingredients left the fields they were recognisable. The same cannot be said when they arrived on ower plates. God what a mess. Do you know what happens to sago pudding when half a hundredweight of blackcurrant jam is added? The mere sight is enough to make one vomit. Anyway. To go on. I was being 'docked'. Not a very satisfactory state of affairs and the reason I now needed to find other ways to supplement my now, meagre, daily allowances.

I earned two pounds from my 'job' at the butchers. This princely sum was scooped from my hands by ower mum almost immediately upon receipt. I was then given my 'spence', a nominal ten shillings in return, to 'fritter' away with gay abandonment at my leisure on whatever took my fancy. It wasn't in my opinion, a reasonable return, a fact I remember once have the temerity to voice openly. She who must be obeyed pulled me to one side, by my earlobe, and went to great pains, I know because I was the one in great pain, to explain to me the household's present circumstances and that as 'number one' son had 'chosen' to stay on at school, we, those of the 'working' fraternity must make greater strides and sacrifices. I know where I would have liked to 'stride' and who at that particular moment I wanted to 'sacrifice' and it wasn't me. But that's the way it was. 'Mugging' I think they call it in today's parlance. But quite legal then!

'Rock Around the Clock'. The name of the main feature at the Regal Cinema. Bill Hayley and The Comets. An American 'rock' band and very popular with all us budding 'males'. The place was heaving. In fact it was jumping. How the 'aircraft hanger' ceiling stayed in place I will never know. I half expected something to 'give' with almost the whole of the audience out in the aisles 'jiving' away like demented North American Indians on a whisky binge. The walls were rocking.
A 'sea-change' had occurred. From the 'forties' Vera Lynn war songs and the crooning wail of the Dickie Valentine love ballads a new and totally different musical sound had hit ower town.

Rock and Roll. Johnnie Ray, deaf as a post, so were we after listening to him, but 'boy' could he belt it out. Eddie Cochran, Elvis Presley – in time to become the King of Rock and Roll and many others including Bill Hayley's Rocking Riots (Comets). For that is what happened the first night when three-quarters of the town's teenage population stormed the 'Regal' cinema foyer in a bid to see their idols and were refused admission. It was standing room only. For everybody. About three thousand managed to get inside with the rest, another ten thousand, ripping the signs off the bus shelters and tossing them at the cinema doors in growing frustration. The town police were called -.

- - They were called pigs, Nazi's, blue-bottled t- - - 's, fuzz bearded ar - -h - - - s. In fact they were called more names that night than I had been privy to in all my young years in the town. They were not amused. I can't say that I blame them. It really was awful language. And who likes having litter bins thrown at them. Nobody in their right mind. Mind you, we didn't consider anyone in his right mind joined the police force in the first place so perhaps that explains that? Ower Kid got nabbed. One of the cinema ushers accused him of assault with intent to occasion actual bodily harm. Ower Kid had hit him with a 'pole', so the police report said. The 'pole' in question turned out to be the usher himself when later questioned at the police station. He was from Warsaw, could barely speak English and hadn't a clue who had hit him with the cinema seat and had consequently just pointed at the first two 'lads' he saw when he came 'round'. Ower Kid and his illustrious mate 'Hoggy', (so called for his name was Hodgkinson and he reminded us of an hedgehog). The groan that escaped the Station Sergeant's lips when this became known was sufficient in itself. Ower Kid and the illustrious Hoggy walked free. But not without a body full of bruises from the previous hours in the cells.

It didn't do to end up in the cells without witnesses. Anything could happen and quite often did. But it was pointless making a complaint. Nobody cared. The old woman just said "And what was you doing being there in the first place?" Which didn't really answer anything and certainly didn't enhance ower respect for the law or its well - recompensed much over-rated servants.

But that was the way it was in them days. Nobody wanted the hassle for a few bruises. You had to be 'killed' first. Then they had to take some notice because there had to be an inquiry and the coroner had to be called. "Eh by gum and what's occurring 'ere then -? Is it serious -? Yon fella dead then is he -? Eh by gum. Can't be doin' wi' that tha' knows. Messes up the place. Couldn't you have taken him across the boundary an' dropped him in Owdham. I wus goin' t' Bingo. Wife's not happy tha knows. Not 'appy at all.

It was following this 'town centre riot', as the press referred to it, that the powers that be, in effect, the local council, decided in their infinite wisdom to make some provisions for the 'youth' of the town and remove them from the streets for the rate payers protection. 'We shall build a network of 'clubs for the young adolescents' and guide them on the paths of righteousness, for ower own sakes.' And so that was decided upon forthwith. Sure enough over the next twelve months a number of these 'Youth Clubs' sprang up in the most strangest of places. Generally miles from any decent bus-route and not within rocket distance of a decent pub. Thousands of the town's kids attended these 'establishments' and stayed just long enough to leave again quicker than they had arrived. I'm not one to 'knock' the efforts of others just for the sake of it but whoever organised this 'debacle' of 'good intent' had the brain of a pigeon but obviously thought they flew backwards. Rules and regulations are not the most sought after desire of the young 'adolescent' and to be told (a) one must 'join' and become a 'member', (b) no 'music' to be brought onto the premises, (c) no alcohol allowed or consumed beforehand, (d) no dancing, (e) no fraternising with the opposite sex, was NOT repeat NOT a recipe for success.

'Well what can we do then?' 'Oh lots of interesting things. We have basket ball, billiards, tennis, football, cricket nets, chess, ping-pong.' There was an awful lot of balls involved but nothing a genuine street-wise adolescent would look twice at. The average twelve to sixteen year old was interested in the opposite sex (or the same whatever your preference), dancing, listening to his/her music, drinking (whether soft or hard) and generally 'pea/hen cocking' (showing off one's individuality).

None of which was possible at one of these well intentioned 'youth clubs'.

Needles to say they were a failure and did almost nothing to sweep the streets of the 'undesirables'. Or to put it more plainly – we of the long hair and loud clothing. And so (surprisingly) it was back to the drawing board to try again - .

'Au God tha' gift ta gi' us ta see oerselves as others see us'.

"So I hit him -." The front row of boys looked at me in astonishment. There was a pause before the cheer went up. Three lads from the second row got up and chanced their arm at a kind of 'Dervish' jig. Suddenly the room was a buzz of whispering conversations. 'Chinny' had yet to return. But none of the class were taking chances. The buzz died down to a feint murmur as I ambled quite peacefully to look out of the classroom windows and up towards the Gothic spire of the town hall clock. He, Chinny, was coming back with the headmaster. He could have been coming back with a brigade of the Coldstream Guards for all I cared. I was well passed caring by now.

It had begun some weeks previously. In fact some months if the truth was known. I was three months away from my fifteenth birthday. The legal minimum age limit for leaving school was fifteen. However. Due to my old woman's 'insistence' that I become academically intelligent and having gained a place at ower illustrious school the rules here restricted pupils leaving before their sixteenth birthday without the payment of a large termination fee. I assume this 'contract' of sorts was to encourage pupils to continue with their education to acquire higher grades, G.C.Es. (General Certificates of Education) and to ensure the higher funding given to these schools was not wasted. In ower town, only four schools received these levels of funding. The remainder, the Secondary Schools, were considered to be one step up from Reform Schools and it was in these that three-quarters of my generation were allowed to languish before being shooed out into the multitude of 'unskilled' jobs that were still available in those days. We won't talk about 'class', for even a dossier full of 'O' or 'A' levels from a pupil from any of these four schools wouldn't get you passed the doorman at a Civil Service Office.

The accent was wrong for a start. But I had no intention of 'staying' at this 'place' any longer than was absolutely necessary and had saved up the 'termination' fees in lieu of the 'big' day. The old woman wasn't pleased. But even she eventually could see the 'pointlessness' of it all. I had no intention of learning any more from people I considered had little to do with teaching and more to do with 'going through the motions'. I had a good job waiting in the wings and had been spending more and more time at the 'abattoir' and the home of the local meat inspector who was teaching me the rudiments of the trade. I was ready to accept the mantle of one of the 'workers'; school was just getting in the way. And I wanted out -.

It originated from the 'Potting Room' Incident. A very famous tale that has since been recounted elsewhere. But for those not acquainted, the 'Art' Mistress was a 'cracker'. And no it's not true I 'tailed' her across the potting wheel. Regardless of the rumours abound at the time. It had nothing to do with sexual encounters – so if that's put you off turn over the page.

Miss Barnes was a 'temporary' teacher. Doing a stint between teachers training college and a probationary teaching post somewhere in Manchester, at a 'real' school, so she informed me. I knew what she meant. To say that to a fourteen-year-old she was as fit as a butcher's bitch was a grave understatement. She was loaded. Boy was she loaded. But as always it was in 'my dreams' young man. You can look but don't touch. Wasn't that always the way of things?
Gosh I didn't half 'fancy' her. There were times my 'art' work suffered greatly as I spent most of the lessons beating down the sentinel snake banging about in my underpants. I got some knowing smirks from others around who were having the same problems. But it paid one very remunerative dividend.
Because she knew of my 'interest' in her, personally, she proved to be most amenable when it came down to extracting small favours. Like being allowed to use the 'potting room' during the morning and afternoon 'breaks' instead of being slung out into the school yard amongst the other roving hordes of budding academics, or illiterates, depending on which side of the school window panes you were standing. To practise throwing pots, (no not at the wall, throwing the clay onto the wheel and moulding pottery). Fortunately she never ventured into the 'potting room' during these interludes.

If she had, she would have found the blackboard with the horse's names and that days odds displayed prominently on the wall alongside in green chalk. It was another way of getting the lads to put a few shillings into my now depleted coffers. Until Bernie Ratigan lost one shilling and two pence on some three-legged nag at Haddock and grumbled that much about it he was overheard by one of the teachers. So that was six of the best. 'Don't' Gamble on school premises - unless the teachers are in on it. It was this punishment started the ball rolling.

There was six weeks before the next mid-term break. I decided I was going to take the 'break' early, make it eight weeks instead of two. I was into the fifth week of my 'French leave' and arrived home at the usual time of seven-o-clock to the smiling face of the old woman. I knew instantly I was in trouble. That smile always suppressed a budding magna flow, a veritable torrent of flailing talons, flashing red tinged eyes and verbose dialectic curses. In other words – she was about to lose her 'rag'. Upps!

"Good day at school today -?" she crooned maliciously.
To answer 'Yes' would have provoked a swingeing right hook. To answer 'No I didn't go', and I might get off with a mild crushing of the windpipe. But I was getting fed up with all the violence and hassle. I threw caution to the winds.

"No. I haven't been to school for the last couple of weeks." I replied. It wasn't the full truth. That's why I still got the swingeing right hook.

"Four weeks yer bloody liar. Four bloody weeks so they tell me -."

I was grounded. No going out after school and finishing work, for two weeks. The following day it was directly to the Headmaster's Study and don't go past go. It was unavoidable because the old woman had me tightly pinioned to her wrist by the scruff of the neck and was frog marching me at the time.
There followed a lengthy discussion, the old woman, the headmaster, the old woman, the headmaster. I might as well not have been there. Only neither of them thought that a wise decision at all.
After the old woman left I was given twelve of the best and threatened in no uncertain terms that another episode of similar misbehaviour would result in my expulsion from the school. And that is what annoyed me.

The headmaster had promised me the 'last' time I played truant that he would expel me this time.

Not next time! Had he forgotten? I lost no time in hopefully reminding him of his previous promise then fled as his face went a dark purple and his body swayed drunkenly in my direction. After all had he keeled over with a heart attack I would most definitely have got the blame.

"It's that skinny blonde haired smart-Alec from 4c – what the devil is he called -?"

"Atilla?"

"Eh? Yea. That's the one – King bloody Chaos. Gobby little wretch!"

So, with yet another broken promise from the top honcho of our academic souls I launched myself into a period of non-conformity, or to be more precise, I upt- the anti-. I hadn't been a conformist since year three, ever since ower illustrious PE teacher had used my head for bouncing his medicine balls on. I had a headache that time for three days. Seriously. But that's just one other story I missed out previously.

Ower form master this, my last term, was Slim (he with the misguided aim) Fielding. I have spoken of him before. He made a lasting impression on me by shredding his cane in a dozen pieces on the back and sides of my head. I can't even remember now, why? But the scar tissue on the back of my head is still there fifty years on. He used a board duster to staunch the seeping wound before wiping the blackboard with half a gallon of my body fluids and cursing me for the inconvenience. Very strange behaviour if you ask me.

"You have no lock on your desk boy. WHY?"

"There's nowt in it worth nicking sir." I ventured in reply. CRACK!

"You have your school books in there -!"

"Yea. Like I said sir. Nowt worth nickin'." CRACK!

"Tomorrow there will be a lock on your desk boy-." CRACK. "Do you understand boy." Smack! A final tap with the thin bony palm and now I'm deaf in both ears.

"Oh. Yes sir." I hear myself reply somewhere in the middle of my brain.

It's tomorrow   - already.

"You have no lock on your desk boy. WHY?"

I looked at the well-chewed woodwork that held the twisted hasp and staple. The man was right. There was no lock there.

"I have no idea sir." CRACK. Wrong answer.

"I thought I told you to get one put on -."

"No sir. You said there would be one on it tomorrow, which is today sir. But there isn't sir – look -." I was looking at the area around the non-existent lock when the world went into a kaleidoscope of colours and whirling abstracts and an anguished scream rent the dark matter somewhere beyond the edges of my present universe. I don't think ower form master was very pleased with me. Such a shame.

"You're about as much use as a chocolate teapot boy. Get out of my class you cretin. Go and stand by Mr Clegg's form-room." Being sent to stand before Mr Clegg's room was the code for – go away and get a thrashing you moron -. This I knew. For I was privy to all the entire strange goings on in this establishment.

On my way up the flight of stone stairs that led to the 'B' corridor and 'Chinny's' Den, the 'B' corridor cloakrooms, I went over my plan for the coming event. Somewhere from amongst the anger and frustrations whirling around in my youthful brain came the answer. It was quite logical to my way of thinking and might just mitigate the punishment I knew was coming. Who's to say I could afford the money to buy myself a new padlock for my desk – Hmm? What am I. Rothschild? I wasn't on a teacher's salary. In fact I could pretend that I wasn't earning money at all. Should he remember one previous occasion when we had discussed at length my various 'modes of employment' I could always claim having been 'fired'. 'Chinny' wouldn't know that – or would he? It was weak, the excuse, but I wasn't really caring. I decided I would allow him four strokes. After that -.

There isn't a doubt but that I have some of the old woman in me. Not the academic side more a propensity towards parameters. I have always been one for drawing lines in the sand across which others must never step. Not that I have ever thought out what I would do if they did. And it's that small matter that makes all the difference. He reached stroke four. My excuse of not having the money had no influence whatsoever on this chisel faced little man who stood a good six inches smaller than yours truly and squeaked himself up on tiptoe every time he raised the cane skywards to deal a blow.

"What! The 'Fagin of 4c' no money. Pull the other one boy. It's got bells on it."

"Right hand." he squeaked again. I'm afraid I looked at him and remembered my promise I had made myself. My right hand remained raised but with the fingers clenched tightly shut.

"Open your fingers -." he sang, quite unperturbed and definitely unsuspecting. The fingers remained clenched. He looked at me. It was the first time he had bothered to do so since the thrashing began.

"I said – Open your fingers. I can't cane you with your hand like that." I looked at him in disbelief. Why not? It wouldn't have been the first time it had been done across the knuckles. But it wasn't that fact which surprised me. What surprised me was he hadn't realised that I had no intention of opening my fingers. My temper had been slowly rising since I first set eyes on him in the corridor and his sneering greeting of -. "Hmmph. You again. What have you been up to this time." I was aware that my episode of painting the 'Boys Grammar School' and the schools inability to prove it was me was a festering sore in the sides of the schools authorities. I also suspect that it was with this in mind that produced the dislike a number of them had for me. But hey. Come on chaps. You can't have it all your own way!

He tapped the cane across the knuckles then, when that produced no movement, raised it and flicked it savagely across my face. I'm afraid that was it. God - that stung! The line in the sand disappeared in a surge of red mist. I remember launching myself at him with my hands raised in a claw like fashion, his body hitting the cloakroom wall and a tearing noise as the collar of his tweed jacket ripped apart on one of the metal coat-hooks. He said I lifted him up onto the coat hooks on purpose and that I hit him. I don't think so. I think that as he fell backwards, in astonishment, he flung his arms backwards and upwards and that it was this singular movement that hung him from the coat-hooks. Furthermore, I did not hit him. I went for him and sort of pushed him. Well that's my story and I'm sticking to it. He was not a happy-bunny when he finally found the rent in his collar. He was ever so slightly miffed. But that was the end of the proceedings. One look at my scowl, which I have to say, is very similar to that of ower old woman's, and he knew better than to push it any more.

"Wait in my form room." he commanded. "We will see about this."

I was still looking up at the town hall clock when the headmaster appeared followed closely by his raggy-jacketed minion. The form room went quiet. The 'boys' of 5a held their breath. What on earth was going to happen now? No one had 'chinned' ower 'Chinny' before, well not in ower living memory. Mr Lewis moved across the wooden parquet floor almost sloth like. His tread making no sound on the worn wooden blocks. I turned. He stopped. We looked each other up and down. He of the fifty-five years, grey moustache and almost white swept-back hair, me of the almost fifteen years, thin, pale and now having replaced my scowl at the sight of the grinning dwarf jigging in anticipation to his masters rear. I felt like I wanted to get at him again. Four years he and his kind had tormented the life out of me but now, now I no longer cared.

It seemed also neither did ower headmaster.

"When are you leaving us boy?" he asked, knowing full well I had put in my papers and paid the termination fees the month previously.

"End of term sir." I replied. Biting back the urge to add, 'but it's not soon enough.'

The Headmaster nodded. Gave me an almost quizzical smile. Coughed gently and turned away.

"That will do for today I think Mr Clegg. Let's get on. Shall we?"

The deputy headmaster's grin dropped away like a slab of heavy concrete. He had at the very least expected me to be expelled or put in the stocks or the gallows or at least something very, very nasty. And here was his superior telling him enough was enough. Do you know something? I couldn't have agreed more. For once Mr Lewis and I had something in common – a little bit of sanity prevailing. God that there could have been more. What a massive world of difference it would have made all around.

And then there was 'potting' of another kind.

I haven't yet worked out if it was Ower Kids' idea. You know the kind of thing. Big brother showing off to little brother – hey up, look what I can do. Or if it was one of Ower Kid's mates who suggested it.

We arrived in the bleakness of the West Yorkshire moorlands one Saturday morning in the back of a green Austin van looking like aliens from another planet.

"Yer gonna need some old clothes." said the team leader. That wasn't much of a problem. Even new clothes looked liked hand-me-downs once draped over my skeletal frame. "We'll supply the rest." The 'rest' turned out to be a pit helmet that fitted my fleshless skull like a large coal bucket and a pair of 'hiking' boots that had seen much bigger feet.

"Wis goin' pottin'." Ower Kid had said.

"Why?" said I. Thinking of revolving wheels and large lumps of soggy earth?

"'Cause wis a 'Rescue' team that's what wi do," he replied, a scornful look etching a course slowly across his face. I remember saying, "Can I come?" and expecting the usual "Get knotted." But instead he replied that he would have to ask the 'team'. I thought no more about it until the Friday night when following a scuffle on the cellar stairs he snarled. "Any more crap and yer won't be bloody comin' tomorrow -."

The moor was covered in a deep layer of frozen snow. I remember getting out of the van and feeling both my legs stiffen like beanpoles. Having a distinct absence of body fat sub-zero temperature was not on my list of creature comforts. I felt my testicles retreat up into my groin and thought I was in for an unexpected sexual treat. No such luck. They knew perfectly well what they were doing, even if the rest of me didn't. Bugger that for a tale they motioned as they disappeared in the direction of my kidneys.

"Reet. Gather round." growled Mustoe, him being the leader of the pack. We shuffled into a circle and tried to appear intelligent. Somehow I managed to get jostled into the middle. It was warmer there.

"First off wis going t' ferckle the initial crawl, then down wi' ropes to the first thingy and then there's a wire wotsit, down that and then it's a belly squirm before wi come out onto yon oujarcapivvy and from there there's water up to yer watsits for about half a mile. The rest I can tell yer later." I know I should have said "Pardon?" Or words to that effect. I hadn't understood a word he had said. Not that it mattered.

"Hey young Atlas. You follow your kid." Ower Kid glared at me and that was that.

The 'pothole' went by the name of 'Alum Pot' and, as I discovered some time later, was part of the 'Gaping Gill' complex of underground caves that stretched for miles across the Yorkshire Moors. They are not for the uninitiated and have been known to claim the life of many an amateur potholer over the years. And 'I' was going down them -! But nobody mentioned this at the time.

I was soon sweating like a stallion on a promise. The narrow funnels and crawls of damp rock hugged and buffeted the body as we snaked slowly downwards towards the first 'pitch'. From the dull yellow light of my miners lamp, fuelled by a huge six volt battery dangling in the space below waist level usually reserved for something else, the furthest ones eyes pierced the gloom was about ten yards. Which was just as well as I grasped the rope and began to descend into the dark. Slowly hand over hand I descended and descended and descended. It was only after about five minutes that I began to realise we were journeying into the centre of the earth. Had someone said the first descent was five hundred feet with no safety net and if you let go you will die I might have volunteered to stay with the equipment, in the van.

I reached the bottom to be met with Ower Kids smirking features.

"Just a little one," he grinned sarcastically. "Yes you have." I felt like replying, "And I know 'cause I've seen it." But I didn't. Team Leader Mustoe wouldn't have taken kindly to his 'men' scrapping like demented school kids in the bowels of the earth. We moved on.

The next 'pitch' was by an 'elektron' a wire ladder. A far safer method if you ask me, then off along a 'crawl' half full of mud and water to our next 'port of call'. I say 'port' because all I could see in front of us was a never ending stretch of water and what I thought at first might have been large black salmon bobbing up and down in the water.

"Where's the boat?" I asked expectantly.

Nobody took the bait. Least of all the 'black salmon' who it turned out were three men in wet suits, either that or they were wearing those close fitting black tights. – Well you never knew in those days -?

The water only came up to our necks. I could see the look of disappointment on Ower Kids' face as I tried to smile against the flow of muddy detritus seeping into my mouth.

This went on forever. Like a huge anaconda we snaked towards the far darkness, yours truly hinged in the middle with Ower Kid and one of his mates dragging me up by the scruff of the neck every time I sank beneath the folding waves created by those who had gone before. By now my boots were so heavy I felt like a deep-sea diver plodding the seabed. It should be remembered I weighed considerably less than a bag of potatoes and was prone to getting washed away by the slightest of swells. Eventually we made wet land; there was no dry land here. Hard certainly, but not dry.

"Halt." cried Mustoe, fumbling in his breast pocket for the 'map'. MAP! Now he shows us he doesn't know where we are -! I had assumed this 'rescue team' was conversant with these 'caves' into which we had entered with such gay abandon! Now we are looking at a 'Map'!

Never trust anyone who tells you he is a 'professional'. Lesson for this day. If he says he knows, check his credentials and then get a second opinion.

"I think we are here. Station 3."

I look around for a sign bearing the letter '3'. Nothing. I can't even see a platform let alone a signboard.

"There's a funnel somewhere here abouts." Mustoe declared with the confidence only someone of high intellect could muster. I frowned. I was beginning to worry the folly of putting myself in the hands of these, Ower Kids, mates. Maps. Now funnels. A steamboat perhaps? Couldn't possibly be a train, not down here – could it!

The 'funnel' turned out to be a vertical climb of a few metres that should have been accomplished by 'crabbing' ones way up it. As I only had four limbs and not six they resorted to pulling my meagre six stone up the narrow tube on the end of a rope. I emerged through the neck of the opening into a large humongous 'gallery' dotted with thick columns of fused stalactite and stalagmite formations shaped by the granite rocks never ending filtration of the moorland surface water high up above our heads.. By the light thrown off of our half a dozen lamps and the odd carbide fuelled mirror-light the place looked like something from the imagination of Tolkien's 'Lord of the Rings'. It was indeed breathtakingly awesome.

"OK. There's a 'siphon' next but before that it's 'smoko time' fer them us needs it." Ower illustrious leader was a non-smoker himself, him being of the 'early' clean environmentalist type. I think he was a vegetarian as well. Other than that he appeared quite normal, give or take his map reading skills.

Mustoe knew it was essential to give the smokers a quick 'drag' otherwise nerves tended to fracture and that wasn't good three hundred feet below ground. A 'siphon' eh! Hmm! What the hell is one of them? Whatever it was it was going to be as unpleasant as all the rest of them, that's for sure, I thought!

We emerged into a late afternoon sky some three hours later. The cloud cover had fallen; well collapsed might be a better description. It lay on the ground about six inches above our feet and whispered around looking for something tangible to come to grips with. The temperature had dropped too. I was soaked to the skin. I suppose so too was everyone else but they all had a layer or more of body fat to help keep out the chilling cold.

"So that's agreed then is it?" Mustoe counted hands. Everybody raised a hand so I did to. "Good. I will go down first. If I can find a way to climb I will signal with the rope. One tug for 'yes' two tugs for 'no'. Everybody clear." There was a mumble of agreement. To be truthful I hadn't a clue what the vote had been about. I was too busy trying to keep my teeth inside my mouth. My jaw was vibrating like a demented woodpecker on 'speed'. God was I cold. My fingers had begun to turn blue and my nose, the most prominent part of my anatomy – well most of the time, a darker shade of black. Slowly and with great care ower leader began to descend down and along the surface of a frozen waterfall. I gasped. One slip and it would be 'farewell Vienna'. For some obscure reason the rest of us held the rope now attached around the boy's middle. I didn't, although I was supposed to be, mainly because I couldn't feel the dam rope never mind grip it.

"What the 'ell is he doin'?" I wheezed to Ower Kid.

"Lookin' fer a new way in." was the reply I got.

"What, down a solid ice sheet to nowhere? Is he a fuckin' lunatic?" I'm afraid I couldn't help myself for apparently this 'entrance' was not recognised as such and most certainly didn't appear on the 'map'.

I can't say my outburst made all that much difference. It's doubtful anyone present would have cared what the 'sprogg' had to say. But only moments later, and after a 'bollocking' from Ower Kid for not holding the rope properly, ower illustrious leader thought better of the 'folly' and clawed his way back to the rim of the 'pot' where thankfully it was decided we should 'call it a day'.

Personally it felt like a 'fortnight'. I was thoroughly soaked, thoroughly frozen, thoroughly knackered and thoroughly determined never to go on the moors with this bunch of lunatics ever again. 'Pottin' indeed! Should have been turned over to the local S&M Club for inclusion in their nightly programmes if you ask me -?

'West Yorkshire Moors' 1958.

And a 'potting' we did go. Alum Pot 1958. 'Ower Kid' searches for a helmet small enough to fit me. No chance 'brother dear'.

Note the snow in the background and the sexy motor with the 'nick as much as yer want petrol cap' fitted to the top of the boot. – Groovy.

Subsidence, Sex and Snooker.

Ower house, as I've said previously, stood atop the canal locks on the main road to Manchester. It was a pre Crimean War stone terrace whose stones had now turned black with industrial grime and whose roof of heavy flat grey slate sagged dangerously inward under the ponderous weight on the ageing oak beams. Two storeys at the front, three at the back and with a brick extension annex forming a 'T' shape, which held the majority of the extra rooms, added to the original building. The 'extension', probably erected around the end of the First World War.

Ower Kid and me slept in the back bedroom in the original part of the house with ower slanting sash window overlooking the lock. The noise was tremendous with the falling water rushing over the permanently closed lock gates. I say permanently because the last time anyone had opened them had to have been in the 1920s at around the time the mills ceased sending their cotton wares by canal boat and began instead to choke ower valley's fair roads with their fleets of diesel billowing motor-wagons.

We became acclimatised to the house 'moving'. The canal bridge over which ran the main road was less than ten yards from ower front door. Whenever a wagon or a double-decker bus hit the bridge, and by that I mean drove over it, the ground shuddered like a mini-earthquake. We had learned to put the crockery in the kitchen cupboards leaving a full inch gap between the piles. Otherwise everything came out chipped.

In the middle of my dream, she was just about to whip off her knickers, the whole bed shuddered and leapt across the bedroom. I remember it was a 'Rumble – Thud – Rumble – Crack! I whipped back the bed sheet and sat bolt upright. That was no bus. It had to have been a 'tank' or something much larger. Ower Kid, who it has to be said was less aware of 'things that went bump in the night' than yours truly, also stirred and struggled up on one elbow.

"Fer fuck's sake. What's the matter wi' yer? Go play with yerself will yer – and move yer bloody bed away from mine – Pillock!" And with that went back to sleep. I looked around. That was no ordinary nocturnal event. I listened. Suddenly there came a sound of movement from the direction of the window. A rattling sound followed by a hollow thump. Throwing caution to the wind and ignoring for once the icy cold linoleum I swung out of bed and went to the window. The annex had disappeared. All I could see was a furling cloud of dust that billowed against the wet glass covering the whole with an opaque sheen.

"Hey! Kiddo! Hey. Bugger me!" I called.
A snort came from under Ower Kids bedclothes and a mumbled, "You'll be bloody lucky. Piss off," erupted from within.

"No. I'm serious! Look at this! The bloody house has fell down. Look!"

"What! What the heck are yer going on about yer twat?" I stood at the window looking out at the slowly descending yellow cloud of mortar dust and debris that was becoming ever so slowly less dense.

"The bloody house has fallen down I'm telling yer. Come and look fer yerself if yer don't believe me -.!" I yelled back irritably.

Now I know ower bedroom was in the house and that was still standing so it wasn't that much of a surprise Ower Kid didn't believe me, not that he ever did most times anyway. But I knew what I thought I was seeing was the genuine article. That was no earthquake, that was ower house, collapsing, falling down, splat, on the deck, not there any more, gone, Puff! With that ower bedroom door opened and the old woman is standing there arms folded defiantly across her large bosom.

"What the bloody 'ells going on now?" she crooned sweetly, no that's a lie, she didn't at all. Boy was she in a mood. That scowl was reserved for 'hanging' offences. I took one look and immediately –

"It wasn't me mum HONEST!"

We surveyed the damage from ground level. It was about four-o-clock in the morning and the dawn was but a glimmer on the far horizon above the distant mountains. Ower house was still standing – just.
Tacked on to the end of our living accommodation was a double storey workshop and garage – only it wasn't tacked on any more. The 'tacks' had gone, in the night, whoosh! Now it was on the deck.

Reminding everyone present of scenes from the Manchester 'Blitz'. A huge mountain of bricks with the odd oak beam jutting sideways from within. The owner of the garage, ower next door neighbour, stood staring at the 'mound' his peaked night-cap with roving bobbin flapping agitatedly to and fro across his dust-speckled face.

"My car's under there. And the wife's anniversary present. She'll go 'spare'." For a moment I felt like saying 'Don't tell her then.' But this wasn't just some small occurrence. Half the passage way and yard areas were impassable unless one was a mole. Even a diminutive Welsh miner, and I knew of at least one, would have had a mornings work tunnelling through the chaos that lay on all sides.

"That's a bit of a mess that." said the old fella, never one for the over-statement. "Dus't have any insurance lad?" Ower neighbour, who went by the name of Horace, looked at the old fella as if he wasn't right in his head.

"Insurance. Bloody insurance -." We all stared aghast. Horace didn't swear. Not ever had any one of us heard a bad word pass from between his lips. "Who in the right mind would insure this lot of rubbish?" he whined plaintively. "They'd have to be out of their heads." Which prompted a thought in my mind as to why he had risked putting his car in it in the first place, knowing it wasn't in tiptop condition, so to speak?

"What sort of car is it?" asked the old fella.

"Fucked." offered Ower Kid in a low murmur hoping Horace hadn't heard him.

"It's a Wartburg." said Horace.

"Pardon?" replied the old man. "Tha what?"

"A Wartburg."

"What's one of them?"

"A car. They come from Czechoslovakia. Iron-bloc." replied Horace, (he had meant to say Iron Curtain). The old man adjusted his cap and scratched at his forehead.

"It makes no difference what the blocks made of mate, it'll need to be made of more than bloody iron under all that lot -." Horace looked at him sideways and mooned both eyes. This wasn't just an inconvenience this was a disaster, and still in the making!

It was the weight of the grey slate. Grey slate by the way isn't made of slate. It's thinly cut Yorkshire stone.

Usually about half an inch thick and it weighs a ton per slate sometimes, well perhaps not that much but it's not light any-road. The wall-plates had succumbed pushing the brickwork outwards whilst the roof had collapsed inwards like an express train. Whoosh. I had heard the 'whoosh' and I was mightily impressed. I thought it was a German land mine going off. Not that I had ever heard a German land mine go off. But you can imagine it can't you. Whoosh! Then silence. Because the explosion has made you deaf. If it hasn't killed you in the first place. Anyway. Like I said, it was a mess and Horace was in no mood for smart-Alec remarks from useless teenagers.

We weren't so useless when it came to removing most of the rubble from the yard so we could get to ower back doors. No. See? Not so useless now Horace? Eh?

The Captain wasn't impressed. In fact the Captain was never impressed with anything 'civilian'. He lived next door but three to the right where he 'ran' his 'woollen shop'. Captain Lawson. He wasn't a mister.

"The names Captain Lawson to you boy. I didn't get to be where I am today by having plebeians call me 'mister'. Captain." He tapped his shoulders with his metre rule.

"Didn't get these for nothing you know boy." I looked at his shoulders and frowned.

"Why, what did yer have to pay for them?" I asked curiously. I glanced at my own shoulders. I got mine fer nowt. Or at least the old woman hadn't mentioned anything. The Captain looked me over trying to ascertain if I really was that 'thick'.

"They had to earned laddie. Hard graft. Teaching boys like you to be men. Hard men. Soldiers. You get my drift laddie – Eh?"

I got his drift all right. Another arsehole. Chances were he had never been near the 'front' in his life. And if he had it was the 'front' of the queue when they were handing out 'creep' medals. God! These people were everywhere?

"Can't be doing with all this mess on my lawn laddie." The Captain pointed at the heap of rubble spreading outwards from the huge mound of brickwork from Horace's 'folly'.

"Well I didn't put it there -." I replied huffily. Typical. Something wrong, blame yours truly.

"Don't care how it got there laddie. Move it." the Captain bellowed. I surveyed the small area of lawn now buried three feet deep in brickbats. I noticed the metre rule he was carrying in his hand.

"Is that a measuring stick tha's got there?" I asked innocently. The Captain took a step backwards and brought the ruler up to eye level. "Yes laddie. I do believe it is. Measure's exactly one metre or three feet and one quarter on the reverse."

"Dus't think yer could measure one of them full size bricks for me then -?" The Captain looked surprised but seeing nothing wrong with my request bent forward from the waist and placed the ruler along one of the bricks.

"Nine inches by – four and one quarter inches by – two and one half inches exactly laddie." he sniffed, pleased with his performance.

"Very good. You should be able to get a full one in that mouth of yours then shouldn't yer." I snapped sarcastically. Then I went like a bullet over the monstrous pile of debris for the safety of ower yard. Selfish swine. He was the sort who wouldn't see a person starve to death. He would just shut his eyes. Hard faced bugger!

Ower house fell down. Ower bedroom stood just behind the remains of the single stack chimney to the right in the picture above.

Ower yard after the collapse of the end of Ower house. That bloke on the left bum to bum with yours truly is known to me. Otherwise I don't think my posture would have been so relaxed. Well yer never know d' yer -!

'4C' -Form-room. Ower School.

There was a buzz of excitement running up and down the raised steps of the form room. Ower 'form room' was the only one in the school to house tiered levels. Like one might find in a large lecture hall. I suspect we of the '4c' had been given this room in order that each and every single one of us could be instantly seen from the point of view of the teacher far below. A particularly insidious practice if you ask me. Not a level playing field in today's parlance. We, the pupils, were at a distinct disadvantage and with 'Slim Fielding's' dubious eyesight almost anyone could get accused, sentenced and flogged for even the most innocuous of physical movements. Like blowing one's nose.

"I saw you Butterworth. Smacking your papers on Whittaker's head. Have you nothing else better to do boy? Get on with your work you idle wretch -."

"But I was blowing my nose sir."

"Don't you argue with me. Get down here NOW -." THUMP. CRACK. WHALLOP. "Now get back to your desk. Impertinent wretch." Butterworth had been blowing his nose, but it didn't matter. He had come under the gaze of the avenging angel Saint Retribution, the guiding saint of lower grade teachers, better known as budding aspiring 'wannabe's'. There was no escape from them once your card had been marked.

So what was all the excitement about. 'Nature' classes. Oooooo!

"Err. What's them when wis all at 'ome?" asked Simpkin's. 'Simmy' wasn't the shiniest spoon in the cutlery drawer. Then again he wasn't the dullest either. It was just that sometimes he tended to miss the point, especially if he came in half way through the conversation. But he was game for a laugh and could be relied upon to try the patience of a saint, which in this case was just what we needed.

"Sex." said Turnip. Simmy's eyes lit up like two Belisha beacons.

"Oooo. Sounds great. When d' they start?"

"We don't know. That's the problem. Somebody needs to ask Slim." replied Turnip in all seriousness.

"Oh! Hmm. Who's going t' ask him then?" Simmy looked around ower sea of faces. Nobody spoke.

"Somebody will have t' ask him wont they otherwise we can't put it on ower 'period' lists can we?" Nobody spoke. The die had been cast. 'Snowcap' (Mark Heywood by name) was 'Simmy's mate and the two were very well known for some of their more 'outrageous' pranks.

"I suggest we toss for it."
We tossed and 'Simmy' lost. 'Snowcap was using his 'double-headed' coin again. 'Simmy' never knew his best friend had the 'coin' in all the years I knew them both. It was the two of them who had filled 'Chinny's' car with half a ton of hardcore whilst it lay parked up alongside the playing fields one day. Ower illustrious deputy headmaster was not amused and threatened all kinds of 'whackitus' on the culprits should they ever be exposed. Nobody took up the 'reward' offer to be made up to a 'Prefect'. 'Prefect' (otherwise known as 'snitchers') badges, were two a penny. And who in their right mind wanted to be permanently despised by the rest of the pupils anyway?

And so it was that 'Simmy' ventured forth into the jaws of the beast his young, innocent, uncorrupted body an adjunct for the poisoned saliva and broiling fires that nestled within.

"You blithering cretin -." snarled the Science master his shoulders sagging visibly. "Do you seriously think we would teach you idiots to procreate? Isn't it enough that you lot are here without adding to the problem later on by teaching you lot to 'spawn'! What do you think we are – Lunatics?"
Yes. Would have been my answer. But 'Simmy' hadn't quite figured out why the form master had gone into an epileptic fit when asked the question. "When are we startin' the sex lessons sir?" It might have been the wide grin and the gesticulations 'Simmy' made when broaching the subject that sent the poor chap overboard? Who knows?

It was couple of days later 'Simmy' drew me secretively to one side and said in a low conspiratorial whisper. "What did he mean 'Procreate'?" This might have been the first time I got the inkling of what ower teachers sometimes had to put up with. Not that I was ready then or even now to forgive their mindless reactions.
Nature classes. Nothing more exciting than an addition to the self-same classes we had at ower primary school. Birds, flowers, trees and bees. And that's just what we got.

Text books full of pretty pictures. It later transpired the school authorities had wanted 'Biology' adding to the curriculum. But nobody had wanted to teach the subject for fear of being drawn into the aspect of 'reproduction', a subject some of the more forward thinking of ower society deemed an absolute must to reduce the burgeoning pre-marital, unwanted pregnancies now becoming ever more evident in ower rapidly expanding society. Victorian values were fast melting away. A new dawn had broken over them thar hills. And the 'powers' that be were mightily worried. We never did get 'Biology' or anything like it. With a curriculum already containing twenty subjects it was thought 'impossible' to take on more. The 'Nature class lasted for one term then suddenly disappeared faster than it had arrived. Much to 'Simmy's' disgust. He attended religiously still hoping 'Slim' had been joking. 'Simmy' had a thirst for knowledge little knowing however much he drank from the pool he was destined never to slate it. Like a lot more of us. It didn't go in. It circulated around and around like a London roundabout, round and round and round and spun off drunkenly in some obscure direction never to be seen again. What the good Lord hath determined shall not be – shall not be – regardless of all the good intent.

I had a good record for 'staying' power when it came to the more practical 'hands on' approach to ower curriculum. I completed my 'boomerang' coffee table in under three years in my 'Woodwork' studies. My steel callipers in Engineering in less than four years and my 'collage' for the Art and Crafts remained behind when I finally left. It had taken that long the canvas was rotting away at the seams and the frame had contracted woodworm. But it's the thought that counts. I thought I was wasting my time being there and eventually so too did the teachers. We were all correct. It was about the only thing we all eventually came together in agreement on.

Only I thought of it first. So there!

Dinnertime, (lunchtime if you come from down south) was 'snooker' time. The 'Temperance' Billiard Hall stood less than fifty yards from the side school entrance and it was to this tantalising den of iniquity we would repair for to rid ower bodies of the rigours of the morning's violence induced 'edification'. To immerse ourselves in the game of 'snooker' and its many wondrous variations. As I have already said, we were pretty useless at the game, not that we thought so at the time, but it helped to take us out of ower misery for that short period and stood us in good stead for what was to come later in the day.

Wozzle was reasonable, Turnip passable, yours truly getting there and Seth, absolute crap. Not that he ever let it get him down because as he was often heard to say, 'When it came to balls he could knock the rest of us into a cocked-hat-.' And he was right. I had never seen a fourteen year old with 'balls' as big as his.

Now you might think how did we know that? Well it's simple really. We didn't have any hang-ups where sex was concerned. If the situation warranted we were quite happy to 'prove' ower claims. Seth had maintained he had bigger testicles than the rest of us and so put them on display to prove it. Admittedly it shouldn't have been in the middle of Woolworth's; he could have picked a more 'selective' venue. But at the time he made the claim we was 'shopping'. Not with money you understand. That wasn't the object at all. Anyway be that as it may the proof of the pudding was in the eating. They were huge. God knows how he got them. Turnip was impressed.

"D'yer have any trouble runnin' with them buggers banging about?"

Seth thought for a moment.

"No. Not really. They can be a bit of a nuisance when I'm swimming. Keep draggin' me under-." replied Seth tucking his shirt lap back in and turning to me with a wicked glint in his eye.

It reminded me of the story of Ezra and Clementine and their day by the canal.

(Dear Diary.)

Ezra and Clementine were from Nigeria. They lived on Ramsay Street in a small terraced house and were deeply in love. It was during the summer of '56'. The month of August had suddenly come alive to a scorching heatwave. A very rare occurrence in ower town and one to which the residents had little knowledge of how to respond. Sitting on the front pavement, on a rag-rug, with a knotted handkerchief banded around one's head, a bucket and spade in one hand and an ice cream cornet in the other, went some way towards it but didn't seem quite right somehow. After all there was no sea, no sand and no donkeys. None that the rag and bone man would let you ride anyway! And you couldn't buy a 'kiss me quick' hat for neither love nor money.

So Ezra and Clementine decided they would find a quiet spot and go skinny-dipping.

The nearest water was the river. But it was only four inches deep. So that was out. The 'lido' had closed after the First World War and had no plug in it. So that was out. The Municipal Swimming Baths was closed for the holidays. So that was out. That only left the canal.

Ezra and Clementine arrived on the tow-path of the canal just in time to get a spot mid-way between the lock gates. Anywhere else would have meant removing the rusting prams, bicycles and a multitude of rubbish before attempting to get in the water.

"Er. You know Clem. There is sure an added problem honey" said Ezra.

"Why Ezra sweetheart what do you mean?" replied Clem.

"Well honey, You knows how long I is. If I goes in dat there water and I swims across I wus be dragging weed -."

"Oh Ezra sweetie pie. D'at's alright. You just turn over honey and you swims on yower back."

"Yea. Sure honey. Dat's fine t' begin wi. But what about dem low bridges - huh?"

(Packer Spout 1959.)

Ower Grandma. The old man's old lady. 1960s just before she saved us havin' another party for her 95th birthday. See over.

Ower town centre in the background with the trams tracks, the river and the cobblestones all tarmac'ed over. To hide the history.

Families, Familiarities and Familiars.

The family was organising an eighty-fifth birthday party for Grandma. Nobody had ever lived that long before in ower family so all us 'kids' were sent round to have a look at her. I thought she looked reasonable. A bit tatty here and there and she smelled a bit as well but on the whole not too bad considering she was a 'coffin dodger'. It wasn't that 'old' people were revered in ower family, more astonishment the old beggar had managed to stay alive that long. So it was 'ordained' that Grandma would have a big party every year from now on seeing that we didn't expect she would last much longer. She wasn't ill or anything like that. But we thought she was better not to push her luck – so to speak. Well you never know do you?

"I'm doin' the sausage rolls." said the old woman. "I want ten pounds of sausage meat – lean." So I did. I always did what the old woman commanded. It was safer that way.

"Ten pounds! Who are we feeding, Fred Carno's Army?" I asked in astonishment from my angled position.

"The usual count is about two hundred and twenty. But yer Auntie Lilly's not been feeling too well and your second cousin Billy twice removed has been removed again - by the 'rozzers'. He's doing six months. So that'll bring the tally down a peg er two."

It's true we had a very 'extended' family. They were everywhere. It didn't matter which street one walked down there was bound to be a relation lurking somewhere in the shadows. Not a good idea if one wanted to associate with the 'wrong' kind. Word of your 'indiscretions' travelled fast.

"Who wus that girl you were with last night?"

"What girl?" Here there is a pause whilst the old woman decides if she is going to clout you one or not. Today she decides not.

"Down Charlotte Street. You were seen. Messing about with one of them 'Sidebottoms'. Bad lot them is. Yer stay away from Charlotte Street in future. D'yer hear? Eh?"

"Yes mum."

It was pointless saying otherwise. Even if you did think Gladys Sidebottom had a very nice 'bottom', one you wanted to get both hands around, it was better to drop the whole idea and make for pastures new. Otherwise you could end up not sitting very comfortably on your own 'bottom' for a number of days.

The 'party' went down a treat. We hired the local Conservative Club (as usual), hired a dance trio (as usual) and provided all the 'eats' from within the family regiment. - Well it could hardly be called a circle could it, if we all joined hands and tried that we would have stretched twice around the town boundary and back. Grandma had a 'ball'. Uncle Fred gave it to her to keep her amused whilst the rest of us got drunk and scrapped with one another outside in the street. They didn't allow fighting inside – after all it WAS a 'Conservative Club' not one of your 'Labour/Socialist places'. Mind you the biggest Labour Club in ower town could only get about fifty people inside it. Somebody's front room on Smith Street I think? Then we all got tired and some were already asleep under the chairs, so we all went home. It was a good night. We said hello to everybody we hadn't seen since the last party and gravely promised we wouldn't see them again until the next one, Grandma's eighty-sixth or an engagement or a wedding or a twenty-first or an eighteenth birthday party or if one of the family came up on the 'pools', whichever was the soonest. It was a good way of keeping in touch and finding out how many had been added and who had died since the last time. Every year the figures kept going up. Without the odd fatal accident or two it was evident the time would come when some, preferably the stingy ones', would have to leave town – permanently – the borough was fast running out of space to house them all.

And talking of 'accidents' -.

I didn't drop the block of ice on 'Slims' foot on purpose! And that's a statement of fact. It was an accident. Honest. He kept me there in front of the class that long praising my efforts and awarding me a gold star (the shame of it can you imagine) that my fingers went quite numb with cold and it slipped to the ground. Well, not quite to the ground. It crushed his foot first, then hit the ground.

He wasn't pleased. The reason being he was in a great deal of pain at the time. Quite understandable. It was a very large block. I was glad it didn't hit my foot.

I lost my gold star and did two nights detention. I spent that much time in detention my employer was under the impression ower school didn't finish until gone 5pm. He never did find out the truth.

It all began with a Science experiment. Mr Fielding wanted a block of ice and could one member of the 'form' provide one. In those days nobody has fridge's or deep-freezers. Keeping food fresh was a matter of 'using one's noggin'. A cold stone in the larder being the usual method. But yours truly worked at a butcher's where we of course had such 'facilities'.

"Splendid, boy." Slim looked at me over his rimless glasses with more than a modicum of suspicion. It wasn't like me to 'give' support to his daily toil without an ulterior motive. He waited to see if I was going to add conditions to my gracious offer and seemed genuinely disturbed when nothing more was said.

He couldn't possibly have thought I had intended to attempt to cripple him from the outset. Could he? No. Surely not!

And what was the experiment? A suspended weighted wire left on the block of ice would cut through the ice emerging underneath and lo and behold – the block of ice would remain intact. Wow. Earth shattering that wasn't it? 'Simmy' thought the Science master had sneaked back into the lab during 'break' and stuck the two halves back together with some 'Bostick'. But then 'Simmy' would -!
(Simmy became a first class joiner and carpenter in later life. But it had nothing to do with ower school. He failed his woodworking exam after losing it with the Woodworking teacher and 'dobbing' him with a piece of 4 x 2).

I decided it was time to remove my photo from the school's 'Hall of Fame'. What! I hear you cry. Is this a wind up?

No. Believe it or believe it not my photograph, taken at the school play in the winter of 1957, was still in pride of place near the 'Staff Room' on 'A' corridor. I was twelve, going on thirteen at the time and the 'Arts and Culture' teacher, Miss Halstead, she of the religious fervour, required a pupil to enact the role of a 'deck-boy' for that seasons school play. I was chosen for my 'art and dexterity', my clarity of projection and my youthful angelic looks.

The part consisted of my entrance, right stage, doffing my forelock, being grasped violently by the scruff of the neck, being thrown to the ground and picked up and then being hurled across the stage exiting stage left on my stomach. And my cry of 'Aaarrrrrrrrrrgh' as I plummeted swiftly out of sight. Miss Halstead said she had never seen anyone capable of such violently flowing movements without doing themselves an injury in the process. She was quite overcome. Had she any idea just how often I had ducked, hit the deck, dived for cover and thrown myself rapidly out of harms way in the past, she would have better understood. On the night of the play I smacked the deck that hard half the parents stood up and began protesting. It wasn't until I reappeared around the curtained wing of the stage and waved at the old woman, who knew very well how good I was at 'faking' it, that they sat back down again. And so I got my photo in the 'Hall of Fame' and now I wanted it 'out'.

"What? Which photograph? This one? Why this one?"

"Because it's me sir." I replied innocently. Mr Ashworth, the Technical Drawing master, peered in through the glass.

"Is it!" he replied in astonishment. "Are you sure -?" It was because he couldn't possibly equate me with 'Hall of Fame' status. 'Hall of Infamy' perhaps – after all the whole lot of them had had it in fer me for years.

"Positive sir. I was younger then – sir."

Mr Ashworth peered across at me and grunted.

"Yes laddie. It's truly amazing how you've managed to survive until now. I would never have believed it myself." He wasn't on his own.

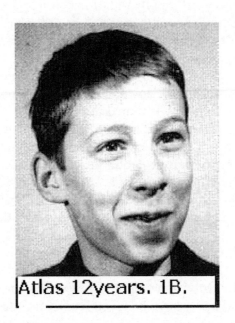

Atlas 12years. 1B.

'Deck-Boy' taken from school play in the year when they had yet to discover I had an independent nature - and didn't like being 'beaten' with large sticks., wooden dusters, chair legs and large bibles. The year was 1956.

'Fun, Frolics and Freedom'

The morning at the slaughterhouse had gone off without incident.
Big J. Poke had gone to his maker in the sky and everyone was still
watching their 'Ps' and 'Qs' following a lecture from the Health and
Safety Officer/ Meat Inspector regarding 'attention to detail', i.e.
make bloody sure the beast is unconscious before attempting to slit its
throat. As had been shown, they could get quite obstreperous about
things like that. (*See – Slugs and Snails & Ower Darkling – same
author*). I'd spent the morning scrapping pigs. Not unpleasant with
the morning being very frosty. Working over the steaming vats of
warm water stopped ones blood from freezing, but my feet were like
blocks of ice whilst my hands were like those of a leper, waxen white
and crinkled with bits peeling off the edges. Still, it was all good
training for later on.
We, that's the old man and myself, spent the afternoon stacking
bricks, thousands of them. We were going to re-use them for making
good the end of ower house, the bit that's missing. Horace, the next
door to the left neighbour, had extricated his 'Wartburg' with its iron-
bloc and the wife's anniversary present, albeit seven days late. He
was right. She wasn't at all pleased. She didn't want a large tin of
'Sanatogen' pills for the over fifties and it didn't matter it was seven
days late. She wasn't fifty for another twelve years. Or so she told the
rest of the neighbourhood. Horace just shrugged his shoulders and
ducked. He spent the rest of that Sunday afternoon erecting a small
bell tent in the back yard. Very strange behaviour? But then again
perhaps not all things considered?

Later that same day Wozzle called and wanted to go on a pub-
crawl. We started off at the 'Citizen' a well-situated libation hole on
the edge of the town centre. Here Wozzle lost a shilling at 'Brag',
which didn't start the night off well. Then on to the 'Navigation' so
called because after a pint or two of the landlords 'secret' brew you
needed a compass to find the next pub. We never had more than a
quick 'gill' otherwise ower legs gave out before the end of the night.
Next it was the 'The Ship' and then off across the town to 'The
Shakespeare' up on the 'Pavilion Brow', a particularly scruffy 'dive'

where the police never ventured unless a platoon strong and clad in riot gear. A very 'salubrious' hostelry with large fanlight windows in the Gents loo for scrambling out of in an emergency. Fortunately we never experienced a 'raid'. Wozzle would never have fit through the escape hatch. He reckoned he would. I knew he wouldn't. But I didn't have the heart to disagree. He would have had to stay there and get arrested. I wouldn't. You could have got two of me through the window light at the same time and as I have already made plain, I was a 'slippery' customer at the best of times. Wozzle wouldn't have 'grassed' me up. He was made of much stronger stuff than that. Going to work and then school the next morning was never a problem. I never wanted to go to the school any morning so Monday's held no extra dread than any other school day for me. I would take the same very slow trudge the mile or so down the cobbled hill fully expecting to arrive late, get beaten up and given another detention which had to be 'booked' by now on a calendar because the form master had lost track of the totals. It was all very sad and silly by this time. What was needed was an 'arbitrator'. One of those 'cooling off' periods would have gone down well. Instead it was constant battle. Me versus the 'system'. Ridiculous. But that was how it was. They wouldn't 'give' and I had nothing left to 'give'. And so it went on, ad infinitum.
Until the day of my 'release'.

I thought the noise in my ears was Elgar's 'Pomp and Ceremony'. A triumphal cacophony of tubular bells and strings. No. Wrong again. It was the school bell for the end of term. But it didn't sound like that to me. I had never before or since heard such a wonderful sound. I should have been in detention but today's detention had been cancelled in my honour. I fully expected the form masters to line the cobbled expanse alongside the school to applaud my departure, those of the lower strata not The Headmaster or his Deputy of course, but no, not a sign of anyone. Still, it didn't detract from the cloud upon which my feet slid away from the place nor did it make me look back. There was nothing, absolutely nothing, would have made me do that. I remember emptying my school satchel over the railings a little lower down the hill that stood opposite the 'maths' form room. Maths was my very 'worst' subject.
'One out of hundred for getting his name right'. A very memorable examination result from year 'three'.

I'm afraid they lost me at the fractious – sorry - 'fractions' stage. What on earth logarithms, algebra and calculus was I have no idea. I could barely 'spell' them let alone make them do anything else. I'm sure somebody somewhere liked 'them' to play with. They did nothing but confuse me and waste a lot of ink and paper. Still. It wouldn't do for us all to be the same, would it? As I often tried to tell the maths teacher. He used to get very angry. I think we went through about half a dozen different 'maths' teachers over the years. They had no staying power some of them. Some. And there were a few, couldn't bring themselves to thrash' us for 'denseness'. They had to leave. Sadism was an absolute 'must' at ower school. If it wasn't on an applicant's CV. No chance. Some just pretended then gave it up as a bad job. You couldn't get away with that. A cane, rubber strap, boomerang board-duster and hard rubber marbles were all essential accoutrements to a form masters wardrobe. Prof. Brown (Buzzer) had the lot and – a water pistol and a potato gun as well. A lump of potato can sting at five paces, especially if it gets you on the back of the neck. Ow – bugger!

"Acceleration and trajectory boy. The study of 'Projectiles' and their nuances. I can see your body. Is your spirit with us today as well?"
I am absolutely certain it wasn't just me!!!!!! It couldn't have been? It really, really couldn't have been? – Could it?

The working week began at eight-o-clock in the morning until seven-o-clock at night. Six days, Monday to Saturday and Sunday from 10am until 1pm unless I was going to the abattoir then it was 7-30am until 1pm. A working week, less dinner-breaks, of sixty hours a week or thereabouts. I received apprenticeship wages of five pounds a week plus another two pounds of free meat on a Saturday. A grand sum of two shillings and fourpence per hour. Not bad wages in those days but hardly a fortune when one considers that eighteen hours were supposed to be overtime. Of which nobody spoke, including yours truly. It didn't do to upset the 'boss'. You could be thrown out on the spot, at a moments whim and have no redress or procedure of complaint. It was always best to trust to discretion.

But it mattered not. I liked the work immensely and couldn't have cared less how many hours I did providing I could stay on my feet.

Christmas time was the worst. I remember working a one hundred-hour week on more than one occasion. Every 'bird' was farm reared and required dressing. Some, especially the turkeys were delivered 'live'. Have you ever tried 'screwing' a turkey neck? It's like making love to a telegraph pole and just about as arduous. God they were strong. Mind you so would I have been if some raving lunatic came at me with hands the size of dustbin lids and tried to throttle me. Very understandable. Still. It had to be done. Mrs Winterbottom, the Police Superintendents wife wanted her turkeys 'fresh' and still warm. So we popped them in the oven for her on a low light for half an hour before delivering them. She was non-the wiser.

There were numerous ways to keep the meat fresh looking and smelling sweet. For mincemeat we had a powdered preservative that turned the meat a beautiful red colour. Most mincemeat will turn brown an hour or two after mincing. If yours is red. It ain't kosher missus. Bacons and hams had a habit of sweating. Producing a film of a sticky mucus like covering. A quick wash in salt water removed it and no one was any the wiser. Checking your fridge now are you? Very wise. Chickens turn out much better in colour and odour if given a similar treatment and hung up in the top of a cold room to dry slowly. As I say lots and lots of methods. Some of which I will not divulge here for the sake of the 'meat' trade and a sudden stampede of the population into vegetarianism. But every trade had its 'little secrets' so don't be fooled into thinking otherwise. And we knew them all.

It was an imperative in those days that nothing at all was wasted. Profit depended on as little 'waste' as possible. We had dustbins for the bones of which each and every single one was inspected beforehand by ower Fred or ower Ruby. Any sign of a sliver of red meat and it came out of one's wages. 'Sliver's wus money'. As Ruby was fond of saying. The bones went to the 'Bone Man' and for glue, the other bits and pieces, gristle and rotten pieces to the knackers yard for rendering down for dog meat and domestic oils. Not a single thing, chicken heads, lamb's horns, pigs tail's or bulls willie's, was thrown away. You all think that you have never eaten a bulls willie?

Yes you have, believe me. It was all recyclable one way or another. And went back to the public in one form or another. You have no idea what some of you women put on your faces believe me.

You don't need to buy expensive rejuvenating creams, just whack yourself around the chops with a bull's willie a few times a night.

It has many of the same properties. Honest!
Them African's do it all the time! Well, some of them anyway.
The Australian aboriginal makes walking sticks from them. Knob-
ended. But then come to think of it they would be wouldn't they?

The secret of a successful trader in the meat trade was cleanliness,
politeness, good display and quality. People buy meat with their eyes.
They were a very peculiar lot round ower way. Most other people use
their hands. But being serious. It was always the way the meat was
displayed. The trimming of fat, the removal of gristle, the care taken
when removing the bones to keep the meat whole, the double
stringing, the tight rolling. All were vital to the final presentation.
And yours truly intended to be the best at it or if not a close second to
my 'boss' Ower Ken Master Butcher of ower town, now that I had
finally 'escaped' from that – educational 'institution'.

With so much of the days taken up with work I began to see less
and less of my 'mates', most of who were still at the school (no – not
'whom' – the majority hadn't taken their brains with them -!). I did
continue with the nights at the billiard hall and the odd pub-crawl and
looked forward to the Friday night when the 'lads' got together for
the local 'dance' known as the 'Carlton'. Primarily because that was
its name 'The Carlton Ballroom'. Friday night was Rock and Roll
night baby. The night of the week when you could show them 'bints'
all yer tackle and get told to 'dream on scab-face' or 'are yer talkin' t'
me sweet-pea 'er chewin' a brick'? Such darling little things the
opposite sex. Especially when in large numbers and half 'cut'
(drunk). But then so were we. They looked so much better through
four pints of bitter. A lethal combination. Beer and sex. The former
cut out the latter even if you were lucky enough to be on a 'promise'.

"And what the bleedin' 'ell d' yer think you are goin' to do wi'
that-?"

"Eh! Oh I thought as how you'd like t' talk to it for a bit – yer
know, get it excited – a bit?"

"Looks to me like it's had enough excitement for one night. It's a
bit like you. Can't stand up straight."

"Eh? Oh. It's not done that before. It needs some encouragement."

"Encouragement! Needs a bloody bargepole strappin' to it more
like. Put it away before yer get arrested. I'm late fer the last bus –
Tarraaa -."

Dead romantic it was.

But the dancing was good. Using up what little bit of energy you had left after a week's 'grind'. Providing you could keep out of trouble.

"Hey you! What d'yer think youse doin' chattin' up my bird - eh?"

"Yer what?" The gorilla in the bright red and blue monkey suit is all but surrounded by a dozen of his tribe, each one similarly decked out in knee length jackets, beetle-crusher boots and bootlace ties. There's that much varnish lacquered hair on display it's difficult to make out individual faces. You look for one you might know. To appeal for quarter. There's only you and Wozzle and that don't constitute an army. But there's never a friend in sight when you need one. You can either say "Oh sorry mate. I didn't know she was yours." Or. "Was I? Gosh my mistake. She's that ugly I thought no one would want her." Then all hell broke loose.

I've seen bodies thrown from the balcony, tables uprooted and cast iron seating hurled around like so much confetti at an Irish wedding, you wouldn't believe it. A Teddy boy fight had a habit of being a very nasty affair. Home-made knuckle-dusters with spikes, bicycle chains and flick-knives. A lethal combination at close quarter. I avoided them wherever and whenever possible. But it wasn't always possible in the early days.

No - . There wasn't a friendly face to be seen anywhere. The gorilla did a sort of Zulu dance the long overhanging stock of jet-black hair almost plucking his own eye out. He came to a stop with a shudder and groped around trying to keep his balance. Beer and the sudden gyrations having an adverse effect upon his already befuddled brain.

"Who told yer yer could mess wi' my woman?" he snarled.

"That bloke down there." I replied quick as a flash and pointing over the balcony.

He believed me! He actually went to the balcony railings and peered over!

"Which one-?" he demanded to know grabbing hold of the brass rail and swaying dangerously back and forth.

I looked down amongst the two or three hundred sweating couples scouring the surface of the dance floor below.

"The one with the red hair." I pointed to what from this distance resembled an outraged orang-utan displaying its genitals from a half-nelson position.

"Gibby. I might er known. Bastard. Little creep I'll kill 'im. Come on -." The gorilla swept half his tribe aside in his rush for the stairwell leading down to the dance floor. Suddenly we were alone again, save for the constant stream of revellers passing back and forth in aimless abandonment. Wozzle still had his mouth agape in surprise. He felt sure we were going to get stomped to death by the gorilla and his band of half-cut followers.

"Wha – what do wi do now?" he stuttered.

"Leave -." I replied decisively. "Unless you think it's wise not to-?" Wozzle glanced over the balcony to assess the gorilla's progress then looked back.

"No. I think that's a cracking idea – Can we make it very quickly - Please?"

I shouldn't leave this tale without telling of another incident when 'Ower Kid', yes, I repeat. 'Ower Kid' came to our rescue on another similar occasion. Well to be precise 'Ower Kid's mate'. He was known as 'Little Joe' (Joseph Hesketh). Little Joe got his name because of his diminutive stature. He was all of four foot tall. But perfectly proportioned. Stocky and muscular. Almost the exact opposite of yours truly. Wozzle and I were in trouble again. It had nothing to do with either of us, but that mattered little in those days. In fact such was generally the case. Being in the wrong place at the wrong time seemed to be a forte of mine. It was that curiosity thing again. Oh well. Never mind eh?

This time it wasn't over a woman. In fact it wasn't over anything at all other than too little room to get passed the crush of bodies coming down the balcony staircase. I pushed he pushed we both pushed and became very close friends in an instant – only he wasn't that friendly. When push came to shove I shoved and he didn't. When he got up from the bottom of the stair landing he wasn't a happy bunny and grabbed me by the collar as I walked passed. As usual he had a gang of his mates with him and I, as usual, I had Wozzle – only.

"Who d' yer think you are smart arse -." The youth snarled angrily flinging me back against the wall. "Want sum wellie d' yer?" Wellie was a term for a good battering – of the painful kind. I decided to play dumb.

"What! What's this all about?" I was playing for time. Wozzle was running his eyes over the rest of the opposition. There were four of them. That was four too many. He tried to pretend he wasn't with me and began studying the flock pattern on the red and gold wallpaper above his head.

"Who d' yer think yer pushin' -?" said the pock faced youth himself trying to assess his quarry (me) and not quite sure if he could handle what he had begun. He needn't have had any fear on that one, I was about as far through as a lathe and punched like a girl guide, a female one, not them other ones with the moustaches -, I was no match for him let alone his four mates. Wozzle had by this time retreated a further three steps down. Wise man.

"I wasn't pushing anybody!" I replied trying to feign as much surprise as I could muster. Well it was better than saying. "Bog off yer freckled face freak-." That wouldn't have got me anywhere but dead would it?

"I wasn't pushing anybody – Ooo don't we talk nice -." parroted the youth. "Cum from a posh school then dus one?"

I was about to say 'You must be joking' when a voice came from behind.

"Hey you! W-w-w- what are yer d-d-d-oin' t- t-t' my m-m-m-ates b-b-b- Bollocks b- b- brother -?" I looked around. Below me. Considerably below me stood 'Little Joe'. Behind him and almost barring off the staircase was 'Ower Kid' and the rest of his 'small faces'. Six in all.

"Y – y-y-you t-t-touch him an- an- and I' –I-I'll b-b-bloody m-m-m-molly c-c-crush yer." he eventually said. You will have gathered that 'Little Joe' wasn't only very small, he had a very bad stutter as well. This made it appear he was of the nervous type. Nothing could have been further from the truth. He was a wild cat, as Ower Kid had found out one day when he tackled him over some 'problem' or another, with a very quick temper and a swingeing right hook. He was handy with his feet too. Essential when up against the teenage youth of the day.

The freckled face youth took a long look downwards and lost some of his freckles in the process. Now he was on very dangerous ground himself and – he knew it. Little Joe clawed his way up the staircase until he was nose to belly button with the boy. I didn't see the fist come up. All I heard was a sharp grunt and my freckled faced tormentor sinking rapidly from my line of vision. Little Joe turned and looked up at me. He grinned a huge grin from ear to ear.

"They forget they got balls. What use it is putting yer hands up t' protect yer face I don't know. Stupid if yer ask me." When I looked about the remainder had fled the scene helped along it seemed by a few quick slaps from Ower Kid and the rest of his entourage. It was the one and only time when I was aware of any kind of protection I received from 'Ower Kid' and then I'm not so sure it would have happened had not Little Joe recognised me at the time. I didn't much care for Ower Kid most of the time but his 'small faces' had some good lads amongst them. Handy too.

A couple of snapshots taken around that time. Not Ower Kids lot. His mob where known as the 'small faces', a term given to snappy dressers and more 'in the groove' than your average run-of-the-mill Teddy Boy.

'Pubic petulance & Pediculus corporis'

'Ower town'! The Forgotten City. In truth it was a very big town come the end of the 1950s. Most of the countryside surrounding the valley slopes was still evident but the valley itself had become lost in the sprawl of 'urban' development. So much so that the surrounding 'towns' had begun to merge as the whole became one huge pan-tiled patchwork of conurbation. All that signified your exit from the town was a single road sign which said 'Hey up – Going somewhere?" The reason for this stemmed from the town's history. For countless generations families were born, raised and worked within the confines of the 'borough'. To 'leave' the town had quite serious connotations. You were either 'off to klink' or 'doing a moonlight' (running away from the rent/debt collectors). Only during 'Wakes' fortnight, when the town emptied for the annual holidays was one's absence justified. For aeons the 'Cotton Barons' had run the town. Most lived in a 'mill' house, went to the 'mill' Sunday school and worked at the Mill itself. Son followed father, daughter followed mother. All worked for the God 'Cotton'. For 'He' was the provider of everything. Including an early death – but nobody spoke about that. Not out loud anyway!

But by the end of the 1950s cotton's hold on the town was waning. The industry was dying. Foreign competition known as 'Empire Made' goods were flooding the markets. Hong Kong mainly and a number of other Far Eastern territories were importing the 'finished' article at less than a quarter of the price it cost to produce the goods locally. The mill owners were quick to see the value and began stripping their assets abroad as fast as the dismantlers could take it apart and export it. God Cotton was moving on, his rape of ower gentle hillsides at long last over. He had found more lucrative 'slaves' to do his bidding.

How I came to be involved on the tail end of this mass exodus comes from the old woman's 'pride'.

Not that she had anything to do with it, personally, but who else was I going to blame for the 'genes' that imbue me with a peculiar stubborn streak that infrequently manifested itself in times of being 'taken advantage of' or in the present vernacular 'used'.

For the full story we need to go back about twelve months. I was sixteen. Not at all spotty (unlike Ower Kid who had begun to erupt all over the place in countless 'Vesuvius' type zits) and beginning to feel as if I needed a bit more of a challenge to my daily routine. Ower Ken had his eye on empty premises near to ower house. A butchers shop who's owner had gone 'to the wall', which wasn't quite the same as 'bankrupt' more 'not making ends meet' so to speak, leaving Ower Ken and Ower Ruby to make the poor beggar an offer he couldn't refuse. The price still sounded more like a telephone number to me so I didn't press the point.

"We'll do it out and you can run it fer me." said Ken.

"OK." said I.

"It had better be." said Ower Ruby throwing me one of her looks. I think she had reservations about increasing her own workload. Two shops, two sets of books (always assuming she kept any), two delivery areas. There would be problems if the new business grew to any size. Most of which Ruby knew would fall on her shoulders one way or another. She didn't trust her better half passed the chopping block. So nowt different there then?

We opened the new shop in October and slowly began to receive the attentions of some of the local residents. It rapidly became obvious that the previous owner had liked his 'tipple', so much so that on many occasions the shop had remained closed when it shouldn't have been, sending the prospective customers to other 'butchers' in the area. I mentioned this to the old woman who frowned darkly, nodded her head slowly and suggested I put the kettle on for a cup of tea. Now. I don't know how much the reader understands of the Northern mentality but, when somebody from ower town looks at you gravely and tells you to put the kettle on – it's serious.

A cup of tea is the northern panacea for all ills. If you don't know what to do about something, you put the kettle on. If the situation is grave, you put the kettle on.

If someone's dying and the doctor's already at the bedside, you put the kettle on. If someone has dropped a bomb on your house and you are still standing amidst the smoking ruins with one of your arms blown off, you use the other one to put the 'bloody' kettle on -. I took the 'nod' and went in the kitchen to put the kettle on.

The old woman had been in business herself for nigh on ten years. First with the bakery and confectioners in ower previous house down by the 'Arches' and now with the drapers shop here on the canal lock. She knew a bit about the nuances of 'customers' and aspired to the old adage that the customer was always right until they weren't. (which with ower old woman was pretty often). But she knew that they were creatures of habit.

"How long has the shop been closed?" she asked, when I passed her the warm water and milk through the serving hatch. (She rarely drank tea).

"Eighteen months I think."

"How long!" There was more than a hint of surprise in her voice. It was almost as if she thought I was fibbing again.

"Eighteen months. So Ken said anyroad." I repeated.
The old woman shook her head.

" Oh yea. Hmm. And how many customers have you had in this week -?" To be truthful I hadn't actually counted, but it wasn't as if there had been that many I couldn't have taken a good guess.

"Oh probably about – thirty, thirty five perhaps. Not many. Not as many as we had hoped."
Again she shook her head.

"Eighteen months! Eighteen months is a long time. People get used to going elsewhere. I'm not surprised things are slow. You've got a job on yer hands if you're expecting them to change back from what they've got used too. It's never that easy once you've lost them."
And she was right. Christmas came and went. We put on a wonderful display which included a real Highland bull's head complete with horns the lot, and pigs heads with apples and turkeys on the run. It was a wonderful show and drew quite a crowd, but unfortunately very few of them came inside to make a purchase.

Spring came and went. I tried various sales ploys and even included opening at nights for hamburgers and hot dogs in an effort to draw in some passing trade. It was hopeless.

Short of giving the meat away nothing was going to attract the old customers away from their new 'shopping' grounds. Things were looking grim.

"Thar's got tha fortnights holiday comi' up. When is it?" Ken asked one day during a flying visit. "In a few weeks time." I replied. I had been wondering would he want me to work it on double pay. Considering I had already agreed to go to Butlin's Holiday Camp with Wozzle and a few of his mates. It was a tricky situation.

"Aye reet. I've got someone in mind fer then. T' take over like. No problem." Ken smiled one of his best Saturday smiles and drove off. Oh dear. That wasn't a good sign at all. A Saturday smile had about as much sincerity behind it as an Amazonian crocodile's. What on earth was he cooking up now?

'Pwllheli'. Butlin's Holiday Camp on the sunshine Riviera of North Wales-look you. Pronounced Puckelly it means either salty pool or briny pit in English, not that we cared a fig or even knew where we were. All that interested us as we piled out of the train and on to the siding was 'where was the booze and the women'. And 'how many coppers did the local police force have'? Not that we were in any way a danger to the local populace, for we soon discovered we weren't allowed outside the parameter's of the camp once they got us in.

B - - - - - -'s! Only children with parents or guardians were allowed beyond the confines of the wire. Children? How dare they. We were sixteen or thereabouts. Hardly children. Not that ower protestations made the slightest difference. "Go out and you stay out." was the warning at 'Reception'. Nobody wanted to do that. We had paid for ower chalets and were looking forward to turning them into 'mini' brothels for the duration. Regardless of the 'regulations' or the six foot thirteen inches tall 'Bluecoats' that roamed at will peeping through half curtained windows on the look out for 'illegal' bonking. As far as we were concerned we had 'paid' for ower potential 'bonking' and to hell with the rest of it -! Eh what?

Seven days of total freedom. Well – almost. The first night, after checking out the beds in the chalet, we went to the 'Pig and Whistle' and got 'blathered'. It wouldn't have mattered had we 'scored' that night.

None of us was in a fit state to even know we had.

'Ratty' (David Radcliffe) ended up in the swimming pool, in his suit and trousers and only survived the 'drowning' because his jacket billowed up with air as he crashed over the edge. It acted as a kind of life jacket and we were able to grab him by his upturned feet as he floated by. You would have thought with a name like 'Ratty' he would have been in his element. I think we made the dinner-gong the next day although I can't be sure. It's all very hazy now. It was so then as well, only moreso.

We were four. Wozzle, Ratty (David Ratcliffe) –one of Wozzle's mates, Turnip and yours truly. And a very 'merry' bunch of ner-do-wells as you've ever seen. Not that we thought so at the time. In fact we thought we were the 'bees knees'. Young, virile, dashingly handsome and 'tooled up'. The women were sexy, virile, the right age and it didn't matter what they looked like as long as they were 'up for it'. No good could possibly have come from it – and I wasn't wrong either. Nothing did.

Mine was very large, wore National Health glasses and hadn't got past the primary school toilet stage. I forget her name, thankfully. Coming, as she did, from ower town you would have thought she should have known something about 'coupling'. If she did she was very clever about acting 'dumb'. I don't think I have ever been so frustrated in my life? In fact I know I haven't. It was awful. To go on any further would be too traumatic so let's leave it now. Which is what I did the very next morning before breakfast. I cut her dead, dead as a door post, as she and her friend, the vivacious Louise ,Ratty's bit, came to ower chalet. As she entered I left, which didn't go down at all well with the rest of the lads.

"That's no way t' treat a bird tha's slept wi -." screeched Ratty getting angry and poking me violently in the chest. I didn't want to fight about it but I was still very angry from the night before and wasn't prepared to leave it by walking away.

"What the 'ell d' you know about it?" I snapped back narrowing my eyes and giving him the thin lip treatment. He stepped back. I wasn't known for losing my temper and he was more than a little surprised by my reaction.

"You was there was yer? You know all about it then do yer, smart arse eh?"

Ratty pulled a face. He wasn't sure of his ground but for the sake of the two girls he didn't want to be seen to back down.

"I don't care what happened. You can at least talk to her." He growled back defiantly.

"Talk to her!" I looked at him in astonishment. "That's exactly what I've been doing all bloody night. It didn't make one jot of a difference. She did nowt. Lay there like an Eygptian Mummy. Stiff as a board. I thought she'd bloody well died once over. Talk to her. No thank you. I'm bloody hoarse enough as it is. Not t' mention half bloody stir-crazy. Bog off." And with that I turned and left the scene for the 'Pig and Whistle'. There at least I could look at something with 'potential' even if it was only wistful thinking.

Relations between the four of us went downhill very quickly after that. I told Wozzle the full story and he, to a degree, understood'. Falling out over a 'woman' wasn't going to break up the friendship we had had for nigh on five years or more, even if he did think I had been a bit harsh. I had. But I needed to show my acute displeasure and at that age it seemed the best way. Like a guillotine. Whap. End of story. Ratty never forgave me and though I employed him in later years (as a bricklayer) and he became a good friend of Ower Kid we never really did hit it off thereafter. Then again I never felt I had the need to explain myself to him then or later. It was my 'disaster' not his. Turnip kept his own counsel. It's pretty certain had he been in my position he would have found a way of encouraging the young maiden to become one less so, he was good at 'persuasion'. As for me - well, I was far too much the 'gentleman'. I blame the 'old lady'.

My second disaster came the next day when I discovered someone had 'lifted' a five pound note from my wallet, which had been left for safe keeping under my mattress, leaving me with less than three pounds to spend for the rest of the week. At the time we all assumed it was down to a chalet maid, women who cleaned out the chalets at the end of each weeks' occupation, as they had keys to enter chalets to check them out. Fortunately Wozzle had brought a little extra cash with him and 'saw me right'. Just as well really otherwise I couldn't have stayed the course. (It would be many years later when I would eventually discover the truth behind the 'theft' and forgave the real 'thief' instantly. Real mates do that - Or at least we did.)

The week shot by like a herd of fleeing antelope. Zip – gone. It was Saturday morning and time to go.

The days had been one long merry-go-round of snooker, booze, fun fair, booze and hoping for a 'sniff'. We 'sniffed' until we caught dog-fever but little all else. We spent a fortune, five quid a day. Seven weeks wages in one big blow. And now the train was pulling in to take us back to ower town. Take us back to the smoke and the grime and the grey dismal streets with their grey dismal people and their grey dismal lives. Such joy. Such joy. Pwllheli had been an eye-opener. It had taught me one very valuable lesson. All that glitters is not gold, but it was a dam sight better than the pig iron in ower streets back home – for all its other failings. We vowed to return to the holiday camp the next year. This time we would be ready for it. Not just tooled up. But a year smarter and this time we wouldn't bring more blokes with us. After all, they were only more competition! You would have thought we should have known that wouldn't you? We did now.

Wozzle found himself a mate in the Pig & Whistle!

And speaking of 'missing' monies -!

"Er this is – er – I want to ask yer –. Have yer – er - ." Ken was getting nowhere fast. It wasn't like my illustrious employer to be reticent with words. He was always quick enough to give me an ear-bending whenever it suited. Something was up! Ruby had been giving me peculiar looks all morning. But then that was quite normal. She wasn't much into men no matter what age they were. Daft buggers was her usual complimentary comment. This was before my taking over the 'new' shop and just one more of those sad, pointless incomprehensible idiotic instances that proves ower species to be questionably desirable in the greater scheme of things.

"You er – you haven't been upstairs this morning have yer?" It wasn't a normal every day question. The toilet was situated upstairs in the living quarters so a journey up the staircase was required at least twice a day as a minimum. It so happened I hadn't. I'd taken a quick piss in the bone bins early that morning. It was easier than taking my boots off to save the stairs carpet, another of Ruby's little foibles. "No-." I replied. And that was that until a few days later.

"There's money going missing." said Ruby one morning after the deliveries and we were taking ower usual half hour break for dinner. I nodded, then thinking I should say more added. "Where from?"

"Tin ont stairs." The 'tin' was the receptacle used for the loose change to supplement the small change in the till.

"How much?" I ventured knowing full well by this time I wasn't being informed of the incident for the benefit of my own health. Now it wasn't that I didn't normally handle the shop monies, on the contrary, I handled vast amounts of the shop and meat delivery takings every day and had done so for nearly three years. Which was probably why I was being 'asked' about the missing money and not being accused of theft outright? However we were not a big organisation there being the owner and his wife, myself, the trainee boy and the cleaner.

Unbeknown to me the cleaner had been asked about the thefts and had gone to great lengths to 'finger' yours truly as the only possible suspect due to my 'past' record. It transpires my past 'record' had been as a result of her son's opinion of me. He was a fellow school pupil but from a 'higher' strata.

An 'A' form prima-Donna. When I was later to discover this information I was flabbergasted for both he and I were 'coupled' as major boy soprano's in the school choir and although he wasn't in ower 'group' so to speak (not that he or his mother would have wanted him to be) I didn't think too badly of him for being one of the 'swots'.

Following my vehement protestations of innocence, duly coupled by my old lady's somewhat dubious assistance namely in the shape of -.

"I don't know what to say to you about him. Strangely enough I believe that this time he is innocent. He is not acting the way he would if he was lying. I know. I've lived with his shenanigans for the last sixteen years. Somehow this doesn't feel right. If anyone can believe that!"

Which didn't over-fill my employer with the greatest of confidence but was the best my mother could do at the time. The police were called for.

Sure enough the trap was set, sprung and the cleaner carted off to jail in one day's work. Not the brightest of criminals. To go on 'nicking' money from the 'tin' after she had been questioned about it. Unless of course she thought that would add credence to her 'blackening' my good name – well reasonably clean one anyway. Ken was all apologetic, Ruby not so much so. But like I said, Ower Ruby thought all us men blaggards; the fact that this time a woman was the guilty party must have thrown her equal-rights attitudes to pieces somewhat.

Ken left his next 'pearl of wisdom' until the week after we closed the new shop down. Whilst I had been away on holiday a new temporary manager had been brought in to 'manage' the shop during my absence. Unbeknown to yours truly the new 'temporary' manager had been paid fifteen pounds a week, which was just over double that of my weekly wage. (Had I worked the same week I would have been paid fourteen pounds, a whole one pound less). I suspect Ower Ruby had a hand in it. They were trying to see if a 'new' manager might give better returns. As it transpired he didn't. In fact the 'takings' were nearly half that of mine for the two-week period and he wasn't as good a butcher, in boning and cutting terms, as was I. After all Ower Ken had taught me better.

It was around this time in fact some months before when I got stabbed. It wasn't intentional. His knife was just bigger than mine. Thus proving that 'size' does matter.

He had hold of a steak knife, which is about a foot in length and yours truly had a boning knife, which is less than half the size. I know the lad was hot tempered. He was younger than me by about a year and had a look of a gypsy about him. Dark black hair, dark green eyes and an olive tan to his skin. His accent put him local but beyond that I knew little about him. Which was why I shouldn't have called him a 'lazy bastard'. I think it was the 'bastard' bit that upset him. So he stabbed me. Just to see what effect it would have on me. I can tell you I wasn't pleased. As the blood, mine, sprayed out in his face he changed colour. Yes. You got it. Red. But underneath he went a creamy white. I thought he was going to feint. That annoyed me even more. Here am I standing with a knife protruding through my right arm, spraying blood everywhere and he wants to feint! I think not indeed.

"Well don't just stand there. Go down the cellar and get some muslin's. (No. Not 'moslems'. Cloth - used for wrapping lambs for transit). " And make sure they's clean." I removed the knife from my arm and grabbed it tightly to staunch the blood. It was making a terrible mess on the floor and guess who would have to clean it up later? At that moment ower Ruby walked in. I have seen her shocked before but today's was a 'pearler'. Now there's always quite a bit of blood around in a butcher's shop which is why some premises used sawdust on the floors to soak it up and to stop the workers from slipping on the stone surfaces. The boning room was floorboards and any blood showed up immediately. Mine was very fresh and ever so bright red in colour by now.

"Bugger me! What the bloody 'ells goin' on! Whose all that blood there?" I knew her well enough to understand the question had been 'What's all that blood doing there'. It's the Derbyshire twang with the slant on the indecipherable.

"Mine." I replied. And removed my hand to show her the spray. She went quite white.

The young knife-wielding buck reappeared at the top of the cellar steps wielding a handful of lamb muslin clothes saw ower Ruby and dropped his head in shame. He stepped closer and pushed the bundle of clothes at me, which I gratefully accepted knowing I could now tie my arm back together before it dropped off completely.

Talk about harmless. I nearly was and he bloody-well wasn't.

 It was a few weeks later he was 'fired' for threatening to smash ower Ruby over the 'bonce' with the sausage machine funnel.

He wouldn't. He would never have been able to lift it high enough. But it was as well he went. He really was quite dangerous without giving him the equipment to help him be moreso.

Ower Ken had stopped a passing motorist and got him to drive me to the 'Infirmary' where someone who had been in the same trade as me at one time or another put fifteen stitches in my arm whilst I watched. (Ken couldn't close the shop for an hour or two, as it was Wednesday, one of ower busiest days.) I knew the surgeon chappie was an ex-butcher by the way he used skewers to hold the flesh together whilst he stitched. Afterwards I was given an injection and told to go home whereupon I promptly returned to work. Well. The shop needed cleaning ready for tomorrow didn't it?

With my arm in a permanent sling I continued on until five days later when I woke up one morning to a very muscular right arm. I knew instantly it wasn't mine. I never had any muscles to start with. It had gone 'septic' and the injection was penicillin, which didn't work on me. I told you I was 'unusual'. They had to send off to America for some foreign stuff, which arrived five days later. Meanwhile I was in agony so they gave me some 'happy' pills to shut me up.

But to get back to ower Ken and his 'pearl of wisdom'.

"I've decide we shall all have to start at 7-30 in the morning from now on." All, of course meaning 'me'.

"Trades not been too good of late and ower little foray with the other shop has left things a bit lean – unlike some of the beef we had in last week- ha-ha." His little joke didn't impress me. But I tried a smile all the same. Now. My wages had gone up to the seven-pound mark. A pound a year as it was. But it was hardly a fortune and I already worked a sixty-hour week on average. I thought I should venture a question. A 'probe' into the inner workings of my employer's mind, or Ruby's, whichever?

"And how much is it going to add to my wage then?" I was nothing if not direct. Primarily because I couldn't work out how to put it gently.

"Wages! Oh. No. No. I wasn't thinking as we could afford any more money. The object of the exercise is to get more done to boost the taking's. When wis done that we can talk about wages can't we?" Can we? Will we ever? Who's kidding who mister?

I suppose the fact that in a years time I would be finished as an apprentice and would then require full pay might have had a

bearing on this latest of Ken's schemes.
I didn't think that at the time because we had been together for a very long time, five years getting on six. I knew I couldn't learn any more for he had nothing more to teach me in the art of 'butchering' but the fact he would 'instigate' a problem in order to replace me with a new apprentice at the princely sum of three pounds a week hadn't entered my head. Looking back of course perhaps it should have. Still, isn't that the way of things? I said no and he said take it or leave it. I said I would leave it thank you and he said OK and that was that. I left in the March of 1961 for pastures new. His parting comment as I bundled up my coats and aprons and my working knives was – "Whatever you do don't go working fer the CO-OP, you'll get a bad reputation -!" Huh! And you won't? God, they broke the mould when they made Ower Ken and Ower Ruby so they did. Not only 'broke' it they 'buried' in a deep mine shaft somewhere – One hopes!

I had been home about fifteen minutes. The old woman was busy with a customer in the shop and the old man had not yet returned from helping one of his 'mates' change the chimney pot on his roof. I made the compulsory 'cup o' char', for stressful situations and settled my bones across the sofa in the living room. The old woman entered. "So. That's it then is it -? she said moving to her favourite chair and plonking herself down left foot under her posterior right leg dangling over the top. Her feet never touched the ground when sitting. They weren't long enough. It gave us an advantage if she made a lunge for us. She could never get to us fast enough. That's why her aim was good with whatever she had to hand at the moment of her anger bursting forth. But today, she was cool -. Too cool. Not like her at all.
    "Yep. He wasn't for budging. Told me 'not to go working for the Co-Op. As if I would -." I replied and took a careful sip of my tea whilst watching for any reaction.
    "So. Last wage then today is it?" I fished about in my apron pocket and tossed the small envelope across.
    "No meat this week-end I'm afraid. He didn't offer and I weren't askin'." The old woman just shrugged her shoulders. She hadn't expected it to be otherwise, knowing the situation.
    "So. What yer going to do now then -?"
Now I know I had 'lost' my job and I fully intended to remedy that fact, but I had only lost it an hour ago. This was no time for 'adding' to the problem by giving me a third degree on the subject.

But I wasn't allowing for my old woman being anything else but herself.

"Don't know." came my answer.

"Well I do-." came the swift reply. "Yer can drink that -." she motioned towards the cup of tea, " – and when tha's done that yer can get out and find another one. If yer think yer living here free gratis you've got another think comin'." And with that she unslung her left leg dropped to her feet and departed.

"But it's Saturday night -!" I called after her. I might as well as saved my breath. She knew what day it was. It was her way of telling me she was not a happy bunny at me 'giving up' my job, albeit on principal. (On the basis that 'principals' are a rare commodity and don't cook very well.) And that principals or not she expected me to pay my way regardless. I could have said, 'tell that lazy pig of a brother of mine t' stop playing silly buggers at Art School and help out here once in a while'. But that would have got me a slug behind the ear and another lecture on 'education, education, education' and all its shining principals. (There's them principals again – the buggers get everywhere). I took another sip of tea. It was suppose to help. Perhaps it did. I don't know. I do know I went out after it and made my way over the Lock Bridge and towards the big cotton mills that lay either side of the sluggishly rippling canal. The noise emanating from inside them was deafening even from here. A constant never ending rumble of clanking spindles and flapping leather belts. The mills had started a system of continuous shift working. The only time the machines were disengaged now was on a Sunday morning. The 'Barons' still believed in the 'Lords Day', well morning anyway. The new bands of coloured immigrants had no hang ups about working on a Sunday, unlike ower lot, so that solved that problem straight away. It was known as the 'Cocoa Shift'. I can't think why? But I was soon to discover, quite surprisingly, it would fit quite nicely into my plans in the months to come.

I began work again on the Monday. The Era Ring Mill. A huge four-storey red brick monolith not more than a few hundred yards from ower front door.

"An what makes yer think you'se an handy lad then -?" asked Old Jack the Winding Room Manager?"

"Well I only live around the corner." I replied cheekily. Old Jack spied me from the corner of his turtle shell glasses. He grinned. A little suppressed but a grin all the same.

"Young bugger. Ok. Monday. I need another bobbin carrier. 7-30 an' don't be late."
So that was that.

Monday morning and I was on time. I got up at twenty minutes past seven and tried running. Old Jack was hovering in his office as I stepped out of the 'hoist'. He looked at me and in the same instant pressed the button that sounded the 'klaxon' throughout the room. Instantly the machines sprang into life. It was like the sound of an underground train approaching down the tunnel but with no intention of stopping. My ears gave up after thirty seconds. People were moving around. Old Jack appeared at my elbow. He smiled and proffered a long steel hook, which he latched under the metal handle of the nearest skip then dragged it towards him.

"That's what that's fer -." he mouthed. I looked at him stupidly. He tried repeating what he had said then gave up. Turning he touched the shoulder of a huge man who had been emptying the bobbin filled skips from the doorway of the hoist. Something passed between them and the huge man nodded. Old Jack gave me a passing grin as he walked away.

The huge man it transpired was 'Ivan'. He was Polish. There were lots of Poles in ower town from before and after the war. Some were refugees from Hitler's rampage others had escaped in the chaos after the war ended and were fleeing from the Soviets. Needless to say they were acceptable having white skin and fleeing as it was from persecution. I'm afraid the same could not be said for their darker skinned brothers who would come to ower town and who would have a far harder time of it as the years went by. Ivan barely spoke decipherable English. It was bad enough trying to learn ower language without the Lancashire twang and slang that accompanied it. During the first tea break Ivan tried to explain the job.

"Is every person is not like. Da number is not like. Da number is da number on da skip. Da number is da number of da person. If da person has not da number he get bloody mad and he cross. Understand!"

"Er – No." Ivan puffed out his cheeks and rolled his eyes. And in his best English too. Now he was stumped. In desperation he 'collared' one of the women. The mill employees were mostly women. The men were used for the heavy work, carrying, lifting etcetera. But when it came to working the ring-spinning and winding machines women's finger work had proven the more dexterous. More efficient.

Scotch Mary was known for her fiery temper but with us 'lads', the younger ones, she had a kind of motherly patience.

"Ahhhh. And you be startin' today laddie will yus?" I gave the old lady my best beam of a smile. She would have been about mid-forties but that was 'old' to me. "And nobody's teld yer what t' do?" I shook my head helplessly. Scotch Mary took hold of my arm and led me away from the 'brew' bench.

"Well it's like this you see -." she began, casting a glance to her rear to see if anyone else was within hearing or seeing distance. (It was important nobody could see her lips moving as they were all proficient in long distance lip reading.) " – it's very important each frame gets the correct bobbins. All the skips are numbered. Usually thirteen to twenty-five. The higher the number, the tougher the thread. Everybody of course wants those with high numbers. The thread doesn't break as easily and they get more done. More done equals more money – Get it?" I nodded. I wasn't absolutely sure I was fully trained with such scant information but I was prepared to accept it didn't take a genius to work in a cotton mill, otherwise how come half the town worked in them? But Scotch Mary hadn't finished.

"Now. What is very important is that you keep me stacked up with loads er bobbins all the time. It doesn't matter if there are others on the same number. Just you look after me and I will look after you. Got it?" I again nodded because it seemed the appropriate thing to do. I got the distinct impression there was something of a 'war' going on between the frame operatives and that this old lady was trying to get me 'on side' so to speak. I wasn't used to old lady's propositioning me. Hurling abuse. Yes. That was fine. I was used to that. But 'seeing me right'? What did she mean? I soon found out.

The number 22 bobbin flew the full length of the top spinning room and felled Doris Braithwaite on the spot. She went down like a sack of spuds! Splat! Old Jack was not pleased.

"It's her own fault, bitch." hollered Scotch Mary from the middle aisle of her machine. "It was my turn fer that next skip an' she got the lad to give it to her. Well, she wanted one, now she's got one – a flying one –. Cow!" Doris Braithwaite was carried off to the first aid room and had two stitches applied to her cracked skull. Old Jack docked Scotch Mary half a shifts pay for damaging works property. No body seemed 'mathered' about Doris Braithwaite. Perhaps she was a known troublemaker? Who knows! Hey Ho -! All in a day's work.
And that, as I would soon find out, was just for starters.

The cotton mill was about eighty years old. One of the more modern structures and less likely to those peculiar 'outbreaks' of devastating destruction from fire. As the industry weakened and became less profitable, more and more mills were succumbing to accidental fires, well 'fires' anyway. I have given previous description to the 'holocaust' of a cotton mill fire in my other 'ramblings' (See Ower Darkling) so for those not familiar, tough titty you'll have to read my previous scribblings. This mill wasn't likely to self-combust in the dead of the night as it still had a full order book and a compliant work force. So my employment was safe, at least for the time being.
The mill was 'sectioned' – (or at least it should have been) – with the ground floor holding the boiler rooms and warehousing, above there the Carding Rooms, above that the Ring Spinning Rooms and above that the Winding, Creel and Beaming Rooms. I worked on top. The whole thing connected by a winding stone staircase or if you wanted you could put your trust in the ancient 'hoists' of which there were two, one either end of the sprawling elongated structure. The noise, as I have mentioned, was constant and tremendous, the air, breathable but dangerous. Masks were available. Cotton pads held against ones face by an elastic band, totally useless the minute they got wet from ones laboured breath and consequently rarely worn by any other than those in the Baling Shed next to the warehouse.
To breathe at all in the Baling Sheds, the air was that thick with cotton fibres, it had to be filtered to get any! I've seen men's faces go grey after an hour in that environment.
 But the money was better so it continued to attract its required complement of victims. Tea breaks were taken, ten minutes, one in the morning and one in the afternoon, at ones 'post'.

It was my job to light the gas boiler and brew the kettles in readiness for this event. Tea, milk and sugar were 'pooled' from a weekly whip-round. Everybody had to contribute, even if you didn't drink it. We were all comrades in arms. United we stand, divided we fall and all that. I didn't perceive much comradeship when it came to doling out the work. God help the floor 'manager' from the wrath of those on less than an 'eighteen' wind. (That's a hard 'i' not a soft one). Old Jack must have had an arse of iron to put up with all that from that pack of half demented women. There was nothing, absolutely nothing, like a woman scorned or in this case – left out of the high numbers. I got so that I stopped looking at the 'winders' as I replenished their skips with bobbins. Eye contact could get your eye put out with the blunt end of a wooden bobbin if the 'winder' had been on 'fifteens' all week.

"Oiii. Bloody 'ell. What did yer do that fer? Christ - - !" I became very adept at 'bobbing and weaving'. Now I know where that saying comes from if nothing else!

The highlight of the week was pay-day. Old Jack would dole out everyone's 'tally', a metal disc showing your works number. At three-thirty on the Thursday afternoon the whole 'room' trooped down to the main office to stand in line to exchange 'tally' for 'packet'. Everyone had to open their packet before leaving the hatch and check the contents. Half the workforce couldn't read, most of the other half couldn't write but not a single one of them couldn't count, money that is!

"Oy thar's 'apenny short 'ere lass. What tha 'trying t' do? Get me 'ung. Tha' missus won't like it -."

"Why's that Billy. You bin givin' her one then?"

"Piss orf. Am talking about this 'ere money tha' daft clot."

And so it went on. Until everyone had checked their respective packets and passed muster. Then it was across the road to the corner shop and stock up on 'goodies'. Fags, sweets, cake and next weeks 'brew tackle'.

Smoking in the workrooms was forbidden. Toilets were situated on each level. To pass them one needed a respirator. Almost everybody smoked. The staircase landings were like small enclaves of a Manchester smog. Old Jack, a non-smoker, swore it was having to extricate chain smokers from the loos that had given him his 'dickey' lungs. It couldn't possibly have been thirty years working in the mill itself now could it? Eh Jack?

Saturday mornings were 'overtime'. Only the 'bobbin carriers' went in to give the 'room' a weekly clean. This was to remove all unwanted fibres from the walls, floors and machinery. Each frame had to be brushed clean and oiled ready for the next weeks shifts. I wasn't complaining. With the overtime I could push my weekly earnings up to twenty-one pounds a week, three times my butchers wage and for fifteen hours less work each week. I was classed as a labourer. Labourer's got the going rate – permanently. Skilled tradesmen, like butchers' assistants, got three times less? Can anyone see anything wrong with that? Ah but. It was the old woman who tried to answer the question logically.

"As a fully qualified butcher you could get twenty-five pounds per week and a bit more in some places -."

"Yes mum. But the average working week for qualified butchers is fifty to sixty hours."

"Ah yes. But you'll be known as a semi-professional person wi' a trade under yer belt. You'll be more respected."

"Wow mother. Really?" Gosh. I don't know how I'm going to live not being respected. Huh?

To be truthful the job at the cotton mill was, in my mind, only a temporary situation. I had other 'fish to fry'. Fish I wasn't about to tell the old woman about until I could find a more propitious time to do it -. Hmm? That wasn't going to be as easy as I had first thought.

She had a displaced hip and a displaced face but at the time she wasn't walking and I wasn't looking at her, well not directly in the face anyway. My nose was buried deep within her thighs and my tongue was elsewhere. Can't say I was over the moon about the taste but then again I have to admit it wasn't the first thing on my mind just then. More poignant in my thoughts was the tingling sensation coming from my nether regions and the slurp, slurp, slurp of her mouth and tongue roaming around my crotch.
Her name wasn't that important either although if I recall correctly she was a Janice. Her father worked at the mill so I had been careful as to where we went during the dinner break. She had all the requisite accoutrements and I was 'gagging' for it. It had been a very long time. Too long and I was getting fed up of trying for 'something' I liked. I didn't like Janice and I'm pretty sure she wasn't over the moon about me.

But 'needs' must. She had one and I had one and to hell with all the rest of the nonsense. We managed the 'whole' routine or to be fair all that we knew about. I hadn't done it in that position before and to be truthful, seeing as I didn't have to look her in the eyes whilst I performed, it was pretty dam satisfying all around. Most of the dinner break had gone by the time I groaned a climax for the third time. I don't really know how she went on. She was pretty quiet about the whole affair which considering the warehouse lads were only a few dozen yards away was perhaps as well. I couldn't say just how much an impression I had made of things. Good, bad or indifferent. To be honest I couldn't have cared less. I wasn't there for her enjoyment albeit I wouldn't have minded had she said something along the lines of 'Wow. That was a blinder'. Instead of 'Have yer finished yet 'am losing the will t' live.' Still, it served its purpose and I was feeling a dam sight better than I had for ages.

It's no use pretending that we males are in full control of ower faculties. Any that say they are, take it from me, they're spinning you a line. Between the age of twelve and forty-two the crotch rules OK! And in many cases long after that too. I don't know of one 'male', and I've met thousands, who hasn't been 'screwed up' one way or another or at one time or another by the 'snake' in his pants. It's the 'male' curse. But where would we be without it?

"Who've yer bin with -?" Oh dear I knew I should have kept my gob shut. The old woman took another long look through the large magnifying glass and then began drumming the table top with her fingers.

"What d' yer mean?" I tried innocently. Her eyes narrowed.

"I know yer think I'm thick and old fashioned but that there's not someat' you've got from not bathing properly. Who've yer bin with?" I stood with the hem of my pants furled down sufficiently so the old woman, who had seen my very obvious discomfort, could view to top of my crotch through the large bulbous lens of the magnifying glass at close quarters. It was useless to try another tack like, 'Oh I fell into some nettles'. Or, 'Oh I've been spraying it with some of that there new deodorant stuff'. She wasn't going to fall for any of that. The old woman had done nursing in the war and was pretty conversant with most of the 'unpleasant' side of 'social' problems. You could always tell a wartime nurse by the tender way they treated you. 'Slap,rip, Arrrgggh, Next'.

But we won't go into that here. I tried a diversion. It was the best I could come up with at the time.

"Why. Is it one er them things tha' gets off toilet seats then?" Well it was better than nothing. I was only seventeen! Crikey! What do you want- blood?

She transfixed me straight in the eyes with her cobra like stare.

"If it is. It's the first time I've come across 'crabs' that can leap three foot high-."

"CRABS!" I stared down at my crotch aghast. Now at sweet seventeen nobody had told us about anything, apart from how to tie up ower shoes laces proper, and the word 'crabs' was a confusing word to juggle with. I had heard of 'clap' and 'nits' and 'fleas' and the 'dreaded pox' and to be honest 'crabs', but 'crabs' in the context of testicles and penis's and sexual intercourse, sorry, that was a blurred canvas. It was obvious these crabs must have been very tiny because I couldn't see them. That they must have had claws was equally obvious by the movements they were making, which was driving me up the wall. Now I was really worried.

"Pubic lice. Crabs. You've bin with some dirty 'trollop' somewhere or else my names Betty Grable-!" The icy stare held its hypnotic hold on my face whilst inside my brain whirled desperately to come up with some plausible explanation. It was no good. I was all out of ideas. This was one of those times I would have to ask for a truce and get the problem sorted out.

"Er – Yea. OK. It was some woman at work." I replied at last. The finger tapping ceased. The old woman shifted in her seat and cleared her throat.

"Right then. First off you get to the doctors. He will give yer some ointment. Then you're going to have to shave -." she gestured, "- all round. Back, front, chest, only that won't be a problem-." Cheeky mare just because I hadn't a single hair on my chest, "- under yer arms, 't'ween yer cheeks and around yer bits an' pieces." I looked at her stupefied.

"Oh it's alright. If you think you're going to have difficulty I can help you do it. It wouldn't be the first time tha' knows." WHAT? I have never shaken my head so fast in all my life.

"No thank you. I'll manage." The old woman cracked a smile.

"Hm. Thought as you might somehow. One more thing. This 'woman', as you call her, she needs telling.

She must have known she had them or if not she will by now. She needs de-fumigating before she goes and passes the bloody things on again. The doctor will give you a card for her. Don't tell him anything about toilet seats, he won't see the funny side of it like what I did. Tell him the truth. Meanwhile I want all your clothes. Everything you've worn this week or since the day you 'defiled' your body on the 'trollop'. Everything has to be boiled. To kill off the eggs. Get moving -." She jerked her thumb at my waistline. "Change now and make sure I get the clean ones back again after you've shaved and treated yourself." She got up from the chair and moved towards the kitchen door. She stopped. Turned. I got another look that held somewhere in the back of it a weird sort of smile or grimace or something! What the hell was going on in that brain of hers. Mothers – I don't know? You can never win with them. Well you certainly couldn't with mine -!

'Making Moves & Merriment.'

Wozzle couldn't believe his ears. Turnip just fell off the bar laughing.

"WHAT! The bloody Navy?" There was a silence as the two of them gathered their composure.

"You couldn't follow orders if yer arse was on fire – You'd still have t' ask why before puttin' it out?" I was offended. Cut to the quick I was. I'd never heard such drivel in all my life. Who? Me? Can't follow orders? Rubbish! Turnip looked up at me from the floor.

"Now I've heard everything," he said smiling in his usual cocky way.

We were all a bit breathless. Having run like bats out of hell the last half a mile and finally being granted sanctuary in the Tap Room of the Red Rose public house.

"Fuzz on yer tail then?" asked the landlord as we piled in through the back door a tangle of flailing arms and legs.

"Eh?" replied Turnip innocently, as if we always entered pubs looking like we had just spent a month in the 'trenches'. In truth we were escaping from the clutches of the remnants of a big 'barny' that had taken place alongside the cinema gardens a short distance from the town centre. Two local gangs of 'teddy' boys had decided to have a 'showdown' naturally to see how many of them were intelligent enough to stay away in the first place. It appeared to the three of us considering the numbers that were involved few if any had given the subject any thought at all. We estimated the numbers to be around forty or so with more dribbling in as the fight swayed from one end of the gardens to the other and as the 'body count' steadily rose.

It wasn't dangerous to walk around the streets of ower town. Then again it wasn't that safe either. Under twelve year old was relatively safe, unless you met up with a victim of a previous 'bonny' raid then it was best to 'leg' it. Thirteen to thirty was the dangerous age group to be in and it was usually from someone of the same or similar age group.
Teddy boys, fifteen to twenty five years of age was the worst possible accidental meeting for it was this age grouping that tended to be the most violent and ignorant.

One wrong look could get you branded with a knuckle-duster, a bicycle chain or given a spot of facial surgery from a blunt cut-throat razor. A lesser 'towelling' and a few cuts, bruises or a broken rib or two from a dozen size thirteen 'beetle crushers' might be the result. But the trick was to avoid accidental meetings and most certainly not to go 'rubber-necking' at an all-out massacre. Which is just what we had done. Doh!!!

The word was out on the street. The 'Syke Mob' had challenged the 'Cutgate Mob' to a 'whosoever is left standing takes all' shindig. Madness of course. But then we had no wars, no riots and conscription had ended – so what was one to do? We was all young 'bucks' – well I nearly got that right didn't I -? The upshot of the early evenings entertainment was a few of the 'combatants' had mistaken we three as cannon-fodder and set off after our lithe young bodies in a bid to trash ower brains out. What they hadn't reckoned on was just how fast we Tech School lads could run when pursued by a screaming mob of lunatics brandishing enough 'armour' that would have put Attila the Hun to shame. Like gazelles on the African plains. Boy did I 'motor' that night. I certainly haven't run for my life that fast since let me tell you. Hey-noddy-no! And that's not a lie.

This was the 'fish' I had to 'fry'. After a bout of light conjecture I had decided to leave town. No – there was no 'force majeure'. The 'fuzz' had my number but they weren't for phoning me. I didn't owe the local 'sharks' and I wasn't doing a runner from some woman's old man. Quite frankly and not to put too fine a point on it I was 'pissed off' with the 'whole' routine. The town, the pubs, the work and the family. It was also abundantly clear that there was another world out there. One free of all the boring routines and the staid confines only close knit communities can engender. I wouldn't venture to put 'down' ower town and its people. Taken all round they were good people or as good as I knew anyway.

But that was the problem. I didn't know any others. The furthest I had ever ventured alone since my early childhood was to Oxford to burn down the Scout Camp (See Ower Darkling – Night of the Flaming Woggles). It was hardly Darkest Africa. I had seen a couple of black men but that was on Fridays when the coal delivery came and they were only black from the neck up.

Not quite the real thing! But first I had to get it all passed the old woman? That might not be the easiest project I had planned for that week.

"WHAT! The bloody Navy?"
Why was everyone so negative? It didn't matter who I approached with the idea they all seemed to come up with the same reaction.
"WHAT! The bloody Navy?"
I was beginning to think I might have had a bad idea – for some obscure reason? It seemed to send everybody else into hysterics? Did they all know something I didn't?
"Yea. I can just imagine you in the Royal Navy. You would have sunk the bloody ship before it managed to get out of port. God help 'em!"
Ah! The Royal Navy. No, no – oh dear me no. Not on your nelly.
"Not the Royal the Merchant -." I replied rolling my eyes. "Give me a bit more credit than that can't yer. Even I know I wouldn't last two minutes in that lot –Jeez."
That seemed to do the trick. Everybody started to relax a little. Even the old man had put down his newspaper at the news. One less mouth to feed would have been rattling around in his brain and less hassle in the household. Him and Ower Kid had been at loggerheads now for the past three years over the 'education' the old woman was insisting should continue, come hell or high water.
"I was thinking as how I would apply for a job as a steward wi' one of the shipping lines. Most of them come into Manchester. It's not that far." The old woman looked at me.
"Yea but they don't just stop in Manchester, they bugger off all over the place, for months, all over the world, places like China and America and – and them sort of places. Why? Was yer thinking you could come home at night fer yer tea -?"
Daft bat! I didn't reply to such a silly comment. Of course I knew they went away from Manchester. They went up and down that big canal they have there to places like Liverpool and Wallasey and Ellesmere Port. What did she think I was, an idiot? Hmm. America eh! That sounded a very good idea. I wasn't too struck on the China bit. I was never that keen on rice although they did do a fair bit of 'tea-leafing' come to think of it.

"How soon yer goin'?" That was Ower Kid. Obviously. He would be thinking his 'ship' had come in. No younger brother to give him pain and the bedroom all to himself. He was forgetting the money he managed to scrounge out of me each week to supplement his 'nil' income. He'd remember soon enough knowing Ower Kid. What's betting he taps me up for a monthly credit drop on my wages from the shipping line? I'd put a 'fiver' on it – and I'd probably win!

They sent for me eventually. They, being the Merchant Marine Recruitment Board. I would be offered a placing in the 'deck' section there being no present openings for stewards available. I agreed and sent back the multiple forms signed as required. I had to go to Liverpool. A medical. Oh dear. That was a 'bummer'. Ower Kid thought it highly amusing.

"Next! - - I said Next! - - NEXT! - Oh sorry. Didn't see you there. Will you please face the front and stop turning sideways. Nobody can see you when you do that. – Speaking of NO-BODY la -. Are yer serious about this?"

"Get knotted." I snarled angrily. Why I have no idea? People had been extracting the urine regarding my physic for as long as I could remember. I was used to it by now. But Ower Kid's sarcasm frequently rankled which I suspect came from deeper reasons than being subjected to it from the lads at school or work or elsewhere.

M.N.T.S. (Medical) Centre. A collection of porta-cabins under the shadow of the Liver Buildings, a large neo-gothic structure that sits near the waterfront and has a 'ruddy' great statue of a weird bird hovering on the top of it. It didn't do anything for me. I thought it quite grotesque, almost threatening and somehow out of keeping with everything else around it. Everyone else seemed to think it was wonderful. I suppose it's whatever turns you on -?

I had a number of concerns. Un-aligned 'bollocks' for one. I had the regular complement of 'two' but one had to rummage around to find the other one because it spent most of its time hiding behind the one on the longest string. My scrotum never had that aesthetic quality about it. Not that it was the most appetising feature of the male anatomy in the first place. Mine certainly wasn't. But no. That didn't seem to faze the man at all.

He placed a fish spatula in the desired position and said "COUGH." I coughed.

"Something wrong wi yar lungs laddie?" he enquired softly. I shook my head. "Voice gone as well has it?" I began to get the measure of this man.

"NO." I boomed in my best parade ground manner.
My lungs were the second worry.

"Well yer's got a shadow on yer left lung. Always have had. Pleurisy. One of them things that was wrong with yer in the early days -." The old woman's eyes went misty. I hadn't wanted to prompt a re-telling of the story of those 'early' days but there was nothing would dissuade the old woman once given an introduction to the subject.

- - "Well you should have seen it Ethel- ". Ethel was Mrs Ethel Speak of number 23 Hope Street (See Ower Darkling). " – it wus like a stick er Blackpool Rock. All bloody colours other than what it should have bin -." Ethel beamed her wide smile over the flag-yard wall and inhaled slowly from the cigarette dangling from between her crooked teeth. She had heard this story maybe a half a dozen times but Nora told it so well – and anyway there was nowt decent on the radio.

- "I said – What's that?" The doctor said, "It's a boy." I said "Bugger off, I've already had one of them and it didn't look nowt like that thing tha's getten there. Tha's not palming me off wi damaged goods. Not after all I've just been through. Find me something else. I can't take that home. Mi old man will do his nut."

- Ethel disgorged a large plume of grey smoke and half a gullet of flem in the direction of the ashbin-hole. She reminded herself it was necessary to breathe some of the local ordinary soot-filled air occasionally otherwise it brought on one of her 'head's'.

- "He's a blue baby -, said the doctor. "Ay an' red an' green an' yeller an' every other bloody colour under't sun too-," I said. The doctor was most charmin'.

- "He's going to need some help. Nurse will take him away to have him seen to. If that's alright. You're not to worry. Everything's going to be alright."

- "I should bloody hope so. If you don't get him the right colour you'd better keep him. The old man will think I've bin having it off with half the Bengal Lancers if I take that 'ome sais I."

- Ethel nodded in agreement. She stroked at her distended belly. She had had six of her own, so far. Each one was different but all had the same demanding way of wanting to eat, wear out clothes and clogs and of 'nicking' anything not tied down. Including the tar from between the cobblestones on the street outside to make 'jet' marbles or black bubble gum. Like a plague of locust about the place. One of these days she would find out what was causing her to have so many of them – like sausages one after the other -?

- "Well after that. If it wasn't one problem it was another. Pleurisy, Chickenpox, German measles, Mumps, Lancashire measles, Glandular fever, Tonsillitis, on and on. 'Tha's not feeding him properly they said. He keeps losing weight.' Three-foot bloody tall and under two stone. Like a bloody lampost. Only thing you could see of him was his head and that was because of his dad's nose. That was how the old man recognised it was his. One look at the nose was all it took. He was a happy bunny from then on. It was the rest of us that were still bloody miserable. Anyroad like I was sayin'. They took him into the nursing 'omes. He was at one for six months. Another one for four months and that last one up by the park for two months. He'd grown six inches and put on two pounds. That was when they sent him back. Apparently he was eating them out of house and home. Said he was like a horse. All teeth and dung. Anyway they gave it up as a bad job so I took him to Harley Street down in London. Cost me an arm and a leg it did. A hundred quid! A week we was there. Then this posh 'consultant' bloke after taking mi money off me said. 'There's nowt wrong wi 'im madam. Right as rain he is.' I thought – Aye. Yes. That's about the size of it matey. There's only one daft bugger here and it's yowers truly. Muggins! A hundred quid patsy. That's me. Come 'ere yer little beggar. I'll give yer nowt wrong with you. Just you wait while I get you outside. At a 'undred quid a throw there soon will be - - and as fer you Mr Consultant if tha' calls me a 'madam' one more time tha'll get thi' clock knocked round so tha' will -." - - - - - - - - - - - - - - .

"Take your clothes off and stand in front of that screen -." ZIP. CLUNCK – ZIP. "Next!"

My third worry was my colour blindness. It wasn't a chronic case but I had a tendency to see blues, purples, reds and mauves as greys of one shade or another. That was why 'blood' had never seemed to be bright red all the time I was in the butchering. Not that I ever questioned it. I could watch a black and white television screen and pick out all the different 'coloured' balls on a snooker table better than anyone else. It was easy -! No probs.
I passed the 'tests' with flying colours, including those of the 'psychoanalysts'.

"Enter -." I tried the door handle. The door was locked.

"Enter –"I tried the handle again. It was still locked. Somebody was playing games with my head. I frowned.

"Enter -." As I made to grasp the door handle for the third time something clicked inside my brain. Beside the door was a single chair and above the door an open glass fanlight. I stood up on the chair and looked through it. The doctor, in his white jacket, stood directly behind the door with his hand grasping his chin.

"ENTER -." He shouted louder. I tapped at the glass. The man's head shot up. He stared at me wide eyed.

"Door won't open It' stuck -!." I shouted getting down again. The lock clicked and the door opened. The man leaned forward.

"Number?" I was number twenty-six I replied. He smiled.

"Thank you number twenty-six. Please make your way to Room D12." And with that he closed the door and proceeded to lock it again.
What that test proved I have no idea? I don't even know if it was a test? I don't even know what I was sent there for? Perhaps he had a 'thing' about young boys with no clothes on - ? I did know it was certainly turning out to be a very, very long day - - - - .

Meanwhile, back at mill, Stephan apparently wanted to kill me. He was the big Polish chap who brought the bobbin skips up to the Winding Room in the hoist, a very large man with typical Slavic looks.
It was rumoured he had been brought to this country as a POW after the end of the war but no one was prepared to ask him about it because he had a foul temper and his English wasn't that good.
One day in a fit of peak I had smiled at him and called him a worthless cretin.

"Cretin? Cretin? Was ist cretin? He had asked in what I assumed was pigeon English, only later to be told he spoke mainly in German. Not wanting any further 'hassle' I lied. I told him it was someone who was considered to be intelligent and 'please would he keep me adequately supplied with skips in future as my 'winders' were getting restless and I didn't fancy having my eyes poked out'. He smiled, nodded his head and preened the bib of his overalls in a most self-congratulating manner. "Da – no problem. Da boy Da."

I thought that was the end of it. Until some 'bright spark' enlightened him otherwise. Now he was looking to beat me to a pulp as for about a week afterwards he had gone around telling everyone that he was a cretin – and a big cretin at that. To which of course everyone else had agreed. Well they would wouldn't they?

I told Old Jack I would be leaving the job shortly and would give him the proper 'notice' and in the meantime would he issue a 'stop' notice on the big Pole, as I didn't think I would live until the end of the day if he found me. Old Jack was very accommodating but gave me a dressing down for my 'loose' tongue and made me pay for the next weeks 'brew' money. Fair Do's everything considered. Stephan spent the rest of the week glaring at me from the gloomy lit confines of the hoist shaft and mumbling incoherently to anyone who passed by what he was going to do to me if he got me alone outside. Some hope!

I gave she of the displaced hip and face the note from the doctor. She couldn't read. So nothing new there then! I had to explain it to her. Which isn't the easiest of things to do.

"Hey Scabby face. Tha's got thisen a dose of the crabs and don't look at me. I didn't give them t' yer. Who's tha bin with, apart from me that is?" When she had finished listing three-quarters of the blokes in the mill I gave up writing, my wrist was beginning to ache. What a waste of time that was. The easiest way was to keep one's eye's peeled for blokes with their hands in their pockets and who appeared to be pleasuring themselves. Then what do you say. 'Oi. I know what yer doing!" Or, 'Oi I knows what you've got!" You can get in a lot of trouble for that from where I come from. Annoyed ex-Nazi Poles would have been the least of my problems.

I worked at the cotton mill for less than six months but what an education that was. They were just ordinary folk, not very well educated but not as thick as others would have you believe.

They, like all the rest, had the same problems as you or I and not always the means or the skill to overcome them. But they were always 'real' people who wouldn't just shut their eyes so as not to see injustice or cross over the street to avoid involvement. The salt of the earth. Sometimes a little too tangy but never an unpalatable dish. In some ways I was sorry to leave. But it was time to move on – me, on my own, with nobody with me and with my little, now bald, ukulele in my hand - so to speak. Hey ho -!

'Seamen, Semen & Young men.'

Talk about 'Muldoon's Picnic'? I had never seen such an unruly bunch of misfits since the fire brigade was called to ower school to search for a gas leak. Not the firemen, the pupils. I have a good idea of what happened. No – it wasn't me. Honest.

The fire-bell went mid afternoon. There was the usual sauntering to the exits in single file headed by the form teachers all except that is, those boys overcome with the fumes from the Art class. Most of the unconscious ones were being carried out, one boy to a limb. Those not unconscious to begin with, soon were. No one thought to put a fifth boy to support the victim's head. But like I've already said. They have thick heads where I come from. So having one's skull rattled a few times on the stone staircase between 'B' corridor and the bottom exit wasn't considered that important.

I suspect it was Turnip and his daft mate. Every summer Turnips step-dad brewed a fresh patch of 'Poteen' or 'Hooch' as we called it. This was a sort of whisky made from potatoes, raisins and sugar. I know because I used to keep 'cavey' for the lads on the 'Mount' in my younger days, watching out for the 'coppers'. I got threepence a day or a penny for an afternoon. It was a lot of money in those days. The lads used to brew it in the kitchen 'set pans' and run it off through inner tubes into bowls on the kitchen tables. Powerful stuff and apt to put blisters on the throat if taken neat. It was also dangerous in that it should have been distilled at least three times and more often than not wasn't.

Be that as it may, I think Turnip had sold a batch to the boys of 4a in the dinner-hour. They had a two hour period Art class that afternoon and halfway through started collapsing all over the place. The Art Mistress. Miss Barnes, thought it was an outbreak of acute food poisoning or, because of some strange odours, which I suspect, were hidden bags of vomit, a gas leak. So the fire brigade was sent for.

"Eh by gum an' what's occurring here then -? Where's yon fire?"

Mr Lewis the headmaster was at a loss to explain the absence of billowing smoke. Had he have asked me I would have most willingly provided some. But he didn't.

"We think there is a gas leak on 'B' corridor. We have a dozen or more boys unconscious and being sick." The Fire Chief, a man with a vast experience of climbing ladders, sent the turntable unit up Nelson Street in search of smoke with the instruction that if they couldn't find any smoke to make some otherwise people would start complaining about spending the rate monies on afternoon 'junkets'. He was also a man very conversant with alcohol and vomit fumes.

"Whose bin hitting the bottle then -." he croaked hoarsely having bent over a number of the semi-conscious and still legless victims lying about the school-yard. Then the crap hit the fan in a glutinous spray. Mr Lewis was not best pleased! But ower Turnip was a bit quicker off the mark than most. He had his 'mate' do the selling on Vicars Field during the dinner-hour. And his mate didn't go to ower school -!

Like I said. I had never seen such a bunch of wandering misfits since my school days. We alighted onto the platform, suitcases in hand and sporting some of ower best going-out clobber. There was a number of the 'teddy-boy' ilk amongst them. The vast majority of us had moved on to a more sedate classical 'small face' style of three-quarter length jackets with rolled collars and chisel-toed shoes. Even in ower town the 'styles' had caught up somewhat. A large man sporting a naval uniform with two crossed embroidered anchors on his sleeves gave us a look of utter disbelief and shook his head slowly as we milled in random confusion under the clouds of steam billowing from the locomotives boiler. After a few minutes he finally lost patience.

"MV Vindicatrix trainees form a line here." he bellowed. One poor bloke standing close to the man's elbow leapt aside in terror as if half expecting to be set upon by the man's massively extruded vocal chords. Boy could he shout!

We 'yomped' two abreast like a swaying line of eastern European refugees the two miles to the camp. Across a small harbour where a number of rusting coaster's wallowed gently at anchor and on across a wild open plain of marsh-grassland and skeletal trees.

The camp was to our right and lay hidden down below by a tall wire fence whose diagonal mesh had become so infused with masses of thorn and thicket branches it was impossible for the eye to penetrate. Had such been possible we might well have marched back in the opposite direction had we known what our accommodation reposing on the opposite side of the fence was going to be. But we didn't. Nobody 'chickened' out the first day.

We lined up for another medical, a haircut and to be issued with our 'induction' gear.

"Clothes off. Stand in line. Mouths shut."

I don't know if you have ever been to a 'group' medical. But it's a bit like first day at the new nudist camp. It's one thing to romp around in the nude with those you know, it's quite another amongst a bunch of strangers. Ower old woman said to stay away from strange men with no clothes on. She knew what she was on about let me tell you. Anyway. We all stood in a long line against the nearest wall with ower hands cupped firmly over ower 'medals'. Then Third Mate Mr Hawthorn came in.

"HANDS ABOVE YOUR HEADS – NOW!"

Nobody moved, all apart from one small bloke with a blonde crew-cut. As his hands swept skywards this huge python emerged from beneath. We all looked sideways and gasped. Bloody show-off. He was gianormous. I could have got three of mine in the same space with room left for a mouth. God. Where had he got that from? Apparently it wasn't a hernia or a clap test. The wizened old physician, I hesitate to call him 'doctor, was looking for infestations of the upper regions. Nits, that sort of thing, as he combed the inside of our armpits armed with a fine steel comb. It begs the question as to how many of us became infested very shortly thereafter as he used the same implement on the lot of us. I found it strangely sensual as he breathed deeply into my armpits and mumbled gently to himself. I can't say for the others. Most tried desperately to stand still and failed. Much to the annoyance of the Third Mate whose only words throughout were "STAND STILL THAT BOY," in a rattling high pitched nasal squeak.

The medical lasted most of the first two hours. After that the haircut. Amazing how it can change quite handsome looking young men into something resembling the 'missing link'.

Near baldness does absolutely nothing to turn the majority of women on especially when it exposes the under developed human male skull and all the neck zits previously hidden beneath heavily lacquered locks of lovingly nurtured hair. I caught my reflection in the window and cringed. There was one consolation. In a few weeks time some of it would grow back and we would also be issued with our berets. But apart from that we wouldn't be allowed out of the camp for the first four weeks so meeting any 'potential' copulators' wasn't on the agenda anyway.

Finally, and it was getting dark by now, we were given our 'induction' gear. Two blue shirts, a pair of dark blue coverall's, two pairs of dark blue woollen socks and a pair of black boots. Our uniforms wouldn't be given to us until after the sixth week of training. The reason being that any 'trainee' wishing to leave the 'establishment' could do so without penalty providing it was within that period. Uniforms were expensive. Failure to complete the remainder of the course would incur 'costs' which, we were informed, would be substantial. Then it was on to our barracks. Oh dear. A chicken shed. One of those types for 'battery' hens. We were going to be 'battery boys' for the duration. The 'shed' was about thirty feet long and fifteen feet wide with a centre aisle. Halfway down stood a 'Romesy' stove. A pot-bellied coke burner with funnel stove pipe leading up to the roof. This was to serve as heating which was only allowed to be lit between the hours of seven and ten in the evening – thus ensuring the room was reasonably warm for sleeping in. This in the winter months of January, February, March and April and it was already snowing outside. Hey ho. Here we go! We are now thirty four in number. Time to take 'book' on how many are going to stay 'this' course. I did a swift appraisal. Some of the 'heavy' gang, the 'big mouths' would be the first to go, although it was difficult to tell. The mommy-boy types would probably make it through. Such was the way I had found it at school. The bigger and tougher the more likely to wilt when the going got really tough. A strange often puzzling result. But true nevertheless. Outward appearances were no useful guide. It was what was inside that mattered. The will to overcome the difficulties.
I took out my notebook and began furiously scribbling down names.

"What odds are on 'Barky'?" said Big Scouse trying to suppress a smile. I didn't need to look in the 'book'.

"Evens." I replied. Big Scouse gave a sneer.

"Not taking any risks are yer la."

Of course not. The name of the game was to win a few quid. There would be no point otherwise and as any Scouser should know, if you come from the North you're not as thick as you look! And we could look dead thick when we wanted too.

It was our second week at MV Vindicatrix. (My doesn't time fly -?) The Vindicatrix was an 19th century schooner built of a mixed wood and steel construction and lay berthed in a purpose built dock in an estuary off the River Severn on the outskirts of Sharpness near Gloucester. And she stank! What of, is probably beyond description. Sweaty youths for a start. A number of trainees were housed aboard her creaking timbers. Stale food. It was here we ate all our 'meals'! An assortment of previous cargoes? Diesel fuel? Dry rot? Wet rot? Rust and Must? God knows. But mangled together in such a small claustrophobic entity it was powerful stuff and should have been bottled for use at the Government Experimental Establishment at Porton Down. It usually hit one from a distance of about fifty yards and was, as time went by, to become quite inviting and tantalising After that was, one got used to the 'meals', of which there was never enough, and one was wishing the hours in between would go much faster as one's stomach groaned loudly for sustenance.

We lost five boys the first week, one of whom actually went walk-about one night and ended up being rescued by the Coast Guard motor launch in the mouth of Sharpness harbour. Three of them were on my list. I got to keep three shillings. Not a bad start seeing as how we couldn't spend any of it. Six more went the second week. It was the weather. And to some extent the rigorous training regime, which was designed to sort the 'wheat' from the 'chaff' as quickly as possible. Although this wasn't the Royal Navy, in many respects the life we would have to endure hereafter wasn't designed to be easy. As we would come to discover for ourselves later. Life at sea wasn't for the faint-hearted. It wasn't a game – as we were to be often told. Danger lurked around every corner. To avoid the consequences one had to be aware. Alert. Alive to staying alive as the saying went. But first one had to survive the 'Vindy'.

(Readers Health Warning – Turn two pages NOW!)

'It was on the good ship Vindy.
By God we had a shindy.
Up at dawn, bollocks shorn
An' tools all limp and mingey'.

The First Mates name was Horrocks.
By God couldn't he talk bollocks.
'In here we make men, nine out of ten
with the odd one over for 'frollicks'!

The Purser, who came from near Reading.
Said 'Captain, Can you do us a wedding?
With me and my boy and his lively sex toy
and whose bum I'm getting' mi 'ead in -!'

Now the Captain found nowt so amusing
As Pursers and the boys he was using
But to wed the poor buggers, let alone bed the poor buggers, was
something he found un-enthusing.

So the Captain he took it much higher.
To the crows nest, just to prove he's a tryer.
He tried the tossing of coins then massaging his loins
But nowt came from pulling his 'wire'.

He'd have to write to those men in the 'Pool'
Get them to explain him the 'rule'.
To marry male onto male was right beyon't pale
Not to mention a strain on one's 'tool'.

Now the men from the 'Pool made a ruling.
They was having no truck with male 'tooling'.
Permission wasn't granted, male to male being slanted
And who did the man think he was fooling?

Then the order came down 'bout the 'shindy'
"We know there's brotherly love at the 'Vindy'
But bonking one's brother is like bonking one's mother
And that's not only all manky but mingey."

So if you're coming to join us mi dears
Be sure to bring the baccy and beers
And woman by the truckload who are already in fuckmode
Because. By Order. there's bugger else here.

(Sung or recited to the refrain – 'It was on the good ship Venus')
Sharpness. Jan 1962.

My apologises to the author if I got it wrong. Atlas D'four.

(End of Reader's Health Warning!)

    God it was bloody cold. And that was putting it mildly. Reveille was 05-30 hours. Shorts and singlets on the parade ground after five minutes for 'ablutions'. In other words a quick swill in ice cold water from a line of frozen taps and badly chipped enamel washbasins. 'Morning Drill' lasted three-quarters of an hour. After which time you were either on a life support machine (the kiss of life from the Chief Steward -)* or ready to face the day revitalised from the icy northern winds and snow-blow drifts that howled across the open marshlands from the general direction of Northern Siberia. *(- the Chief Steward just like kissing young boys – well, there wasn't a lot of other entertainment at the 'Vindicatrix'. So everybody allowed him his minor predilections).
06-30 hours and it was time to tidy up the barracks. Breakfast was at 0700hrs. Porridge and if you didn't like porridge – more porridge for those that did. To be fair there was also a cup of tea. One large chipped enamel mug for the purpose of. One got used to what one found in the bottom of the mugs and treated these 'delicacies' with an air of wild excitement and wonderment. If the object worked loose during the quaffing of the vile liquid therein so much the better. One could fish it out before it polluting the rest of the unconsumable mash that went by the name of 'tea'. As for the food-.
    "What the bloody hell's this." I looked at the puce coloured concoction on the plate before me and grimaced.
    "Corned beef hash". said a pimply faced youth opposite,
    "Don't yer want it then?" Before I had a chance to prod the obscene lump that was spreading slowly outwards towards the edges of the

plate with what looked suspiciously like grey scale like tentacles the plate suddenly leaped from my line of sight and disappeared. When I raised my line of vision the youth opposite already had his head firmly down in the plate and was sucking up the contents of my meal with the enthusiasm of a road-gully cleaner. "Er – no, I don't suppose so, not now anyway." I replied, somewhat temporarily stunned at the speed of the unsolicited transaction.

Sustenance was that scarce you ate and drank anything after a week or two. That's why there was no leafy foliage left on the beech trees that lined the cinder path down from the camp to the ship's basin on the estuary below. It wasn't caterpillars. They had probably been snaffed by the previous summer's intake of recruits anyway. Lucky beggars.

0800 hours. Following breakfast and a few barterings for 'baccy' and 'paper' and a relaxed 'smoko' as one left the ship and headed back to the huts, was 'cleaning barracks and peripheral areas' (otherwise known as 'Blanco' time). 0830 hours First Mates Inspection. "Locker door not fastened. Jankers." "Blankets not folded properly. Jankers." "Kit not presented properly. Jankers." "That boy is cross-eyed. Jankers." "And what's your name – sonny. Hmm Philip eh. What lovely hair you have. Come and see me before lessons." "Bed out of line. Jankers." And so the inspection progressed. If the First Mate found something he liked the inspection was over much quicker. We spruced up one baby faced blonde-haired sprog from Birmingham and stuck him near the entrance door. Ever hopeful. Nobody wanted 'jankers' if they could help it. As for young Brummy, he would have to take his chances. Every operation had to have at least one participant who was willing to make a futile gesture for the good of the rest. Tomorrow it might be my turn. Who knows? The lottery was held the night before. With a bit of luck I hoped I would never win it.

The rest of the morning was taken up with 'lessons'. Before being allowed to pass out of the training school every survivor was expected to attain a certain standard. From very low to whatever heights ower testosterone ravaged brains would allow. It was supposed to sort out the pretty dense from the ambulance cases, those who under different circumstances would have been gathered up by the little men in white coats and hidden away somewhere.

'Navigation' was today's lesson. 'Cardinals'! Half of us thought they were Roman Catholic wannabe's the other half that it was a floor polish for tarting up hospital wards. In essence they turned out to be the main points of a 'compass'. There's a thing! Half cardinals, quarter cardinals and minor points. Three hundred and sixty points in all.

"So! Let's see. - - - Wilkinson B." The Second Mate consulted his seating arrangement chart and pointed at 'Over and Out' (a nickname derived from Wilco – nee Wilkinson). "If you were standing ten degrees North off Nor,Nor East – Where would you be -?" 'Over and Out' looked at him through glazed eyes, then back at his exercise book. One could tell both actions hadn't been the slightest assistance to his land-locked brain.

"Er – Fuckin' lost Sir?" he proffered hopefully.
The Second Mate held the boy in his steely gaze as if trying to decide why on earth he had ever signed articles to teach these misfits from the four corners of these British Islands when he could have been out on the Indian Ocean playing patsy with giant squid. Squid had more gumption. That was for sure.

1200hours signalled one and a half-hours for lunch. It might have seemed a long break but when the walk back and forth to the ships dinning room and having lunch and the compulsory writing of one paragraph of one's weekly letter home, there was rarely much time left over for having 'fun'. The afternoon was likewise taken up with more lessons, the final lesson finishing at 1900 hours with a break at 1700 hours for tea. Those on 'jankers' (punishment parade) would then report to the guard room for 'duties' whilst others would be 'rostered' guard duties with the remainder given a choice of recreation in the barracks or going out of camp to the local seaman's 'Mission Hall' down by the docks. One third of the camps complement, six week plus, were allowed 'off camp' every other night to throw themselves into the mass merrymaking of the snooker room or cafeteria at the 'Flying Angel', a charitable organisation whose sole purpose was to care for the physical and spiritual well-being of seafarers the world over. But alas women weren't allowed.

"That's a bit of a bummer isn't it?" said Wurzle in his loud Berkshire twang. Thin Scouse bundled him off into the nearest corner.

"Are youse stupid la. Yer can't use words like dha' in 'ere. Bummer. Are yous' mad. They's got enough bumming on the brain as it is. When you get up ta leave keep yer arse away from the open air.

I'm not scrappin' to save yower arse la." Wurzle soon got the hang of things and when to keep his mouth shut. Praise the Lord.

It didn't take too long for those boys of a certain 'bent' to get together. It was however frowned upon and great care had to be taken that such liaisons were not reported to the quarterdeck. To get caught 'inflagrante delicto' got one 'booted' out. To get away with it got one an invitation to the First Mate or the Chief Stewards sleeping cabins, a night's tuition on how to do things properly and a provision of 'safety first' by appointment. But isn't that always the way of things. It's not what you know but 'who' you know – and how closely -. As in all things.

For the rest of us, the hetro's and the bi's it was a case of make do and mend, or bend, if it all got too much.

To keep things in check the nightly mug of 'sludge' cocoa was taken with a healthy 'drugging' of 'bromide'. We all knew about it for the 'cookies' (rostered stewards) made great efforts to invite some of us on board to see it being made. The bromide was added under the watchful eye of the 'duty' mate. Usually the bo's'n (short for boatswain) or his second in command. And was 'added' by the shovel full. A large cereal scoop the contents of which were carefully levelled off with the side of the palm. Three scoops to every batch. About a third of a teaspoonful for every rating in camp. The problem was almost everyone knows what happens to cocoa when left to stand. The grains settle to the bottom. If you were the last in line at the tureen, the sludge was half bromide. Cocoa and a large wadge of brown bread with a thin smearing of jam heralded supper at 2130 hours with lights out at 2200.

For the first two or three weeks masturbation continued. As one would expect from males of such tender years. In fact the hut fair rattled to the gruntings and sweatings as getting it 'up' wasn't the problem but making it do anything thereafter required the strength of a bull elephant and the rhythm of a demented woodpecker.

As all the bunks were doubles, a large twelve stone youth three feet from ones head with only a thin metal mesh between, thumping his groin like a heavy weight wrestler, does nothing for ones own libido or ones assessment of ones own personal health and safety.

One or two did collapse under the onslaughts and it wasn't unusual to find one's mattress frame had been surreptitiously 'switched' by some thieving swine during ones absence and you left with a mash of metal wire held together by numerous bits of string. Survival of the fittest. That was still the name of the game and we still had quite a number of weeks to go.

The end of week six had reduced ower hut complement to eighteen; sixteen of Britain's finest had flown the coop for one reason or another. The main excuse had been the rigorous training.

"I didn't sign on to have mi bollocks frozen off – I need mine 'only' between mi legs – not some other buggers." Or. "If I wanted to put up wi all this crap I would have joined the Royal Navy – this lot are a bunch of psycho's." Whatever each personal reason, slowly as the days passed by ower numbers had dwindled until only the 'thickest' of us remained behind.

I was promoted to 'bo's'n's mate' and had a little red anchor sewn onto the sleeve of my new 'battledress' to signify my importance and 'lordship' above those of my 'crew'.

"Brown 'atter." grinned Wurzel by way of a compliment.

"Creep". scowled Lanky throwing a familiar look of disdain in my direction as I sat on the bunk wending thread carefully around the embroidered edge of my bright new acquisition with a rusty needle.

"Fuck off," I replied uncaringly. Lanky had never liked me and likewise I had never much cared for him.

"Been sniffing around the First Mate then have you? Bummy boy?"

That did it. For one I didn't fancy the First Mate, for two he was at least twice my age and for dessert I wasn't into overt homosexuality regardless of the previous two. I saw the twisted snarl of a smile on Lanky's face through a veil of red and sprang at him fingers clawed. In those days I had a bad habit of biting my nails so instead of red gashes pouring blood from both his eyelids I left only dirty fingerprints as he stumbled and collapsed back across his bunk.

"Shut yer filthy mouth yer long streak er piss." I snarled. The boy's jaw dropped open. Recovering his surprise he pushed himself up on both elbows.

"Yea. Typical. Now you have that badge on your sleeve. You know I can't do anything about it or else I will be on the 'quarterdeck'." I took a pace back. The room had gone silent. The rest of the 'crew' had stopped whatever they had been doing.

A fight. Great. I took in a couple of deep breaths. If I backed off now, which is what I should have done having been promoted to a 'more' responsible position, then my credibility with the others, not to mention my 'hold' over them, would go out the window in one. If on the other hand I didn't and got the worst of the 'battle' or even if I won and Lanky reported the incident, I would be automatically stripped of my promotion and reduced back down the ranks. I hadn't been here before, other than in the days way back when I ran the ' Arches' and 'King's Common' gangs and then everything had seemed so much simpler.

"I don't need to be a bo's'n's mate to kick seven bells er shit out of you arsehole." I replied fiercely. Or at least as fiercely as I could. Quite frankly the very idea of getting into a full-blown fisticuffs with the lad wasn't my idea of fun at all. I was hoping my initial onslaught would have been enough to shut him up. Apparently not -. "There -." I snarled, hurling the jacket across the floor. "No badge. No promo. Come on yer long streak er piss let's see what you've got?" OOOooo! Now I had done it. A cheer went up from the rest of the crew who had merged into a ring around the two prospective combatants. I just hoped they wouldn't start chanting 'Fight. Fight. Fight'. I didn't want to encourage the lad at all. There was a flicker, only momentarily, a definite flicker of uncertainty in Lanky's eyes. Then.

"Oh yea. Sure. And then what. You go blabbing to the Bo's'n and he reports me to the Third Officer. I think not Mr Bo's'n's Mate. You must be joking." O joy. Thank God for that. He was backing off. I stepped forward one pace, but not enough to be intimidating, and scowled down at him.

"No I wouldn't. But in future you keep yer opinions t' yerself. Nobody likes a smart arse -." I paused then grinned. "Apart from the Chief Steward an' he's not bothered what kind of arse you've got." That broke the ice. Lanky snorted a grin.

"Yea. Right." He grinned back the relief radiating around his face. I suppose he must have been as fearful as was I for it took him no time at all to become friendly after that, if not, if my memory serves me well, a little too much as time went on. Strange world.
The truth was I had been granted the promotion through 'good work' in the naval studies lessons. Having spent a considerable time in the Scout movement I was already well equipped with ropes and knots and need add only a few more to my repertoire. Likewise with semaphore and Morse code.

The compass and navigation was rudimentary and the various parts of a ship easy to learn. My maths had never been good but nobody here wanted to know the square root of seven or had even heard of calculus. If you could add up to twenty that seemed to take care of everything else. Lifeboats and lifeboat training had a hint of danger to it. So that suited admirably. The tools of the able seaman were in themselves simple and repairing canvas (why?) and splicing monkey balls on the end of throwing ropes didn't need a 'PhD'. All in all I found the studies rather simple and having no other 'available' distractions I learned quickly.

I had been about to be promoted a second time after the twelfth week to the rank of 'Bo's'n' when I fell foul of Third Officer Hawthorn. Not a good idea at the 'Vindy'.

As previously mentioned here was a man of the 'old' school. In his late fifties and no doubt bordering on retirement and definitely bordering on insanity. But, he was the Third Officer. A status of which we were frequently informed and a status we thought should never have been given to him in the first place. A brief description would be a cross between a regimental sergeant major of British Army renown and Uriah Heep of David Copperfield and Charles Dickens fame. As foul a creature you would wish not to meet on a bright day in the Virgin Islands let alone the freezing foggy wastes of the wind swept marshlands of Gloucester. But we had no choice in the matter.

It was early March and we were making for the lower basin for 'supper'. The temperatures had dropped off the scale. Even the brass monkeys were having difficulty getting excited. As for us 'Vindy' boys, mine had shrunk to the size of two chickpeas and the bit in the middle resembled a dried kipper.

"I'm numb," said Wurzle stating the obvious. Thick as well. But nobody thought it worth while adding a codicil.

"Where's the bloody steps gorn -?" The rest of us had been searching through the thick layer of mist trying to determine the Berkshire boy's thoughts when with a loud cry of despair Wurzle suddenly sunk sideways and disappeared from sight. There was a crash, a smattering of oaths followed by an eerie silence. "Looks like he's found the steps then -." mumbled Big Scouse from within the clouds of steam issuing from beneath the collar of his soaking tunic.

"Good man." We walked on, each feeling his way by toecap to where the concrete walkway dropped perilously towards the river basin a couple of hundred feet below.

"Do you think he's alright then -?" someone asked eventually.

"Fucked if I know -." came back a less than caring reply. We walked on dropping down through the cloying layers of satin water that welled up across the course material of ower clothing and lay glistening in the milky blackness against the backdrop of the dead night. Eventually someone whose catatonic brain still had some life in it stopped and forced the slowly moving column to wobble threateningly to a halt.

"Where's he gone then? - Hey! Them at the top? Is Big Wurzle with you-?" the boy called back towards the heavens.

"No he isn't, you BASTARDS -," came back Wurzles unmistakable tones. "He's fallen orf the bloody cliff an' he's fuckin' dead." Those of us who could see the person next to him looked at each other and nodded.

"No change there then -." said somebody, so we all moved on.

There were two methods of boarding the ship. The right way and the wrong way. The right way was via the gangplank, so called for that is all it consisted of, a single boarded walkway resting on the quayside with a pair of steel wheels attached to compensate for the deck movement in the rising and falling tides. A wooden handrail served as protection from falling into the dock. All trainees had to board and disembark via this one narrow access. The wrong way was via an accommodation ladder. This was a much sturdier affair slung from a pair of lifeboat davits over the sloping superstructure of the ship's side. This ran parallel to the ship's side to a half-space landing and hence again at a right angle to the dock and a mounting board on similar steel wheels. But this was for the use of 'Officers Only'. It was however a much quicker method of getting aboard the ship and by this 'short-cut' one could get a head-start on the queue for the 'anti-wank' supper down in the seamen's mess room.

I was cold, freezing in fact, wet and very hungry and I saw no merit with standing limply in line for the next quarter of an hour with my clothing steaming away my vital body heat all for the sake of a mug of sludgy cocoa and a jam butty. The ladder was empty and displayed no signs of life. Swiftly I deviated from the group and made my way towards it.

I had made the half-space landing and was in mid-air swinging rapidly in a semi-circle for the steps up towards the deck when an anguished cry rent the stillness of the night somewhere above my head.

"Aaarrrrgh." Was what it sounded like. I froze, my landing foot smashing down hard on the wooden step in front of me. The ladder took off sideways, then in protest at my sudden intrusion smashed itself back against the steel plating with a resounding bone juddering crash.

"STAND STILL THAT MAN," came a thunderous roar that rattled down the steps and plunged knife-like into the murky waters way down below. The long line of shadowy figures shuffling tortoise like along the dock came to a sudden stop. Fifty or more pairs of eyes appeared from within damp frozen collars and heads turned to see what all the commotion was about.

"Ahrrr. Now whose fur it Under-BO?" came Wurzle's delighted cry from the bank. I glanced in his direction and made a face. The trouble was he was dead right for above my head and slowly advancing towards me came the Third Mate, Mr Hawthorn, with a face of thunder just oozing anticipatory malevolence.

I hadn't seen it fall, the man's hat, somehow it must have passed me in the gloom. But on looking down the ghostliness of the hat's white covering showed its progress towards the bank where it suddenly tipped nib upwards and slide graciously down towards the depths leaving nothing but a very agitated owner spitting oaths in my direction.

"You little bastard. That's my best dress cap!" Mr Hawthorn shrieked whitish flecks of spittle forming at the corners of his mouth. "My best cap -!"

I looked in the direction of the 'shipwrecked' object hoping beyond reason it might just have resurfaced. No such luck. It had been emblazoned with that much egg yoke braiding it was destined never to see the light of day again.

"WHAT are you doing here BOY -?" the third mate thundered.

"Er – Message for the First Mate from the Purser's Office Sir." I lied.

"MESSAGES! MESSAGES? You don't use this ladder for 'MESSAGES'!" Just then he noticed I was wearing my naval dufflecoat. Sin number two.

"You are out of dress Bo's'n's Mate. Who told you you could wear a coat?" There was no answer to that one, not even a plausible lie. I consequently threw myself back on the sympathy tack. I needn't have bothered. Hawthorn hadn't an ounce of compassion in him.

"I've been ill sir. The Second Mate said I wasn't to get wet sir." I lied again.

"WHAT! Why is that boy – Melt do you -?" he sneered gleefully. The upshot of this small contretemps had me before the First Mate on the Quarterdeck at the next 'janker' parade where I explained the circumstances relating to the wearing of the dufflecoat and my desire to get aboard the ship as quickly as possible due to the atrocious weather. I missed out the lies as the Third Mate wasn't present at the 'hearing'. The First Mate couldn't help the grin that spread across his face upon listening to my explanation. The Third Mate was well known for his 'over-use' of the 'janker' system for what could have otherwise been described as 'petty' offences. The First Mate cleared his throat and tried to look stern.

"Unfortunate you came across the Third Mate, Bo's'n's Mate. It will however have to be put on your record regardless of the er smallness of the offence -." He looked around at the other officers present with upturned palms as if to say 'Why me'! And that put the kibosh on any further promotions for yours truly the rest of my time on the training course. - But isn't that the way of things -? Two steps forward, one step back. And always stick to the 'rules' even if you die in the attempt. Eh?

Vindicatrix at berth in Sharpness 1961. Taken from the 'camp' side. (And that means training 'camp'- not what your thinking.) She is missing two of her wooden masts and was nearing the end of her 'useful' days.

This is not 'Hawthorn'. This is what a 'real' naval officer should look like. Firm but fair. Commander Tovey RN.

Just for fun - - - - -!

'Round Pegs, Square Holes.'

Meanwhile ower world was changing. As an adolescent it's easy to 'miss' most of what is happening on the outside. The teenage mind, especially that of the young male, tends to revolve around sex, booze, sex, mind-bending substances, sex, 'natty' clothes, sex, having fun and did I say sex. It is hardly surprising we 'missed' most of the 'important' things. Unless it had large breasts or a pert bum and was minus most of its clothing it rarely got a first glance let alone a second one.

It's March 1962. The ground is a solid block of ice. The air as raw as an open sabre wound and the bullshits coming from the mouth of the Second Mate as we trudge in shorts and vests around the perimeter of the 'Parade Ground', are like stone pellets from a Civil War blunderbuss. The advice, whatever it is, falls on frozen ears aching from the constant wail of a Siberian wind coming at eye level across the petrified Gloucestershire marshes. We trudge on, pretending to go at a run, although any run left in our aching bodies has long past run out.

I'm knackered. Wurzel, who has amazingly stayed the course, sounds like a pair of garrotted pigs as the steel mesh of the bunk above my head groans in unison with his laboured breathing. What the purpose of the afternoon 'run' was for escaped me, and still does. But one didn't argue the toss with the powers that be. They said 'run' you set off at a boggart as fast as your frozen limbs allowed you - or else -.

"Lock Duty Bo's'n's Mate. You can arrange three on four off and visa versa with the Bo's'n's mate of Hut 16. For the next two weeks". Dam! That was a bummer! That's what comes of getting 'noticed' (a euphemism for 'getting promotion').

'Lock Duty' comprised of standing guard over the lock gates that barred the inner harbour access to the canal on the outskirts of the town. The reason? Simply to prevent any of the 'trainees' from using the lock crossing as a short-cut back to the 'camp'.

Taking 'short-cuts' was forbidden. In the 'Merch' one did everything the 'long-way' around, including walking back from the illustrious

'Flying Angel' to be back at the barracks – on time. That time being 21-00 hours (9pm). The 'short-cut' was about three-quarters of a mile, the long-cut over twice that distance. Taking the 'short-cut' got one a week's 'jankers' - if one got caught. Which is why I was there. My orders were to skulk inside the telephone box set back from the lock gates and spring into action the moment I espied a miscreant. Temporarily arrest the 'wrong-doer' and take his name and number. Who! Me?

I took a long good look at my seven stone, pasty face, which had become a great deal pastier these past ten weeks and mulled over a plan of action. I knew that some of the 'lads' would break the 'rule' regardless of the fact everyone knew not to attempt a 'lock' crossing. Mainly because I had attempted quite a number of them myself. In my case I was lucky for the lock gates were not manned every night as the majority thought they were. But one had to have taken the 'risk' to ascertain such valuable information. Having 'temporarily arrested' a rule-breaker, the boy was then allowed to proceed back the way he came and take the long-route home arriving back at camp after hours. The punishment for that, one weeks 'jankers'. Now any mathematician can work out that this made a grand total of two weeks 'jankers' for any boy caught taking the 'risk'. It was therefore a dangerous occupation to be on 'lock duty' and ordering one's temporary prisoner to return whence he came with the prospect of a 'fortnight's 'jankers' hovering over the boy's head. I looked again at my seven stone in the latrine mirror and tried puffing out my chest. No, that looked ridiculous. What came back at me wouldn't have intimidated a seven-year-old choirboy. This was not one of my best days so far.

The 'youth's', for they numbered three, came jauntily on. From the relative warmth of the telephone kiosk, whose single light bulb one had unscrewed slightly to effect a darkened interior, I weighed up the situation. Two too many. In fact looking at the one leading the group call that three. I stepped out into the crisp night air and bunched up the shoulder pads of my dufflecoat to add width and a hopeful intimidating stance.

"Who's going the wrong way then -?" I boomed startling the threesome from their casual foray. The boys concertinaed together and came to a sprawling heap at the end of the lock walkway a tangle of legs and arms and angry oaths.

"Fucking arsehole -?" cried their illustrious leader extricating himself from beneath the writhing flesh. He paused mouth open when he saw the red anchor on the sleeve purposely turned in his direction.

"No –Unfortunately." I replied. " But owt would be better than havin' t' do this every night. You offerin' -?" The boy gave a sheepish scowl and thought better of making another remark.

"You know you're not supposed to come this way. I need your names and numbers."

"Shit." mumbled the spotty one.

"Interesting!" I retorted. "Is that with an 'S'. Would you like to try again."

"I've forgot it." growled Bucktooth. Whose crooked misshapen dentition hadn't been obvious until he opened his mouth. It appeared two of his front teeth had an acute aversion for one another and stuck out almost at right angles either side of the one in the centre which was twice as long as the rest. Unnerving to say the least.

"Then you had better remember sharpish. You've a long way to go back the way you came and around the right way." I glanced at my watch. "It's already ten minutes to nine. You'll never make it."

"Bollocks. Let us through. Nobody's going to know," said the largest one wiping a large globule of mucus from his dripping nose across the sleeve of his jacket.

In fact such was never the case. Trainees arriving at the camp gates from a westerly direction could only have arrived there from the direction of the locks. The 'guards' on main gate duty would be aware and were duty bound to log the event under the threat of 'sanction' in effect 'one weeks jankers'. So that one wasn't going to wash. If my nightly report failed to correspond with the 'gate' it would be 'me' who would be on the quarterdeck and minus the one stripe I had already acquired not to mention 'jankers' for the duration. Sorry lads, but breaking the eleventh commandment was never without its punishments. The large one of the three weighed up his options and showed his reasonably quick grasp of the situation.

"If we go back and round it's one week's jankers and another if you report us. If we tell you to piss off and put a spurt on it's just your word against ours. I think we will take our chances Bo's'n's Mate – So fuck off-."

My arm was in a sling for the next two weeks. Not broken but badly bruised and the wrist not sprained, but I told the MO it was and so had permission to go on 'light duties'.

I felt myself go down and what felt like a herd of wildebeest thunder over my prostrate body. My elbow smashed a hole through one of the glass panels in the door of the telephone box as the last of the large 'hooves' left its imprint in my right cheek. My captives fled into the darkness of the night, leaving me, lying there, moaning and hurting a bit. I told you I was no good at that sort of thing. It was inevitable faced off by more than one and that would had to have been a small one.

The youth's were 'collared' at the 'gate' and held for my return at 21-05. All received a month's 'jankers' for assault and threatened with 'police prosecution' should they try and vent their anger with any re-occurrence of their 'bad' behaviour'. O the joys of 'promotion'! That's what comes of 'doing well' in lessons! That's what comes of breaking the rules of a lifetime. I knew I had been right all along.

At a rough calculation there must have been between 300 and 500 hundred boys at any one time in the camp, given that so many would 'leave' during the initial six weeks of each course. It must have been a nightmare not knowing how many to 'cater' for from one day to the next. A paradise for 'self-helping' I should imagine.

The Chief Steward must have been privy to such an open-ended situation for his circumference resembled that of 'Humpty Dumpty' but in his case he wouldn't have been capable of clambering up any walls. According to 'rumour' he had a job crawling up on the posteriors of his 'stop overs' let alone anything else. It wasn't that homo-sexuality was rife, more a question of what does one do when so many very potent young males are incarcerated together in such a close proximity to one another. It's hardly surprising that Humpty Dumpty's get around to 'Humping' as a regular pastime. And the rewards, to those lads who didn't mind so much how they got their kicks, the Chief Stewards 'locker' held no end of delightful goodies to help put aside the archaic austerities of camp life.

There is a lot of nonsense dribbled forth by those who have no experience of homo-sexuality and the difference between the 'real' homo-sexual and that of the youth who is just 'messing' around, experimenting so to speak. You would be amazed at how many young lads do want to experiment and for these, the majority, no harm is done. But in the 1960s such 'goings on' was tantamount to severe 'criminal activity' regardless that we were all over seventeen and many a year older.

Whilst the 'practice' went on all the time, the authorities went to great lengths to deny its existence and when and wherever possible glossed over any complaints that managed to come to light. If one wanted to return to 'normal' one avoided the cocoa for a week or two, although we couldn't be sure the 'bar-stewards' wouldn't have spiked something else. But it was a brave man who wanted his raving libido to return under those circumstances with 'Humpty Dumpty, and a number of others, always on the prowl.

The last four weeks, we of the 'mature' student variety (there were now sixteen of our original intake) busied ourselves with 'chores' for the 'Officers'. On one trip across the river we nearly managed to drown Wurzel and The Chief Steward. Wurzel very loudly reminded us from the murky surface of the River Severn the reason he couldn't swim and hadn't put it down on his application form, was that he had only intended to sail on the water. No one had suggested he was supposed to try walking on it. We dragged him aboard the Chief Stewards boat together with a large grand father clock to which he was clinging for dear life at the time. The Chief Steward, arm-locked to the prow against the rolling of the boat, was not amused. His clock was very wet and he very nearly had to account for one portly but missing young 'trainee'. On another occasion we happened upon a gypsy encampment during a foray along a forest trail whilst searching for a 'café' and some light refreshment. It was a Sunday and had been granted permission to be off 'camp' for three hours that afternoon. Myself, Wurzel and 'thin' Scouse. It was a 'real' encampment complete with pony and gaily-painted caravan and best of all a young girl by the name of 'Kizzy'. Unfortunately her brother, some years older than we three, returned from a spot of poaching at a most inopportune moment and quickly suggested we 'move on'. Such a shame – What? Well it's all in the mind you know. Dreaming was all that was available. So why not!
It wasn't all sailcloth and compasses. There were other strange goings-on that kept one interested until the tantalising day for ower release upon an innocent unsuspecting world came round, take 'Sex and Tropical Diseases'.

I suspect the man went by the name of 'Dinglefoot'. Well that's what it sounded like, only his very prominent 'lisp' and 'Oxfordshire accent, for which a Northerners ears are untrained, may well have corrupted the reality coming as it did through the throng of bobbing heads in the gloom of the darkened hall.

"This is a plick - - - ." The man had ower instant undivided attention. Not that we hadn't seen one before, just that his was about three feet long and dangled loosely on it's string binding over the rim of the diagram board.

"And thith - - - ." He flicked the paper over with the end of his small wooden baton, " – ith a vagina." Wurzel let out a groan. It was never difficult to imagine what was going on in that large cranium of his. " – and the object, for the majority of you here tonight is to get this –." He pulled hard on a wire extending from within the rubber confines of the 'plick', which suddenly shot, rigid another two feet or more -. " – into this - at the earliest opportunity and as often as possible." His hand obscured the lower portions of the diagram of the female genitalia. Wurzel let out another low moan.

Professor Dinglefoot had a very pronounced lisp and came from Bristol University and was contracted to put in a regular appearance at the 'Training Establishment' to lecture the 'boys' on the dangers of sexually transmitted and some of the other more prominent tropical diseases. He was without doubt 'superb' as a lecturer and kept the whole room of semi-mature teenagers enthralled throughout the two hours 'teaching'. Yours truly included.

No one had ever spoken to any of us in such a forthright and honest manner in the whole of ower short but not uneventful lives. And in a language we could all understand. He doubled up with explanation as in – 'plick' for penis and visa-versa. No one was in any doubt as to his meanings and the 'seriousness' of his message. For although the hut shook with nervous laughter and embarrassed ribald comments the true object behind the man's 'message' could in many respects be a matter life or death to some of us in the not too distant future. Cholera, Dysentery, Yellow Fever. , Syphilis, Herpes, Gonorrhoea, all the then known 'dangers' were displayed in a diagrammatic or slide form and fully dwelt upon. Truly a man who fully deserved his no doubt 'well-paid' expenses. A fitting climax to what had been a short period of 'initiation' into the wider world of the 'adult' – for all of us. To many I suspect he came as a 'blessing in disguise'- -.

- We stood on the parade ground in full dress uniform with our suitcases aligned in the 'correct' formation before us. The First Mate, with his second-in-command in tow, approached from the direction of the ship's 'berth'. We had already been given ower train warrants and ower 'seamen's papers with 'immigration' photographs included. Mine looked like a mirror image of 'Most Wanted'.

"Stand at - ease." The shrill bark of the Second Mate echoed across the dead landscape. The mere fact we were already thus positioned seemed to escape him.

The majority of us had had little to do with the First Mate or the Captain. The 'work' of 'training' what might otherwise be described as some of the nations 'lost' offspring was in the main part left to the lower ranks. Only the once, when brought up on report, had I spoken to the First Mate. Nevertheless he must have been impressed. Either that or he thought me 'interesting', but one had better not elaborate on that one, for he remembered me instantly.

"Ah. Bo's'n's Mate. Managed to keep the one anchor then?" I smiled an acknowledgement. "Good lad. Did Mr Jackson speak to you regarding 'Officer Training College'?" Mr Jackson, the Fourth Mate had. "You should give it some serious thought. If you need any assistance or further advice you may contact me here – meanwhile -." He turned to ower small gathering and to his second-in-command. "Second Mate."

The Second Mate puffed out his chest.

"Gentlemen. Atten - -tion." he screeched.

Gentlemen! We all looked at each other, then around the parade ground. We couldn't see any. It suddenly dawned upon us that he meant 'we of the passing out fraternity'. A crash of rubber-soled boots hit the frozen tundra almost in unison as we snapped to a frozen pose. We were sixteen in number. Survivors. La crème de la crème – well something like that anyway. We had persevered and suffered the arrows of ower outrageous fortunes and come through the worst the 'Vindicatrix' could hurl at ower fragile tender young bodies and – survived. We are now 'men to be counted', Adonis's of ower age, Britain's finest 'Peggies' (the term given to 'deck-boys' prior to becoming Efficient Deck hands). Square pegs, round holes. Look out world – here we come -!

'Minor- Lull Before The Storm'.

The short walk from the station to home drew some peculiar looks from the few passers by. It was mid-afternoon and the night was already beginning to close in around the huddled sprawl of nineteenth century terraces. It wasn't helped by the fine drizzle and the grey smoke falling down towards the streets from the forest of chimneys in every direction. The 'Clean-Air' Act hadn't yet reached ower town and it would be another ten years before its life-prolonging effects did so. I carried my kit bag (home-made in the 'sail sewing' class) over my shoulder with my battered suitcase in the other. But it was my uniform that was drawing all the strange looks. Hardly surprising for it was without doubt rarely of a dress that was seen in ower town although it did have some resemblance to that of a cross between the 'Boys Brigade' and the 'Sea Cadets both of which had 'establishments' locally.
Nobody had the gall to quip 'hello sailor' although from the strained looks a number of them proffered they would have dearly loved to.

I stood opposite the 'shop'. Nothing had changed. The Perspex nude with the see-through 'Spirella' bra still claimed pride of place amongst its attendant 'Playtex' friends that rested in various poses surrounding it. In the other window was a fine display of 'Ladybird' coats for the three to eight year olds. Quality, but hardly money spinners to the vast majority of ower town's customers who could buy the same article but 'Empire Made' for less than half the price the old lady was asking. It was as well my mother didn't rely on the 'shop' to pay for the essentials. But she had her 'standards' and wasn't going to dump them for the sake of a few extra bob. And to buy 'Empire Made' from her suppliers was helping to destroy the cotton trade here in the town. She was having no part of that wasn't ower mum.
I smiled. Why would I have expected anything to have changed? It was yours truly who was doing all the changing.
Now, would it be brass bands and ticker tape or grumpy looks and sarcasm? When I last saw the old lady she was weeping what I took to be tears of joy at my imminent departure.

The old man was also smiling; having no doubt worked out there would be less of a call on his meagre wages. I suppose I could have mis-read that somewhat confusing departure. I remember thinking if the tears were genuinely an emotional reaction to the thought of me 'leaving' home then they had come a bit late in the day. Hardly surprising teenagers have such a difficult time with parents. One minute its snarls of rebuke the next fisticuffs at ten paces and then tears of remorse or despair? Life can be so confusing at times.

As I clicked the latch and pushed against the rusty old bell above the threshold it came to me that I had only been absent a matter of weeks! That was almost the same length of time when I had last played truant from school. That also ended in black bouts of anger and summary violence. Nowt changes then? Hey –ho!

I awoke early the next morning. In fact it was five-thirty and I was about to hurl myself from the top bunk to the barrack room floor when I remembered I wasn't on a top bunk. The purple linoleum was just as cold and uninviting and the rag rug which served to adorn the sparsely furnished bedroom had somehow progressed towards the alcove over the stairwell. The old man must have been vacuming again. He usually managed to chew bits off it and had taken to rolling it up so the old lady wouldn't notice.

I made the bed and made my way quietly down the stairs. No-one else was abroad. Hardly surprising. Even the dog took it badly for as I went to open the kitchen door the stupid mutt launched itself against the opposite side with a resounding crash snapping and snarling through its tangle of bluish grey whiskers at the would be intruder beyond.

"Piss off yer daft mutt." I growled putting my hand gingerly through the crack in the door and expecting it to sink its finely honed teeth smartly into my flesh. It didn't. Not this time anyway. Which isn't to say it hadn't done so on numerous occasions before. It, the dog, was a Kerry Blue. An Irish terrier of moderate size with a mouth like a 'T'Rex dinosaur and a predator brain to match. This 'thing' was Ower Sapper's replacement. Ower Sapper had reached the grand old age of sixteen. I can guarantee this one won't live to be that age, not if it keeps taking chunks out of my legs.

It was a woman's dog and like ower old woman it had an acute dislike of males, especially the human kind.

Mum had named it 'Rory' and only kept it for one reason, in that she never lost a customer once they had entered the shop. As they entered the dog would sidle around the back and sit against the door moving only if someone else entered and then it would slide quickly back into position again. Woe betide the customer who made a move to leave. Up went the hair and the lips curled back as a deep throated snarl escaped its quivering nostrils. 'Did I say you could move then - huh - huh'? One day the old lady had gone to the bakers down the road intending to return in a couple of minutes. On the return a road accident had ensued to which the old lady gave medical assistance until the ambulance arrived, she having been a war-time nurse so to speak, when she returned to the shop twenty minutes later she could barely open the door to enter with almost a dozen prospective patrons jostling for air amidst the disjointed tangle of mannequin corsets and brassieres.

"Bloody thing wouldn't let us out." wailed one of the distraught women pushing out her handbag protectively as the dog advanced slowly in her direction. "But of course not." replied the old lady scathingly as she bent down to scratch behind the dog's ears.. "He doesn't like people who swear – does u not my little petal hmm?" At least it was good for business, if no bloody good for owt else!

The dog gave me one of its 'Put a foot wrong and I'll rip yer bloody leg off' looks. I gave it one of my brightest early morning smiles, which isn't saying much as they say I take after the old lady in that department. With mum it was best to refrain from questions, smiles, loud noises or breathing until a full sixty minutes had passed and she had finished her cup of weak tea and a couple of 'Black Cat' fags. Only then should one take one's life in one's hands and speak quietly in her direction. I have always maintained that I didn't possess the same malady or at least certainly not to such a degree. Three-quarters of an hour and I'm usually human again.

It was time to take stock. I would have three or four weeks before my papers came through to 'sign on'. I didn't suppose the old lady would mind much the lack of a weekly infusion to the family coffers providing of course I signed on at the 'Dole' Office for the intervening period and turned the proceeds over to her.

I think I received the princely sum of twenty three shillings and eight pence –! Boy – time to 'splash out' on a cup of Corporation Pop and a British Rail sandwich. It wasn't that the 'authorities wanted to see you starve –they usually looked the other way but – hey – if you did, it was so much more entertaining -? So what to do to keep out of her way?

"Hey up. You back then? Didn't drown then?"
Oh felicitations brother dear and a hey-noddy-no warm welcome to you too – dipstick. I grimaced a quick smile in Ower Kids direction the usual sarcastic reply I would have normally given sticking somewhere between my Adam's apple and the tip of my tongue. It was only for a month. After that he could find himself some other unfortunate victim upon which to practise his inane humour. Not that his sarcasm would last long. He would shortly remember his younger brother, the golden goose, he who could normally be relied upon to supply the odd pound or two to keep his gaily psychedelically daubed 'mini' cooper fuelled for his daily jaunts from the town to the college in the big city where he now toiled away his days being creative with paints and clays and any other bits and pieces of industrial detritus the sagging canvasses of his youthful genius would sustain. O – did I forget to mention Ower Kid was an 'artist'? O yes. Picasso, eat yer heart out, Ower Kid's on his way.
"Bloody waste er space. S'all bollocks." That was the old man's verdict. Nothing good come ever come from young blokes 'poncing about' having their 'eads filled wi rubbish'. 'It's that that starts wars tha' knows, silly beggars'. "We didn't spend years givin' that old Hitler a bloody good thrashin' t' have Ower Kids heads messed about by poncy blokes callin' themselves educated." "Educated my arse. Them's as can does them as can't teach. Bloody students." Yes father had his own opinions as to the direction his offspring should go – somebody elses home if it was a case of sponging off him. The old lady thought otherwise and in ower house - well - what can I say!

I found the 'Medici' by accident. By now it was some hours later. It was the sound of loud 'pop' music thumping its way down the flight of stairs and out into the busy street that caught my unhealthy curiosity.

The sign above the arrow painted on the wall said 'Coffee' so I followed the direction of the arrow. A form of natural daylight by way of a number of Georgian inspired window frames gave the large room a sort of comfortable atmosphere, one to feel reasonably safe in, I peered around and spotted what might have been a bar, no stools, just one or two pimply youths with hair hanging down to about waist height deep in conversation with a middle-aged woman behind the Formica topped counter. The woman's head came up. Something had told her money had just entered her domain. I could tell. She had that 'Ruby Taylor' smile upon her heavily painted lips.

"Hi. Nice day. Would you like t' take a pew? We are open."
This was my introduction to Rene Carr and what would transpire to be a long and 'interesting' acquaintance with the Carr's of Liverpool.

The 'Medici' Coffee Bar was the first of the 'Sixties' scene establishments to grace the industrialised grimed streets of ower fair town. There had been others but none that catered for the new generations whose predilections for darkened recesses; stark ultra-violet lighting and voluminous ear splitting music which was a must if they were to be persuaded to part with their hard earned cash. Rene Carr brought the present to what we had always considered to be a back-water steeped in Dickensian tradition. It was like a breath of fresh air to we of the 'new wave'.

"Stick it over there la." Rene's eldest of her two children Michael and don't dare call me Mickey. It may have had something to do with the large pair of 'sticky out' ears that adorned the side of his artificially suntanned face from skull top to chin line but him being four years older than yours truly and a 'Scouser' to boot it was best to let sleeping dogs lie. "How many more?"
We had been lugging crate after crate of 'Coke' from the delivery wagon up the long stairwell and into the back room for what seemed most of the afternoon.
"Quarter of a wagon load." I replied through a vastly diminished lung capacity.

That'll teach yer to smoke thirty fags a day dick-head, I thought, as I grasped the door stile for some extra support.

"And what does that translate in to then?" 'Huh? I flashed him one of my best 'smart Alec' looks.

"Fuckin' Swahili?"

Quick as a flash he replied. "Well ask 'em if they got a dozen er two local bearers we can borrow. I'm fucked." So that made two of us.

The teenage capacity for the quaffing of humongous ridiculous amounts of 'Coke Cola had to be seen to be believed. The 'Medici' was already receiving two full wagon load deliveries of the prescriptive blend each week and frequently had to order yet more. The name 'Coffee Bar' should, in my opinion, have been re-named 'The Coke Bar' but that may have drawn the place to the attention of the local constabulary, who weren't known for there great sense of humour, in fact come to think of weren't known for there great sense of anything apart from indolence and brutality.

Rene's first impression of 'money' on my delicate features proved to be an illusion. I was 'brassic'. Such funds as I had reliant on the goodness of the 'State' and the old lady's compassion – which means 'zilch'. "God helps 'em us helps themselves'. Another of her favourite sayings. She didn't say that when I often came home with stuff helped upon myself from the shelves in 'Woolworth's'. But then she didn't know it was me who had 'liberated' them either. But I soon circumvented my temporary lack of 'filthy lucre' by making myself indispensable. Easy when you know how - and I was quite good at knowing 'How'.

"Five percent."

"Ten."

"Six."

"Seven and a half."

"Done."

Rene raised her plump posterior from the bar stool, spit on the palm of her hand and held it out. I hesitated. Too quick. Had I? Been done? Wednesday nights? Worst night of the week for business.

Most people in the town receiving their wages on a Thursday. Come Wednesday everybody and his wife were normally broke.

Just how much trade was I likely to do on a Wednesday night?

And at seven and a half percent was I likely to come out with anything worth while for my labours? I took the proffered claw and hoped I hadn't made an innocent pact with the devil. Not that it really mattered for within a short number of weeks I saw myself on the prow of some fine sleek liner cutting a dashing burst through the sun-speckled waves on the Spanish Main, ower town being then just a distant unpalatable haze of memory. Boy was I in for shock.

M.V. Saint Merriel. I was impressed as I walked slowly alongside her towering superstructure dismissing the odd splodge of rust-staining to her upper sheer- strake. Seven thousand one hundred tons of pulsating steel and looking for all the world a serious piece of ocean going equipment. This would be home for the next two to three months, give or take a week or two here and there.

One signed 'Articles' for one voyage, but there was a catch. A voyage could last indefinitely. In practice the ship's owners listed the voyage from a home port, outbound and returning to a home port, however, should extra cargoes be obtained en route and the ship rerouted such was considered to be the same 'voyage'. Only after a period of twenty four months could the crew demand to be 'shipped' home, by whatever means available to the shipping company and the crew members be paid off.

'Never judge a book by looking at the cover'. Another of the old lady's sayings. Or 'All that glistens is not gold'. I should of course have known better.

The gangplank was somewhat more substantial than that of the 'Vindicatrix's', broader and with a chain rope looped through metal stanchion posts. It also remained solidly seated as I trudged my way aboard to be met by that familiar odour of stale spices and diesel oil which seemed to impregnate every square inch of the deck. Thankfully this time the deck was made of steel the only wooden fabric in evidence that of the hatch covers a number of which lay stacked alongside the hatch coamings ready for re-covering. I turned aft towards the bridge and to where I would find the First Mates cabin. Until I put my 'cross' on the 'papers' I wasn't going anywhere.

Polish (as in- from Poland). The First Mate's name was Sanker. By God was he a W*****!

To be fair his real name was Kowlinski or something along those lines and was thereafter referred to as the 'Cow'. A huge bull of a figure, typical Slavic features with a toothless grin which I recall I happened to observed just the once throughout the whole four months. I am assuming he was drunk at the time otherwise such an occurrence would not have been possible. A refugee from Nazi or Soviet persecution possibly and hired by the company as a result of his servile feudal background from which sprang his revenge on the human race, his almost messianic observance of ship rules and his consequent draconian methods of punishment for every man or beast to break or slightly bend them.

"Fuck zat. Comen here vis no proper time. Sign vis name Peggy boy."

I signed on the dotted line and instantly knew I would regret this unholy bonding of East and West. A face appeared at the open doorway. A tall weather-beaten youth of perhaps ten years my senior.

"Zis new Peggy. He need to show the ropes Bo's'n," and then as an afterthought added, "Vis the knots."

The man beckoned me forward and disappeared up the passageway. Once out of earshot the Bo's'n a local man from north Manchester introduced himself.

"Jamie, but you will call me Bo. The lads will call you Peggy. No disrespect, all the Deck Boys go by that name so don't try to insist they use your real name." I nodded and heaved my ocean-going suitcase into my other hand. He jerked a thumb back. "Keep out of that arso-, fella's way. He's not a full shilling. If you need any help you come to me, OK?"

My cabin I shared with one of the EDH's (Efficient Deck Hand) a youth by the name of Shover. I got the bottom bunk and the remaining corner of a large wooden wardrobe/cupboard and that was it. The need for other furnishings not a priority on the shipping company's lists. The deck-crews quarters, those of lower rating than the Bo's'n's Mate were situated aft below the 'poop deck' and as luck would have it directly alongside the steering gear housing which groaned and grinched from the minute we set sail until the moment we anchored again, euphemistically called 'steerage class' in 'passenger liners'. Not that it bothered me unduly having lived for the best part of five years alongside the canal lock and the rumbling bridge with the odd minor earthquake of falling buildings thrown in. For what it was worth, this was going to be home for the duration.

As the only Peggy aboard my duties lay for the most part in attending to the seamen's wants. I hasten at this point to explain that did not include 'every' want, purely those of food and drink and keeping the seamen's mess in a respectable condition.

The working life aboard an ocean going vessel is one of duty watch, ship repair and long periods of boredom. That is unless one had a liking for 'overtime' or some other worthwhile pastime in which to while away one's free time. Fortunately I had both. The long working weeks of the 'butchering' trade holding me in good stead and with this my first ocean going journey, boredom seemed a very long way off. I soon discovered the senseless rules and crass incompetence of some people didn't stop on the quayside or even outside the twelve mile limit.

"Sorry? – Lookout! - But wis in the bloody Manchester Ship Canal? There's walls on both sides fer Christ' sake? What are we expecting – to get mown down by a bloody herd of stampedin' cattle'?" I couldn't believe the Bo's'n's orders. I had been allocated my two four hour 'watches' the first of which was as a 'lookout'. The trouble was we had only just left Salford Docks an hour previously. True it was dark, but the 'canal' down which we edged towards Liverpool and the Irish Sea, at a cool three knots, was only one way traffic with large lay-by berths for vessels travelling in the opposite direction. I couldn't believe the Maritime Authority of the day would have a system of 'whoever's the biggest'? Even trains on the same track are properly marshalled and that was run by 'British Rail' and you couldn't possibly get any worse than that now could you?

"Owers not t' question why, do as yer told or get a poke in the eye."
The boson's mate, Curly, flicked a long finger towards the mast housing and gestured upwards. "Crows nest." he snapped. "NOW."

Heights I can contend with, up to about fifty feet. After that I tend to start getting concerned. Fortunately the 'crows nest' was around that height as I puffed my way under and upwards inside its metalled safety rails. It was early April in ower northern climes and had been snowing the day before. My breath crystallized on the wrought iron surfaces of the fore mast.
I stared around in disbelief out and across the vast expanse of

industrial wastelands on either side and the length of the black oily surface of the canal running fore and aft.

What the hell was I going to do with myself for the next four hours? Madness. Sheer bloody madness! "Ahoy master of the watch. Semi-derelict onion pickling factory two degrees off the port quarter." – Well there was f' Pete's sake!!!! Which brainless twat thought this one up?

There were twenty one of us. Crammed into an array of variously decorated sardine tins scattered amongst the allocated sections of the vessels superstructure where we the men of the company's labour force were expected to live. Ten deckhands, four stewards, cookie and six engineering crew all of whom I would come to know in one capacity or another during a voyage that was to last upwards of four months.

'The Captain was a haughty man, of pristine garb and blubber, who tried in vain to keep things sane, the silly looking bugger.'

'The Second Steward a playful chap, blue eyed, blonde-haired and merry. Two steps ahead one's bum one kept so as not to loose one's cherry.'

I could go on as each and every one of the St Merriel's crew had some quirk or another as a direct result of too many lonely weeks of close confinement upon the seven seas of ower small but miraculous blue planet.

Two days later we arrived in London. I wasn't impressed. With London that was. I spent quite a number of weeks in that smog laden city as a young boy being prodded and poked from cranium to anus by be-spectacled old men in a bid to discover which planet I had originated from. The place held few lasting fond memories until I remembered Uncle Tom and Aunty Winnie and young Norman their son, but that had been another life ago. For now we suffered the indignity of being pushed and hauled from pillar to post by a bevy of small tugs in a bid to funnel ower large girth into a small wooden jetty alongside the Ford Works at Dagenham.

Tractors. Dozens and dozens of new shiny tractors for ower French Canadian cousins, the white skinned variety or so I assumed.

Two days leave. Not bad considering I had only done two days work. Good job this – hmmm? So where was the catch?

There wasn't a catch. Two days leave. So I made my way into South Ockenden to visit Aunt Winnie who now lived alone, Uncle Tommy having drifted off this mortal coil some years previously, to present myself to this startled old lady who hadn't the foggiest who I was until I opened my mouth and said , "Hey up lass I'm yon bugger from up North. I was about six years old the last time you saw me." True to form and classic for the true Londoner she grabbed me in a big bear hug planted a huge grizzled kiss on the side of my delicate pasty skin and said. "Cor blimey. Well knock me down with a Pearly Kings jock strap. My you're a big bleeder ain't you. Does your mother know your out on the streets? Come in why don't you." She was a star was ower Auntie Winnie. The likes of which will never be seen again, at least not in my lifetime.

Three days later we left the murky river Thames behind and pointed ower bows in a westerly direction. The big adventure was about to begin, at least it was for yours truly.

The year was 1962. No doubt a great deal was happening throughout the civilised world although most of it passed me by like grass clippings through a ducks anus. I seem to recall we were going to get incinerated by nuclear bombs every other Wednesday and somebody was lobbing a big tennis ball called Telstar into the ghostly firmament that would beam telephone calls all over the place and beyond. Wow – I was agog with anticipation. I remember thinking all I wanted to do was get a shag at the earliest possible moment and considering some of the looks I was getting from half the deck hands I was hoping the same for them to – before they ran out of patience and thought me a second best. Curly fair drooled in anticipation every time I passed his cabin door and the stewards, well, I don't know where to begin! I was going on eighteen but looked a healthy fifteen or sixteen year old with a bum-fluff complexion to boot. Not the best side to put forward under the circumstances. I toyed with the idea of a swift application of funnel soot and grease monkeys sweat to produce an aged shadow on the delicate curves of my lower jaw.
But that wouldn't have fooled them for a minute; it wasn't my face they were interested in. Shit -! Well yes. I suppose that came into it to - somewhere?

This is where knowing all about 'dirty old men' and 'brown hatters' came in handy. There's a huge amount of useful information gained from being street wise at a very early age. It's amazing what 'things' you need to know about to survive the trials and tribulations of any would be outrageous fortunes - Mother dear! And I didn't learn that in any so called stylish 'Technical School for Boys', well not from the teachers anyway.

We hit the storm two weeks out and about two hundred miles east of Nova Scotia. It was then I was informed she 'the ship' was a liberty boat, welded plates and very few rivets. In other words super-glued together with a cheap 'American' Bostik. We inevitably sprang a leak in one of the forward holds.

"The 'chippy' needs this. He's in number two. Pop it down to him."

Curly handed me an extension lamp with a half hundred-weight coil of electric lead attached. I had been down the holds during loading, purely from curiosity as it wasn't in my province to work in those areas whilst in dock, and I thought I knew my way around.

"There's a small leak and we shall need to cement box it." I scurried away making sure to grab a hand hold every few paces on whatever part of the superstructure presented itself. The seas were producing regular forty foot deep troughs and topping the furthest extremities of the foremast with every sideways slide. The wheel man was having a devil of a job keeping the ship bows on a 'head-on' course.

I found the 'chippy' (ships joiner) in hold No.2. He was perched upon a large wooden packing case in six feet of water. I knew it was that deep because the tractor seats were playing pat-a-cake with the surface of the evil looking oily slick that rushed fore and aft with every movement of the ships girth.

"Good lad. Plug it in." shouted the chippy across the darkened void.

I searched around and eventually found a socket. I flicked the switch to the 'On' position and staggered back to the guard rail. We now had to wait for the ship to pitch bow down for the packing case to float within handing distance. I misjudged the hand-over and thinking it prudent threw the lamp towards him. I'm not sure what happened other than there was a large bluish flash and a strangled cry of,

"You stupid fucking bastar-." Before a funereal silence descended over the troubled waters. I looked but couldn't see the 'chippy' anywhere. He surfaced just out of arms length his hair still sticking up like the quills on a defensive hedgehog.

"Who told you to switch the bastard thing on you pillock." he screamed at me. I couldn't see what he was getting all excited about he could hardly use it without the bulb being lit – come to think of it where was the bulb -. Ah! That explains it. I forgot the bulb was still in my trouser pocket. I know what happened. I was so concerned at the depth of water sloshing around in the hold, after being informed it was just a 'small leak', that my mind hadn't connect the two elements together. Water and electric. Then again had he not slipped off the packing case – Well – it's all open to individual interpretation to my mind. And what was he getting so excited about when it was so bloody obvious the ship was slowly sinking anyway? If this carried on the whole lot of us were for 'Davy Jones's' locker,- not just him!

'French style, Doggie Style & like an Egyptian.'

The land mass when it first appeared came via the gloom of an exhausted day. We had been battered from head to toe for three days by a 'north-westerly' but late in the afternoon the winds abated and a feint portend of good weather to come flickered far off on the horizon between what at first had seemed to my uninitiated gaze to be dark low lying cloud. It was in fact the two distant promontories of the St Lawrence Seaway.

"Quebec or Montreal in the morning." growled the Bo's'n's Mate as he took in my eager curiosity to what he knew was my first foray into these North American latitudes. "There'll be a possibility of some shore-leave for a couple of days whilst we lose some of the cargo." To my mind we had lost half the cargo already, I couldn't imagine anybody wanting them there tractors after travelling half way across the Atlantic Ocean under six feet of salt-water. But that wasn't what he meant. He placed a friendly arm across the narrow girth of my shoulders and purred closely adjacent my right ear-hole. "If you want I could show you something you have never seen before, Pegs." Shover, real name, Gary Chivenhearst looked sideways in my direction. I caught the eye movement which said -, 'Not a good idea Peggy boy'. It wasn't politic to answer the Boson's Mate's offer in the negative. Curly was a dangerous man especially after a few beers or more which seemed to have a very detrimental effect upon his eyesight and general direction although in all the time I sailed with him he never fell overboard once, although it wasn't for the want of my wishing he would.

"Yea – well – maybe. It depends -." I mumbled and tried to wriggle my crawling flesh from beneath his muscular arm.

"Aw Peggy boy – never look a gift horse in the mouth. There's a long way to go yet." Curly spat out a large globule of flem from the back of his throat gave a grin of his heavy chiselled features and moved on. Shover watched his retreating back.

"Huh. It's not a gift horse he wants yer to look at, but mouths come in to it alright, dirty bastard." He waited until a respectable distance opened between us and the man's back.

"Has he tried it on wi yer yet?" The difficulty for a teenager being asked such a question was how one should answer. I knew what it was Shover was asking but was not yet adult enough to give an answer that would be both learned and sensible.

"You must be kiddin'. I'd poke his fuckin' eyes out." I cockily replied, which lead to an instant ear-bashing from the young EDH on how to handle the various arse-bandits (euphemistically called) that were aboard or that I would inevitably encounter during a life at sea. To blatantly refuse the sexual advances of persons in whose hands your life resides is one thing, to survive in one piece thereafter is quite another.

"You've got to learn how to keep them off without offending their sensibilities."

"Yer what?"

"Without upsetting them. It's an art. I should know. I've had my share." I looked at him. At a glance possibly twenty eight, twenty-nine years old. In truth he was only twenty-two as I would later discover. "In the main there's nowt to worry about. Nobody's gonna try anything on with the other lads around. They could get fired or even worse. Just stay away from their cabins in your free-time. That's when things can get out of hand. Savy?"

Twenty three days since leaving London we passed by the majestic towering heights of Abraham and glittering spires of the capital of Canada-Francaise the city of Quebec. Our first port of call Montreal. Less French, friendlier or at least so we were led to believe.
Ours was the port side aft-hawser. Shover handed me a throwing line. "Practice makes perfect Pegs."
The reader will recall the trouble I sometimes had with 'balls'. The rope line had a huge one called a 'monkey fist' attached to the end of it. The object was to get the throwing line to the helmeted man on the quayside in order that he might haul ashore one of the huge mooring ropes with which we held the huge vessel snug and tight up against the dock. I steadied myself and hurled the rope aloft in the man's general direction. I saw Shover's jaw drop like a stone and turned in time to see the man on the dock do likewise only not just his jaw, all of him. Shover stared at me aghast.
I was pretty proud at myself having actually managed to reach the

dock with my throw until the other end of the throwing rope suddenly flicked contemptuously skywards and disappeared rapidly over the ships rail. Shover closed his mouth then quickly opened it again from the side.

"Don't look now yer little cunt but (a) that's not the right bloke you just missed killin' wi yon rope. You are supposed to wait until we stop moving forwards. (b) you are supposed to tie the other end of the rope to the guard rail and (c) -," He jerked his thumb skywards. " The 'Cow' saw the whole thing." I looked up towards the ship's bridge. Sure enough Kowlinski's unshaven mongoloid features scowled down at me from above.

"Vot good is zat you doin' Peggs eh?" he hollered his Slavic English bouncing about like a trapped rodent between the ships superstructure and the large grain silo's dwarfing the quayside.

"Ooooo. I think he no like small English boy." I quipped under my breath.

"Huh. You think *he* don't like yer." Shover nodded towards the helmeted figure leaping about the dockside who was motioning with long slashing movements in our general direction with what looked to be a large steak-knife.

"Looks like you've got yourself a welcoming committee ashore as well laddie." He shook his head. "How do you do it. Eh. What's the secret. God man you should bottle it and sell it to the Yanks. They's always looking fer more new deadly weapons. Jesus Christ."

If looks could kill I would be stone dead. Immigration Officials would never get on my Christmas list. Not that I had one. He handed me a slip of paper to accompany my set of blackened fingers. The former announced my personal details the latter in case they came across a line of inky fingerprints at any of a multitude of their local crime scenes. 'It's that godammed Limey from off that old rust-bucket down in the docks. Cage the little shit and lob the key into some concrete foundations. English bastard.' I slunk away from the Chief Stewards cabin observing the golden rule when passing through the Stewards quarters to walk crab-wise with one's butt firmly against the bulkheads.

"Hiya Pegs." I froze; the blood in my vein's washing an icy track down the ribbing of my spine. My feet had barely brushed over the raised coaming of the hatchway. I turned intrepidly towards the voice. With more than a modicum of relief I found the Third Mate, or to be precise, Trainee Officer Hughes who beamed a broad smile before checking his rear and bouncing out onto the deck alongside.

"Going ashore?" he asked.

Trevor Hughes was in his early twenties. Thin, tall like myself but with a shock of jet black hair over a pair of ice blue eyes and the merest trace of a neat moustache shimmering along his upper lip. He was a 'Brummy', from the outskirts of Birmingham and about as far from the sea in 'England' terms as it was possible to be. Which isn't saying much as the widest part of the British Isles is hardly more than three hundred miles across, but to those of us who thought then anything more than a fifty mile trip necessitated an overnight stay, it was humongous. Trev spoke with the usual 'yow-yow' drawl of a Midlands accent.

"Yow going ashore then?" he repeated.

"Now." I replied. Meaning 'no' of course thinking it to be more in keeping.

"Well not exactly at this moment -." He consulted his wristwatch. "Half an hour say."

Oh dear. Never mind eh.

"No Sir. I meant 'No'. The Bo's'n hasn't given me permission – Sir."

He grinned again.

"Not if I wish it to be otherwise Pegs. And stop taking the piss. You 'hecky-thump lot are all the same." He checked his watch again.

"1400 hours." As he moved away he straightened his cap. "And stop all the 'Sir' crap. It's Trevor. Not an officer yet. Don't worry about the Bo's'n, I'll sort it out."

It turned out Trevor was as new to this sprawl of an East Canadian city as was yours truly only he seemed totally unconcerned as we wandered blindly through a tenement jungle of high-rise concrete blocks and litter strewn alleyways.

"It's supposed to be around here somewhere." he wheezed tiredly. We had been walking for about forty minutes and to my mind just going around in circles.

The 'bar' was called the 'Sunshine Rooms' although as a recommendation from Curly I doubted it would live up to its elaborate description. It was however one of the very few places an under 21 years old might acquire alcohol French-Canadian law being what it was. Ridiculous.

"Over here you can drive a car at fourteen years, get hitched at sixteen, join the Army and get your knackers blown off at seventeen and put up for Parliament at eighteen. But woe betide you should want an alcoholic drink whilst doing all that. Not on your bloody Nellie." Trevor was not amused and getting more frustrated by the minute. Out of the corner of my eye I spied upon a wandering local.

"Hey up. Why not ask this bloke. He might know."
The man approaching was of middle-age and wearing a lumber type jacket and one of those kinked-brimmed American linen caps. Trevor crossed to the pavement.

"Excuse me please -," he began. "- Do you know of a bar in this area called the 'Sunshine Rooms." The man shuddered to a halt and stared the uniformed figure up and down then -.

"Comment?" he replied. "Q'est vous ditez?" Trevor rolled his eyes.

"Shit. Trust me to pick a Froggie." He grunted in exasperation.

"Comment?" said the man again.
Now during my few years since leaving school it could not have been said I had dwelt to any great extent upon my incarceration at that establishment nor could it be said I was prone to volunteering without first having given the subject some due consideration. But I suppose like all young bucks (I nearly got that right) I must have been prone to bouts of 'exhibitionism'.

"Pardon monsieur. Mon ami. Il demand si vous connez la direction pour une 'bar', La Salle Soliel s'il vous plait." I asked – in my best schoolroom French. Trevor's eyes widened as his jaw dropped stupidly open.

"Ah oui Monsieur. Si vous allez a gauche ici et allors vous prendez la deuxieme a droit. C'est la." the man replied. I nodded. "Merci."
The man gave a dismissive wave of the hand and walked away.
Trevor took a deep breath.

"Where the 'fuck' did 'you' learn to speak French," he grunted crossly.
I smiled. "Just 'cause I come from the slums of Lancashire and don't speak proper don't mean t' say I's thick –Sir. I chirped back.

"Hey buddy," Trevor turned. The man had stopped a few paces away. "You – the one garbed up like a dogs dinner. Next time you call a man out here a 'Froggie', make goddammed sure he ain't gonna understand you – Ca va?" The man turned and went on his way. Trevor waited until the distance had increased.

"Bloody creep -," he said when the man was out of earshot. "- Bastard understood me all the time."

"Yea – didn't he just. Clever these 'Froggies' aren't they – Sir?" I replied.

Trevor looked over the small amount of 'fried egg' braiding circling the cuffs of his jacket and frowned.

"Who's he calling a bloody 'dog's dinner – bloody arsehole! Smart that is -."

"You'll be the one that's smart if he hears yer calling him an arsehole. You'll smart from head t' toe." I stared up the street. "He say's left on this corner and second on the right – Sir." The Third Mate looked at me trying to decide what under all that angelic mousey blonde hair and innocent countenance posed a problem. I could have told him - but I was getting wiser by the day.

However still not as wise as I might have been but try telling that to any eighteen years old and see what you get in return.

The woman left the bar in a flash of imitation red leather and flowing peroxide hair pieces. The bar was as the man indicated. We descended towards the bowels of the earth to a door simply marked 'In'. I fully expected and was not disappointed when upon entering to find an adjacent door with steps leading skywards marked 'Out'.

The bar circumvented the room beginning on our left and terminating within an elbows width on our right. A litter of small tables with two chairs to each and sporting a lighted candle centre top almost covered the remaining area. Trevor went first. In a straight line and aiming for the centre of the huge bar. The barman, who upon our entrance had been to our left and who at first glance appeared to be crouching down, floated eerily along behind the bar at right angles to us. We stopped, or Trevor did, I didn't and had to extract my teeth from between his shoulders blades. The barman stopped. Trevor walked on. The barman continued to float along keeping pace as we passed the centre of the room. We stopped again. The barman stopped again. Trevor tilted his head in my direction.

"You don't suppose it's my magnetic personality do yer?" he quipped from the corner of his mouth.

"Huh!" I frowned. "No wonder it's taken us four bloody weeks t' get here. I thought we kept going round in circles. Does the Captain know about yer affliction then? You could do t' stay away from't ship's compass in future." Trevor narrowed his eyes then shook his head slowly.

"Twat." he replied. I could see his point so we moved on. Looking over the bar the barman's almost angelic progress was exposed for what it was as he hissed gracefully to halt before us. The man was seated upon a leather upholstered chair that in turn was attached to a small trolley which in turn rested upon what can be best described as a miniature railway track. The apparatus was electrically operated from the arm of the chair by an array of brightly lit buttons. I was impressed, and that was only the beginning.

Art Deco. The style of the bar. Although to be truthful I didn't have a clue what it was at the time. Coloured plastic and steel in huge rainbow patterns covered the back walls and lit from behind with subdued lighting that rippled continuously. I could see that might have been a problem after a bucketful or two of the ice cold beers. Trevor acquired two schooners of yellow liquid and we settled across the bar to irrigate the sandpaper that seemed to be sticking to the back of our throats. After nearly an hour wandering the streets of the city we had in fact arrived back at not less than fifty yards from the quayside from whence we started. It was hot on the St Lawrence Seaway at this time of year, not made any better from the clouds of dust that seemed to billow everywhere amongst the tall concrete building that choked the wharves on the seemingly endless quayside. Two glasses of the yellow liquid and my spirits returned.

"So where can we get a shag?" I said matter of factly. Trevor grinned and quickly ran his eyes over the few couples that lounged amongst the tables and bar.

"Not in here."

I wasn't so sure. From my vantage point I could pick out three or four youngish possibilities. Not bad looking. Not that that really mattered. I was looking for sex not a lasting relationship.

"Why. What's wrong wi yon over there?" I nodded towards a young woman drinking alone at the bar on our left.

"Fuck off you bastard."

I spun about. Either Trevor was throwing his voice or somebody in the vicinity was lip-reading. It proved to be neither.

She hit the man just the once with her purse, which admittedly was the size of my old lady's washing bag, and he took to the air landing a good six feet away from the upturned table where he sat up just the once before collapsing in a heap like a discarded rag doll.

"Bloody 'ell." I gasped. "Did you see that?" Trevor nodded through the bottom of his upturned glass then turned back to the bar. It was at this point the woman stormed out of the bar dragging her red plastic coat in her wake. Nobody moved. The barman who was 'fixed' to his chair tried in vain to observe the proceedings by jerking up and down in his seat like a broken 'jack-in-a-box'.

"Bitch. God-dam it. Bitch hasn't paid for her drinks. Dam cock-sucker. Come back here you tit-less freak." he screamed. It was no good. The woman had scaled the 'Out' stairway like a trainee fireman and was no doubt half way to Toronto by now.

"God. What did she have in her handbag? Half a bloody house brick?"

"Yep. More than likely, replied Trevor. "He was lucky she didn't pull out a machete and cut his balls off before she went. Not unheard of I can tell yer."

I looked at him with more than a little scepticism.

"Bog off. Yer windin' me up – aren't yer?" Trevor finished off the last few inches of yellow liquid from his glass, belched gently and leaned across.

"Listen Pegs. I would suggest we've done OK for today. I now see what the attraction this place has for Curly. But I don't think it's really what we are looking for. You see that one by the bar, the one you had your eye on? And the others. Well let me give you some advice. Don't go sticking your hands up any of them skirts because you will be amazed at what you'll find. And it won't be the number of holes you had in mind, believe me."

This was my first introduction to a 'Tranny' Bar. (Transvestite). Where the 'ladies' are not and the 'men' don't seem to mind. In truth I had heard of 'cross-dressing' but she-males, this was taking things a bit far if you ask me.

The problem was, discounting the first and 'second' glance, I hadn't been able to tell the difference at the third or even fourth glance.

Things can be so confusing at times and it didn't appear to be getting any better as time went on either. It was a pretty strange world out here and we've only just begun. Whatever next!

We tarried in Montreal just sufficiently long enough to off-load the two fo'r'ard holds of Ford Dagenham tractors before casting off for Lake Ontario and the bustling, English speaking city of Toronto. A few days here and following a swift but exciting visit to Niagara falls and the quaint metropolis of Hamilton we set forth ower intrepid bows to conquer the menacing heights of the Welland Canal in a desperate bid to gain Lake Eyrie and the vast Canadian hinterlands beyond. Perhaps I should have stayed in Hamilton?

It was during my little walk-about in that fair city I was persuaded to tarry awhile by a fair dusky maiden of less than good repute. She kept asking me for twenty dollars. I thought she was trying to rent me an apartment. The one across the street she kept pointing at. I kept telling her I wasn't on holiday and wasn't looking for accomodation. Apparently, as it transpired, it was only for the one night and what she was actually renting out didn't come with a Health and Safety certificate attached. This was one of those very, very rare occasions my brain, as young as it still was, reacted in the negative signalling my genitals remain in sweet repose and telling me the cash in the pouch of my money belt should not be exposed in eye-shot of this seductive indigenous prying mantis of the 'board-walk', lest I awake (or not as the case may be) the following morning minus my brain, cash and testicles in that order. Be that as it may -.

Everything was fine until we came upon the next 'Lock', the third in line of a never-ending series of these massive gateways designed to lift ower festering rust-bucket of a Liberty ship up the gamble of freshwater steps to the lake level beyond. The Captain rang for 'Slow Ahead' as we crept beyond the two towering concrete entrance ways to the eight hundred foot long basin.

"Aye Aye Captain." And the bridge of the St Merriel's superstructure slid graciously forwards at a steady three knots.

"Stop Engines." "Slow Astern."

"Aye Aye Captain."

The three knots dropped to two. The Captain nodded approvingly. The lock gates ahead came a little nearer.

"Slow Astern Engine Room." The Captain doubled up on the bridge telegraph emphasising the manoeuvre with a flourish of his large hands. And the massive lock gates came a little nearer and a little nearer.

The Captain looked across the bridge at the Canadian Pilot who had boarded at Lock No.1 and frowned. The Pilot's face took on a look of mild concern.

"Engine Room." barked the Captain into the bridge pipe. He looked up. The lock gates ahead, holding back the entire contents of the Welland canal and Lake Eyrie came nearer and nearer. The reply from below came back commencing with the sound of someone clearing their throat.

"Er – Yes?"

The Captain stepped back from the voice pipe and glared angrily at the path of the voice which seemed to scurry away out the open bridge port.

"What do you mean -. Er – Yes. What happened to SIR?" he growled angrily. "And what happened to my

Slow Astern? First Engineer?"

There was a moment's silence before the voice returned.

"Er-Sorry Sir – but we –er – don't seem to have one."

"Have one what?" returned the Captain.

"Er – A Slow Astern Sir -. It – er – seems to have dropped off."

"DROPPED OFF!"

I'm told no one had ever seen that particular Canadian Pilot move so quickly before in his entire life -.

Meanwhile – Yours truly, not yet sufficiently well groomed to be allowed to place my lithe body upon the deck plates of the Captain's bridge, held my 'docking procedure' post alongside the for'ard starboard winch, working gloves at the ready. When the ship came to a stop it was my job to toss ashore the landing line to which I had attached the loop of the landing hawser and into the hands of the stevedore high up on top of the lock side wall, then assist the winch-man in what was known as 'stabilising'.

 In effect to tie the ship central to the lock walls as the water was pumped under allowing the ship to rise to ground level. But the ship wasn't coming to a halt. And the lock gates were getting nearer and nearer and nearer.

To say 'all hell' broke loose was an understatement. Total panic not even an adequate description. That Canadian Pilot flew towards me like a demented Albatross. I don't think his feet touched the deck twice over the last fifty yards.

"Hawsers OUT." he screamed.

I looked at him dumbfounded. He was obviously on something. This was not the correct procedure, nothing like the last two 'locks' when I had executed two perfect high throws landing my monkey's fists directly into the intended areas. The orders were quite specific. DON'T throw the rope until the ship comes to a stop.

"Throw the fucking line you dumb bastard." he roared at me. I was quite taken aback.

"Yer what -?" I parried. Very nearly getting annoyed.

"Throw the fucking line you cock-sucker." Well! I mean. Well! So I did. Straight at him. In one big heap. Cock-sucker! A cock-sucker I most certainly was not. I know. I had tried. And on more than one occasion. I couldn't reach. In fact I never had been able to. I would have needed a willie twice the size of the one I had to get anywhere near it. Cheeky bugger.

Curly appeared at my elbow with a throwing line and hurled it aloft. Within twenty seconds but what seemed forever the steel hawser was secured and wound upon the winch-drum. It quickly tightened. I remember eye-balling the smoke which began pouring from the drum as the forward movement of the ship strained against the reverse action of the winch. My ears, and still on my head at this moment in time, being youthful, began picking up the singing of the steel hawser as the strain got tighter and tighter. Then a muted pinging noise as the steel reeves of the hawser began snapping slowly at first then like the sound of a chain saw starting up. Now nobody needed to tell me about strains and stresses. I well remember the communicators we used as kids on the 'wreck'.

Two empty tin cans and a long piece of burning bant. Boy did they 'sing' when the bant got over-stretched. Instantly I poised myself for a swift duck and just before the sound of the gun-shot hurled myself between the hold and the winch-housing. With a high pitched crack followed by a deadly swishing noise the steel hawser snapped, the end nearest ower group whipping back through the air at the speed of light as it cleaved a two inch gash through the steel plated bulk-heads of the ships galley some thirty yards away down the deck.

As if that wasn't bad enough the ship immediately began taking on a list to port and down at the stern. Ower seven thousand tons plus a ship-load of tractors was about to be stood on end. And true to form I was on the sharp end. Frantic cries instructed the other three winches to let out cable before they too succumbed to the same disastrous results which a moment later the one on the port stern did. I heard it from underneath my armpits, which were protecting my head at the time, smash its way across the plating beneath the boat deck. That was one lifeboat less. Not funny. At this rate we shall be needing them. Slowly the vessel righted itself. More lines, more hawsers and this time by a series of curt instructions and pure luck the ship eventually came to a stop.

Curly, the Bo's'n's mate, heaved a sigh of relief. He coughed loudly and fished about inside his jacket for his pack of cigarettes.

"Everybody OK?" He looked about. "Where's Peg's?" I heard the question from my foetal position wedged between the winch housing and the second hatch coaming. But before I was going to acknowledge the query I wanted to be absolutely clear the shipping companies attempt to terminate my employment by decapitation was at the very least a question of mistaken identity. Jesus – this was bloody dangerous! I didn't sign on for 'dangerous'. Nobody mentioned 'dangerous' when they asked me to sign the 'articles'. Unless the crafty blighters had put it somewhere in the small print? First of all we spring a leak and nearly sink off the coast of Nova Scotia then very nearly turn turtle in the St Lawrence Seaway. And we're not half way through the voyage yet! I'm beginning to think there might be a Jonah on board. - - - I wonder who it might be -? Trevor bounced jauntily passed a three foot rule clasped in his hand. A minute later he returned.

"Fourteen inches -." he declared proudly.

"Yer what -!" I squeaked disbelievingly. "Not on yer Nellie. In yer dreams Pinocchio.

"Not my dick you dozy Heckey Thump. The prow -." He gestured towards the front of the ship. "Another fourteen inches and the rest of the canal would now be pouring out the end of the Seaway."

"O. I see. Hmm. What d' we get fer that then?

"A year on Devils Island on bread and water if that Pilot fella' gets his way. He's well brassed off. Says we shouldn't come here with bits missing without telling them furst. Silly twat. As if we'd have come up here knowing we hadn't got all ower gears."

"Where's it gone then?" I asked, thinking it a perfectly reasonable question.

"– How the 'ell would I know? But the Old Man's not at all pleased. Keeps muttering about keel-hauling the 'grease-monkeys' with barbed wire bindings. I'm keeping well out of his way for the rest of the week and I advise you to do likewise Pegs." Trevor nodded to the Bo's'n's Mate and returned in the direction of the bridge.

"Fourteen inches – bloody 'ell. We were lucky -." It was just a passing comment; something to keep the grizzled bloke from throttling me which I suspect had been in his mind a few moments before when he eventually discovered me down below the hatch coamings. I should have known better of course.

"Well I can't promise yer fourteen inches but I could make the effort if you want laddie." Curly leered his set of broken teeth instantly reminding me of one Jimmy Redneck of Boy Scout fame and my 'Night of the Flaming Woggles'. But that's another story and I hated Jimmy Redneck as well. I smiled, one of my best 'O how kind of you kind Sir but please don't go to any trouble on my part', smiles. He could see it wasn't getting him anywhere and anyway what a stupid time to pick to start propositioning anyone. Perhaps the adrenalin had 'fired up' his scrotum. I know something should have. Creep-.

Banished. Black-balled. Two small tug like vessels escorted us the rest of the journey through the canal. One to the rear one to the prow, a bit like one of Curly's 'Congo' dances – but let's not go into that here, and across the wide expanse of Lake Eyrie to the North American city of Detroit and the Detroit Canal where we were shackled into a 'lay-by' by 'bonded' chains fore and aft. In other words 'get out of that you barmy English persons'. And DON'T dare move until you've fixed yer god-dammed rust bucket of a ship properly.

For five days we languished in what I can only describe as a small enclave of paradise amongst deep forests of evergreen pines and crystal clear waters. With nowhere to go we naturally assumed (or I did) that we would have nothing to do. Captain Morris thought otherwise.

The temperatures rose into the eighties although surprisingly the nights were deathly cold leaving a fine film of ice coating the ships superstructure until the early morning sun dissipated it and the decks steamed like a tropical forest floor. One of the most amazing (and quite extraordinary) sights I have ever seen happened on the second morning.

I received my 'alarm' call as usual; a cup of dishwater liberally doused over my head, at the appointed hour and went to the 'heads' for a pee. Passing the open hatch door to the 'Poop' I saw what I thought was a coating of white paint along the deck. Curious I ventured forth. The whole of the deck and almost every other part of the ship' superstructure lay coated in billions and billions of large white moths. Now I'm not a great lover of fluttering things and in any other circumstance this would have sent me scurrying for shelter. But I was absolutely gob-smacked. I had never seen so many moths in the whole of my life. The only part of the deck not plastered in such a manner was the line of boot-prints left by the passing feet of the early morning 'watch'. It was whilst observing this phenomenon Shover exited the 'heads'.

"What the 'ells goin' on. What's all this lot then?" I enquired, expecting the EDH, who let's face it had more experience than me, and should have been privy to peculiar occurrences, would educate me.

"Buggered if I know." he replied somewhat snappily.

"Where's mi fuckin' breakfast?"

To obtain the morning crews breakfast I would have to walk half the length of the ship to the 'galley' and back. But my way was barred by a trillion reposing moths.

"And how d' yer propose I do that?" I asked.

"How d' yer normally do it?" came back his disgruntled reply.

"Well I - -." There was no answer to that. Shover wanted feeding, as did the other three just off night watch. They were all tired and expecting to bunk down after a hearty meal of rice cakes, bacon and cornflakes. And don't ask me about the rice cakes because it makes me feel all queasy every time I think about them – I hate fried rice.

I also hate scrunching moths by the boot full. Try as I may I couldn't avoid them all. Carefully picking one's path by stepping into the previous guys footprints whilst three tired angry able-seamen hurl abuse at you and threaten you with all kinds of nasty retributions because you are 'fucking' about with their tray-full of breakfasts which is reducing their 'kipping' times is no joke – believe me.

"Pegs – youse a prick -." Yes Mr Very Large AB from Glasgow and please pull me back up and put me back on the ship where I might drip dry in the well accustomed manner.

The lads were not happy that morning. But I didn't need to wash my clothes that week either.

The moths by the way skedaddled, took off – all at the same time. It was as if someone had rung the going –home bell. There was a sound like a fire door closing, you know the kind of thing, a low drawn out 'whoosh' and like an enormous rippling blanket they took to the air. I swear the ship rose up a couple of feet out of the water as the huge massive blanket slid gracefully out of sight amongst the thickness of the tall pines lining the canal banks. The ten thousand that remained behind were in no position to fly. It reminded me of my 'Blackjack' racing days when a 'squished' Blacky wasn't up to the job. Perhaps as well they were so prolific hmm? (At the Captain's request I spent the rest of the morning shovelling dead moths into the canal and washing down the decks fore and aft. A bit like the 'abbatoir' job I once had.)

The 'reverse gear' has arrived. Flown in from Germany, which lets face it was the last place I expected the shipping company would be buying engineering parts from. But as I was to learn, true to form, the company had been unable to guarantee on the machining and delivery from any British factory and time being money had gone to where the product could be produced the fastest and on time. We would have done better to have lost the bloody war then perhaps my countrymen would have realised the need to apply themselves more diligently than was the present case. But this cannot be the concern of one so young and willing to accommodate everything my peers had to offer. All that is required now is for the Lake authorities to remove ower 'shackles' and we can be on ower way, again.

Back into ower stride we traversed a sluggish pathway across the length of Lake Huron towards St Mary's Falls and Lake Superior the largest of the Great lakes. We were also back into ower usual routine of 'watch keeping' now the need arose. Eagle eyed and in fair weather I can honestly say I enjoyed the journey and was looking forward to another few days of sun and leisurely sailing once in the welcoming arms of 'Superior' herself.

That last wave I swear smashed itself to pieces not more than six to eight feet below me and I was fifty feet up in the air. On the fore mast looking for anything that resembled terra-firma. The sooner I was off this bucking ship (and I nearly got that right) the better.

I was on fifth watch. Overtime. Money. Not that I needed the money. But it was better than trying to lie in my cabin and read a book whilst all hell broke loose above my head and all around me. I hadn't realised just how 'big' Lake Superior was. It was bloody huge. This was ower third day across and we still hadn't spotted land as yet. And now we've run into a force six gale which is whipping the dark grey water into a frenzied maelstrom. One is not amused. Not amused at all. In fact one is very miffed off. How I'm expected to spot anything out there when I can hardly see the deck below for green tidal waves of water which keep making moves towards my person and my precarious hold on the ships superstructure I shall never know. I don't remember anybody, including that miserable git of a Third Officer at the 'Vindicatrix, mentioning it was necessary to be purposely marooned up a steel pole without a paddle in the middle of the foulest of weathers imaginable. What happened to 'radar'? Even my old man's lot had some of it during the war and that was nearly two decades back. Madness. If I get killed somebody will be sorry. Come to think of it that would probably be me. Huh! Typical.

'— it seemed all the cops in the Thirty First Precinct were hot footing it down the sidewalk, but Slade didn't want a beat cop; he wanted a plains clothes cop. One who could keep his trap shut. He saw Brandon step from a squad car. Brandon was a son-of-a-bitch. How the hell could he tell a bastard like that he was shacking up with Big Annie and not getting a stalk on -----?'

I was catching up on my edification. A 'dic' novel. American Detective. Purloined from a drug store in Niagara. The storm had passed on. Thankfully I hadn't. I was still here much to the chagrin of Curly whose latest attempt at 'ringing' me had failed yet again.

Did I want some more overtime? Ironing his dobbying. Hmm, yea. I think not. Arsehole. Yea – well best not mention them eh? "Well perhaps you can do it later. Wis be here fer a couple er days and apart from the 'usual' thar's nowt else. You'll be bored stiff.

Anytime today or tomorrow will do." Yea I think not Bos'n's Mate dear. I think I would rather be bored in the conventional manner – not in the way you have in mind.

We docked in the Port of Duluth on the evening of the fourth day. After tea and a short mooch around the deck I turned in. It was to be the first decent sleep I had had since leaving Detroit.

The following morning after 'duties' I decided to seek out a 'local' record shop. I wanted a copy of 'Acker Bilks' latest top of the pops hit 'Stranger on the shore'. It seemed appropriate as I stepped off the gangplank and realised this would most likely be the furthest inland I would ever get on this North American continent and I was indeed a 'stranger' to these parts. Seeking further amusement I set out for what I thought might be the town centre.

"Excuse me. Could you direct me to a record shop please?" The youth, somewhat spotty of face and short of hair looked at me strangely.

"Yaw whad."

I realised instantly what was amiss. This native of these parts didn't speak proper English, like wot I did.

"A record shop. Is there one hereabouts?" I spoke slowly and with clarity fully expecting this youth, who was beginning to show signs of inter-breeding, might pick up on a syllable or two and come up with a modicum of intelligence from somewhere beneath that razored hair and bulbous skull he possessed.

"Records? What sort er records?"

Yes – well of course he did have a point, apart from the one on the top of his head. I could have meant 'paper records' or those intangibles one finds after some spectacular feat of endurance has been accomplished, but I didn't -.

"Plastic ones -?" I ventured, by way of a clue.

"Plastic!!! Plastic!!! Plastic!!!." I thought for a minute he was becoming one and had got stuck on a needle. Then the penny dropped. "God damn. You mean discs. Music discs. God damn why didn't ya say so? Music discs. God damn."

Now I don't know about you but three damnations in under three seconds is pretty good going even for us sailor boys who are not known for ower cultured use of the English language.

However I thought it wise to let things lie. At this rate the 'Record Shop' would have closed before I got there. I nodded my head and smiled.

"The Disc Store. Yea -." He turned, scratched his chin and looked up the length of the street. "Yea – hmm. Yea – hmm. Yea - ." Oh dear this was turning into a marathon.

"Well now. Hmm. Well now. I think it's on the corner of Fifth and Main. Yep. Fifth it is. And Main -."

I looked along the street. "And this is Main is it?" He stared at me his glazed reflection sizing me up and down. "D' ya see another one?" Well to be honest I wasn't looking for another one and as I had no knowledge of the fair town of Duluth it was a question I couldn't honestly answer. I bade the youth a 'Good-day Kind Sir' which seemed to amuse him no end. He would no doubt spend the rest of his life reminiscing the time when as a boy he had met upon this strange Englishman in his fair town who called a disc a 'record' and spoke like a Shakespearian actor.

Three quarters of an hour later I could have cheerfully strangled the swine. Fifth had meant the Fifth Street off the main Street which was of course five blocks down. Had he explained that each 'block' was almost a mile in length I might have done a swift about turn or looked for a taxi before setting off on what had proven to be half a bloody marathon. Fortunately I relented my vituperative snarling at the 'youths' inadequate information when I found the 'store' to be still open. Only they didn't have any left – Acker Bilks record that is. I purchased one by The Shirelles, 'Soldier Boy' I think. I still have it. Well lets face it I wasn't walking all that way for the benefit of my health now was I?

And talking about 'health' and 'benefits' I wish to God I was less often in the wrong place at the wrong time. Well I mean – come on-.

Eighty four degrees. April 62. At home it would probably be raining and quivering at almost 40 degrees. Did I know my stuff or what? No is the answer to that, because -.

I awoke with a start. On such a clammy night I had decided to sleep on the 'roof' of the Poop Deck Housing. The Poop Deck is situated on the stern of a ship and in those days housed the deck crews' quarters.

The area is used for storage of materials that can be lashed down, normally ship to shore hawsers and the like. As I said I awoke with a start. A scratching noise which under normal circumstances and at sea wouldn't have raised an eyebrow. But here in dock! Rats. My first thought. I knew all about rats. We used to play with them when I was younger. Chopping off their tails, you know, easy lazy day activities for the more discerning and intelligent. Anyway. Rats. I raised my head above the coil of rope inside which I had cast my sleeping blankets. The noise seemed to come from inside the crews 'mess'. Now this 'mess' was my total and absolute responsibility. It's cleanliness, it's tidiness and it's comforting ambience. And there should be no foreign bodies a-scratching at it's pleasant welcoming interior. What was afoot? For the past three days we had been loading grain from the huge dockside silos. If we should be receiving a plague of rats this would not bode well for ower homeward bound consignment.

'Bobby the Grease' we called him. Known to the company as Robert McKiernan. Bobby was the ships 'grease monkey' a lowly position in the 'Engineering' department. A labourer by any other description. I watched through the thickened glass of the starboard porthole from my grip on the steel ladder leading down from the Poop Deck. Something wasn't quite right. In the first place 'Bobby the Grease' had no business being in the deck crews 'mess' room and secondly most certainly not wielding a large screwdriver and attacking my painted surfaces. Bastard. What was his game?

It was wiser for the moment to keep a wary eye on the intruder. Bobby wasn't known for his easy going nature. Working with very measured movements and as quietly as he could the man removed one of the galvanised panels to the rear of the mess room sink, took something from his back pocket which he placed inside the revealed aperture and then carefully replaced the metal panel as before. All this had taken about five minutes and should have been no strain on the legs of an eighteen year old. But I miscalculated and as I went to climb back up the ladder away from the porthole I slipped and plummeted down about two feet landing in a heap on the deck.

"Ouch." That was me banging the back of my head on the ships guard rails. Bobby the Grease appeared in the doorway.

"How's up Pegs. You bin eye-ballin' then?" I groaned a little and rubbed the back of my head, more to give me time to think than anything else.

"What?" I replied, innocently.

But the man wasn't to be fooled. He would have seen me flash by the porthole at a rate of knots and heard the crunch as I landed.

I was about to get up when something hard and very solid cracked against the side of my head. I remember the flash of lights and the sudden sharpness of pain and the face of the grease-monkey coming towards me through it all.

"You've seen nowt laddie. Nowt at all. I wasn't 'ere. No matter what anybody asks or says. Bobby wasn't 'ere'. You got that laddie. Hmm?" The man's breath stank of bad beer. His face not three inches from mine.

"What the 'ell. What yer do that fer. Ouch. Bugger me." I replied, now feeling for the second lump appearing on my head in the last few seconds.

"And that's exactly what I will do laddie and a lot more if you say owt about this. You 'ear? Remember. It's a long way 'ome. People have disappeared. Bang. Just like that. It's a big ocean." Bobby the Grease stuck the end of the screwdriver in my forehead and nudged it. "Shtum mister. Remember." And with that he moved away towards the after-deck turning just the once to point the screwdriver and wave it menacingly in my direction.

I sat for a few minutes on the deck which wasn't uncomfortable it being still warm from the late evening sun. So far I have refrained from mentioning that occupation most if not all merchant seamen at one time or another tend to dabble in. It's called 'Smuggling'. The penalty of which can be anything from having your seaman's papers removed thus putting you out of work to twenty-five years to life imprisonment, pursuant on the nature of the crime of course.

So it was no surprise when a week later I removed the self same panel and took a peek at what the grease-monkey had secreted therein. I wasn't then an authority on illegal drugs, come to think of it I'm still not. However. I can say with some degree of certainty that the packet was very 'illegal' and deadly to boot. Heroin probably.

It certainly wasn't sherbet dip he was hiding and aint that the truth. Needless to say. I have never been a 'grass'. It's just not in my nature and it doesn't pay very well either and so Bobby the Grease had nothing to fear from me knowing his little secret.

Typical of him to hide his 'stash' in the deck-hands quarters where, should it be discovered, no suspicion would befall him.

As it was by the time we reached the shores of good old England I

I had almost forgotten the incident. - - -Well – nearly.

She was Dutch. That's to say. She spoke Dutch with a smattering of broken English essential for the satisfactory progression of her fabled occupation. Not to put to fine a point on it. Prostitution. She was twenty-ish and I was drooling like a five year old. And I was a little – liar – a lot apprehensive. In fact I was trembling. Some in anticipation and the rest in a mild form of terror. Mixed race they would call it today. We used the term 'vanilla-fudge'. One parent white Caucasian the other of an ethnic/coloured origin. But she was quite beautiful, sexy and I was totally and abundantly fired up for it. And if we didn't do 'it' right now my bag of testicle fluid would punch a hole in the ceiling that fast it would knock half the roof tiles off into the street below. In fact why I hadn't blasted a hole through the lining of my trousers before now I didn't know! God was I hot -!

But I'm getting ahead of myself as usual. Truth to say that 'sex' always pushes itself to the fore. Especially where the young male is concerned.
This is Holland. Rotterdam and we haven't left Canada yet. Although we are about to do so much to the relief of the Canadian Maritime Authorities and their attendant 'pilots'.
We slid somewhat sluggishly and with a modicum, on my part, of regret from the Great lakes and the St Lawrence Seaway and hit the open Atlantic. The First Mate 'the Cow' had promised us plenty of overtime in the next three weeks (whether we liked it or not – which I did) and Jamie the Boson had warned Curly off from casting his doleful eyes and wandering hands about the person of the Peggy (that's me). I think the expression was if he wished to keep his job with the company in future to 'put the ship's needs first and not his own' or else.
It worked. Curly's constant presence around the Poop Deck diminished rapidly over the next few days and to be honest I relaxed a little perhaps for the first time since we had left Manchester. I just didn't like him. Nothing personal. He just wasn't my type. He rarely shaved. Seemingly rarely washed and his eyes had a permanent manic look about them, when he wasn't drunk, which was as often as he could be.

At sea the Chief Steward handles the 'bond' that's the 'stores' to you and me. Every day during the mid afternoon watch is the time when the crew can 'purchase' personal items from this store under the watchful eye of the Chief Steward and one of his 'boys'. All purchase are 'logged' against one's tally (earnings) and deducted at 'signing off' (when one reaches a final home port and leaves the ship). Nothing is rationed apart from the purchase of alcohol which in Curly's case was never enough. Two 'miserable' cans a day. Some of the crew used to call him 'Two cans' as he was forever bemoaning his lot. Be that as it may, as I said, he just wasn't my type. End of -.

On the outward journey we had 'de-scaled' the ship from stem to stern (that's chipped off all the old paintwork) and given her the once over with a good layering of red-lead paint. On the return journey we were to apply her final colours. Which turned out to be the same colours as before so I couldn't see the point of any of that at all! I thought – jasmine and a cobalt blue myself. The Boson told me to 'frig off' but he was smiling at the time so I reckon we just hadn't got enough of those colours in store. Anyway providing the weather held and let's face it we were travelling east, which portents bad news, the next few days would be three brushes and a paint pot and "Don't paint yourself into a corner Pegs or work on your knees around the Stewards quarters." Good advice.
Our first port of call was Tilbury. Off-load five thousand tons of grain.
Then out into the North Sea and Rotterdam to off-load the for'ard hold of new transistorised radios and record players a new development in media accessories and one of modern man's first foray's into the new technological age. Ergo – I had to have one. But how -?

'Perks'. Everyone knows about them. Every job is supposed to have one or more. In the case of Merchant Seamen it's 'knocking off the cargo'. Not all of it of course. That would be too obvious. Just a nice small percentage as not to be missed. A bag-full. Oh alright a few bags full. Enough to make it worth the risk so to speak.
The cargo holds, when closed after loading, were 'bonded' down. That's to say the door leading in and the hatches themselves were 'tagged' with padlocked chains and seals.
Broken seals discovered en-route were the province of the captain

and his officers. A search would ensue and the stolen goods recovered in very quick time. There's not a Captain worth his salt who doesn't know of every possible hiding place aboard his vessel. So that's a non-starter. So how is it done?

Simple really. Either when it (the cargo) is being taken inboard or shipped off. For that is the only time the cargo sees the light of day long enough for thieving swine like us to get ower grubby mits on it. With the advent of the 'bonded' container in later years I believe the work became much easier. But that's just hearsay of course. How would I know -!

I had my eyes on a very new strange looking record player that ran on batteries or mains electricity and was portable. Considering the only record player I had as a child had belonged to someone who knew Lloyd George and was operated by cranking a handle and sticking a miniature marlin spike on a revolving wax record whilst the sound strained cat like from a large bugle shaped horn level with ones eardrum, this wonder of the modern age had to be mine. And it played the size of 'disc' I had purchased in Duluth. The two things sort of gelled to my way of thinking.

'Ooops'. 'CRASH'. "Bugger." In that order. First the cargo pallet swayed and dipped dangerously, then the contents slid slowly back down towards the bottom of the hold and bounced around a bit. Many hands moved towards the melee of boxes and as the cargo pallet was again lowered the boxes where re-stacked for a second attempt.

"Shtop!" The 'Cow' glared at the winch man. "Shtop wis the lifting." The First Mate grabbed the edge of the cargo net and pulled the pallet towards him. He stood on the hatch coaming and with embellished gestures counted every box contained thereupon and followed up with a second and a third count. He was suspicious of the unloading crew. Why I can't think. But he was Polish so it was best not to question it. Checking the laden bill on his clip-board he frowned, scowled at each one of us in turn then still not convinced all was in order reluctantly gave the order for the unloading to continue. I got my portable record player. But I will leave you to work out how!

I don't remember a great deal about Rotterdam. I remember being there and leaving. But the bit in between is still very hazy.

I was surprised at how cheap everything was. Like the beer and the women and the cigarettes and the women and the food and the women. Have I mentioned the women? Un-believable. And it was legal what's more. Yer know – Having nookey for money. Prostitution. They were everywhere. Hanging from the doorways, hanging from the windows, hanging from the lamp-posts, from the trees, I found one hanging out of my hip pocket halfway through the night. I left her there. I quite liked her handholds. I had been forewarned of this 'isle of dirty dreams' the moment the Captain had announced ower diversion from Flushing in Belgium, the original destination for the rest of ower cargo, but the reality far out- stripped my expectations. Ooo dear me! They shouldn't put young boys of my tender age into situations like this. I was like a dog in a forest. I needed far more willies than was healthy – so many trees.

And so inexpensive! Five guilders! That's only ten shillings a pop. I could spend twenty quid before I died at that rate. That's forty shags. I checked my watch. Had we time?

This was a situation when I should have listened to what I was told more closely, even though the advice came from Trevor who wasn't that many years my senior. Nevertheless, "Get yerself laid before the bar." He said. No – not in full view of the customers - silly. What he meant was. Get myself a woman and have intercourse first before hitting the bars. Very sound advice as it transpired and had I taken it I would be better able to tell you the rest of the story.

Be that as it may, just for you, I will make an effort to plough thoughtfully through the mists of time and alcoholic fug. If I can -.

The girls, for that is what many of them were, held 'court' in the flats above the numerous 'bars' that dotted the Kattenstrasse. When I had agreed a price, ten guilders, I was taken out the bar and directly in the next doorway where a flight of stairs led up into the heavens. I recall it was mandatory to wash beforehand and afterwards. Heavily inebriated that I was I had no difficulty producing my sentinel stiffened armoury for closer inspection which to my surprise almost doubled in size the second she breathed on it. Not one to brag. I was immensely proud of the end result. We 'frolicked' for ten minuets or so which was why I fully expected to loose all my ammunition before indulging in the act itself. To give the girl her due she was aware of the 'new' boy in her charge and the play subsided for a time although not the chronic ache in my lower regions which was fit to burst.

To cut a hazy long story short my 'mount' did her job properly and saw to it I received a full and fact-finding tour of her anatomy and qualifications before swabbing me down in a final delicate routine of paper towels and antiseptic soap. Boy was I a happy bunny by the time I returned to the bar an hour later.

Trevor was missing and according to the barman was still 'inspecting' his purchase in one of the flats above. I ordered another glass of 'pils' and slouched down to await his return.

It was 0700hrs or thereabouts when the barman woke me. Did I want coffee? From the taste coming from the interior of my mouth something much stronger would be needed. I nodded and looked around. Trevor was present. He was lying full out across the tops of two tables that had been pushed together and snoring like an asthmatic giraffe. Not the tables-Trevor. I remember trying to focus on my watch but the hands wouldn't stay still. It was daylight. That was sufficient enough incentive to make an effort. The 'Cow' would be baying for ower blood if we showed up late for duties. In 'dock' or not, ship-board duties still had to be done and it wasn't as though extra hands could simply be brought in to cover. To illustrate the point Curly, he of the wandering eyes and hands, had been sentenced to three days in the 'pokey' (jail) for persistent drunkenness whilst on 'watch' but due to the chronic lack of 'labour' would serve them by being restricted to ship for double that length of time whenever the opportunity presented itself, like now. It didn't stop one of the AB's from smuggling half a dozen bottles of 'firewater' to him the first day we docked at Tilbury. Now he was permanently pissed out of his head and racking up 'jail' time like there was no tomorrow. Crazy bugger.

On board the 'M.V.St. Merriel 1962. The Merchant Navy Training School uniform and Boson's mate badges. The hair was blonder in reality and the body 'lithe and fair of skin'. That was the problem!

We made Salford Docks in time for ower towns Wakes Holiday's and I was looking forward to a few weeks at home in a British summer before shipping out again. I had decided to pay-off the M.V. St Merriel. Apart from Trevor I couldn't say I took to any of the other crew members and shipping out on a turn-around (a week to ten days) and another voyage with Curly's willie sonar tracking every minor passage of wind from my posterior I 'plumbed' for better things.

Her Majesty's Custom's and Excise came aboard as we tied up. No-one was allowed ashore with kit until all the ship had undergone a thorough inspection. Some hours later I was called from my cabin to the bridge to find 'Bobby the Greaser' and his packet of 'goods' being ushered forcefully away by two fierce looking 'ferrets'. Captain Morris had on his usual serious face but an almost imperceptible wink of his eye signified this wasn't that 'serious' and for me to take it easy as his visitor, a large well-built man wearing the uniform of an officer of the 'ferret squad', cleared his throat and called me by my Sunday name.

"Atlas -?" "Unusual name – You are the Peggy?" I nodded and murmured "Sir -." And felt like adding -.

"Unusual person." But deferred knowing smart-Alec comments might not be the wisest course to take at that juncture.

'I was in charge of the crews mess room?' – "Yes." 'Had I noticed anything unusual with the room during the voyage back from Canada?' "Yes. It was a hell of a lot cleaner than when I took it over in the first place." Which it was. Butchering had left me with a cleanliness ethic rarely encountered in a young buck of my age. 'Had I noticed anything different about the rooms panelling?' "No." 'Did I know Robert McKiernan?' "No -. Oh yer mean Bobby the Grease. Yea. But not t' talk to. Engineering's not my province." The man's eyes went up. Either he hadn't expected me to use the word 'province' or he thought I was taking the 'piss'. Either way I wasn't fazed. 'Some contraband has been discovered behind the panelling in your 'mess'. What do you know about it?'

"Nowt. I didn't clean 'behind' the panelling. Why? Was I supposed to?" Captain Morris leant back in the chair and tried to cover a smile with his hands. The officer-ferret grunted. He turned away. Nothing was going to be gained from continuing this course of enquiry. Of course not. I could have told him that. Saved him the bother. Silly man. Thank you and Good-day to you to – Officer Jobs Worth -. Bobby the Grease was taken away to be penalised for breaking the Eleventh Commandment, 'thou shalt not get caught' - smuggling drugs.

I left the ship after signing off and collecting my pay with my hand-made canvas holdall containing ten thousand contraband cigarettes and my acquired portable record player. A smile from the flat-capped gate keeper on the Dock Gate and for him a sleeve of Marlborough charcoal tipped inside a folded newspaper and I was free to go on my way. The Technical School for Boys in ower town had had some uses! N' est pas? And not just my minimal use of the French language.

M.V. St Elwyn. Sister ship to M.V. St Merriel.

I never got a picture of the M.V.St Merriel. No camera and no dosh.

'In-betweens & Go- Betweens'.

"Witness's." the man said. I gave him a double-take then replied.

"That can be a bit dodgy around 'ere. I'd keep shtum about that if I was you." The two smartly attired young men looked at each other then back at me. It hadn't registered. Totally and completely gone straight over their heads. "Yer shouldn't be knockin' around here without police protection." Then the one with the red dickey-bow tie flashed me a smile. Penny had dropped. "No – Jehovah's Witness's. Messengers of the Prophet -. Not criminal witnesses." I stuck him a stern glare. "Witness's is a bit like grassin' in my book. Yer need t' be very sure of what yer seein' and tellin'. This Jehovah bloke. A good mate er yours is he? What did these blokes nick off him? Aren't you a bit wary they might not like it -?" "Who -!" The young man's eyes had glazed over in confusion.

"These blokes yer being a witness against fer this Jehovah fella. You wouldn't catch me tellin' all and sundry I was gonna be a witness. Not bloody likely – yer barmy, the pair of yer -." And with that I opened the front door of the shop and indicated for them to depart from my presence. Lunatics – I could do without. I've just spent the last seven months in the company of a large number of strange human beings, some extremely strange, and I had no wish to enmesh myself in amongst a set of new ones, not immediately anyway.

I had no time for the 'Godspell' looneys, those purveyors of fantasy and legend. In my younger days the 'church' and all its attendant hypocrisy had left its less than desirable imprint upon my struggle from the 'darkling' and to have idiots hawking its falsehoods into my front room (well the old lady's) was a bit more than I was prepared to sanction, albeit the old lady who would have the last word on that, as always. Was I an atheist? WAS I INDEED BROTHER, and I don't mean 'brother' in the 'religious' sense. Bog off -.

Ninety four pounds, seven shillings and four pence. A princely sum of dosh if I say so myself. Two months wages for the old man. All in one canvas bag under the floorboards in ower bedroom.

All mine. Boy was I going to be popular. The old lady had flashed me a bright smile upon my return and had refrained from asking when I was returning to sea until the following morning. I'm sure it was intentional so as not to give the impression she was pleased to see me. God forbid we should have any more emotional scenes as that displayed when I left the first time. And what was I doing fer money?

"Oo I don't know mother. I thought I might try pimping fer a change. What d' yer think?"
I'm sure she would be quite taken aback to realise just how Philistine her questions seemed to others. She was nothing if not direct and to the point. Just because she was pleased to see me again, and surprisingly still in one piece, didn't mean I could take advantage, mouths need filling with food and services don't come fer nowt. So what was I doing fer money then eh? Because I wasn't dossing in her house fer nowt. NO WAY JOSE.

I signed on the 'dole' the next morning and received a healthy twenty five shillings and sixpence to last me the week. For the uninitiated amongst you – dole (unemployment benefit) twenty five shillings and sixpence (to purchase sufficient methylated spirits to commit suicide by because you certainly couldn't live until the following week on that pitiful amount - but – hey – who cares?) So it was just as well I had other plans and a small nest-egg squirrelled away for the use of.

The staccato beat of African drums drew me once more up the darkened stairwell of Rene Carr's town centre establishment where I was warmly welcomed with open arms circumventing the contents of my wallet. I only had a couple of pounds on me but that was enough to get her interest.

"Gi' us a job missus." I quipped in my best Lancashire twang. "Coffee is it?" she replied. "Same rate as before." I offered. "Espresso or Cappuccino." she replied. "Five percent then?" I countered. "Done." she said smiling that rake of beautifully honed white teeth in my direction. And I was. Just like the last time. But I wasn't fazed. I liked working at the 'Medici' and it had a number of very worth while compensations.

Lily Entwistle. Why I fancied Lily Entwistle I have no idea. One of those 'hormone' things I think.

At the time of which I speak Helen Shapiro had hit the 'Rock' scene with 'Walking back to happiness' and I just loved the way her left eye seemed always to want to join her right. Lily Entwistle's eyes had similar desires which I might have mistakenly interpreted as 'come to bed' eyes – who knows? Lily had a friend, who apparently fancied me, my lithe sleek body and charming good looks of course but that was open for yet more interpretation. Could have been like Rene, the contents of my wallet. They were student nurses and totally brassic. I was a lad about town and a seafarer and everyone knows a sailor's cloth has a silver lining.

So we set about skipping rings around each other making small talk and generally acting like eighteen year olds do when the pheromones are wafting the air like loose main sheets. It took me three weeks to end up with the wrong girl. But – hey. She, Kathleen by name and Irish Catholic didn't believe in sex before marriage whereas I didn't believe in marriage full stop and why sex should be so linked didn't make a lot of sense to me at that time. I just wanted a shag and as it had already cost me getting on for fifty espresso's to get this far – I don't care if you is Catholic - how's about it lass -?

She wasn't impressed. I'm not sure we were on the same wave length after that. I couldn't persuade her to come to the pub, any pub, so dosing her with rum and peps was out. We parted company shortly thereafter, a whole six week courtship. Meanwhile Lily Entwistle had been bonking my employers son young Michael who admittedly was a few years older than me and marginally better looking – but come on, I saw her first - - - yer bastard -!

Location, location, location. A very modern saying but appropriate even back in those days.

" Micky says wis need about sixty sheets. Eight bi four. That's thirty er them there la'." Teddy, another of Michael's Scouse mates, pointed to a large stack of plasterboards set in the far corner. We were six and according to my calculations that was ten trips per couple. Out the builder's merchants shed up the yard and along the garden path. We finished about an hour later. The plasterboards now neatly piled in Rene's new kitchen.

"Time fer a brew -?" More a question than a statement. I sagged down on my haunches and viewed the silky smoothness of the skin on my hands.

Awkward stuff plasterboard and heavy when attached together for storage. My hands had lost at least two layers of protection. Michael arrived with my 'bird' in tow.

"Best we nip and board up the hole in the fence." he said after a brief inspection on the materials. I accompanied him and ower Lily down the garden path where he set to re-nailing the fence boards along the opening that led into the 'builder's merchants yard'.

"You should put a gate on instead of those. Be handier for if we want some more stuff later on." I said working out in my head what would be required to make the access easier.

"Don't think as they'd take to kindly to that." he replied.

"and anyroad we don't want they should know how we got in -."

"Got in?" I looked him and frowned.

"Nay lad. Wake up. Yer don't think I'm payin' fer this lot do yer?" Up until that moment there hadn't been a word said about non-payment. For the past four weeks we had been renovating the big house fronting the garden. Half the rooms had been rewired, re-plastered and redecorated. Every night throughout July ower gang of trusty volunteer artisans had lifted and carried literally tons of building materials from the 'builders merchants yard' at the rear of the property and gaily set about titivating up Rene's new acquisition. Now Michael tells me the owners of the 'builder's merchants yard' have not been included in the massive project, other than as an unwitting charity -!

"You pillock!" I gasped rapidly rushing through my mind the unending list of 'stolen' goods' I could possibly be accused of stealing over the past month.

"We've been nicking this stuff???"

"Eh? No I haven't. You have -. Why – don't they know then?" he smiled cheekily. It's easy to see how my very full and descriptive 'social' record could have quickly become 'criminalised' around my present set of 'friends'. But-hey ho- let he who be without sin - -?

Wozzle had been seriously dating a young girl by the name of Dianne and had forgone his usual pub-crawling activities.

"She doesn't know I drink." he said with a straight face.

"How d' yer explain why yer legs wobble s'much then?" I asked.

"Eh! Oh. Well she's only ever seen me wobbling. She thinks it's normal. No point in upsettin' the lass is there?"

As a consequence and I could see he was greatly smitten by this vision of sexual availability we began to see less and less of each other. We were moving on. He to a greater purgatory (well I thought the idea of marriage before fifty years old well crazy) and yours truly back to the oceans and the far flung mysterious countries of this ower diminutive planet. So - We sailed on the 'Pacific Unity'. My old shipmates and me. And around Nassau town we did roam -. Drinking all night. Getting into a fight. I'm tired and broke up. But I don't want to come home. Sethay -. No Sirrrr -.

'Whisky Galore'.

She was a passenger/cargo vessel. Ten thousand tons gross laden with a crew of thirty four assorted souls and this time we 'Peggies' were two in number. 'Tinkerbell' I called him that for he reminded me of a young gypsy boy who helped the rag and bone man on his weekly rounds of ower neighbourhood when I was somewhat younger. It was his first trip out. Which made me senior 'pegs'. A fact he later came to find quite unacceptable. But we are jumping the gun. For now we are entering the Port of Glasgow to obtain ower priceless cargo of fine Scots whisky. Several thousand tons of it. And that's a lot of 'bottles'.

Four days loading in which time I visited the delights of this grim Scottish city, saw first hand the intricate workings of the dockside male prostitutes and added a dozen counts of HSP (handling stolen property) to my not inconsiderable list of criminal activities. All in all an extremely 'edificating' experience. Lucrative too.

It would be unfair to slight the citizens of this grey city with the tag tea-leafers all, but who wants to be fair anyway. There were certainly hordes of them around the dock areas. I have never been approached with so much contraband in so short a time anywhere else in the world. Bottles of whisky were disappearing from the deck cargo and into ower cabin faster than dropped loose change in a doss-house. The going rate was two bottles per meal. And as Tinkerbell and me had access to an unlimited supply of 'meals' from ower friendly 'cookie' (he of the Jamaica extracshon -) whisky galore wasn't in it!

We were bound for the U.S.of A. Most of it to hear tell – minus the middle bit of course. There were no rivers and lakes big enough to take us inland like in Canada. Pity. I wouldn't have minded a sail through the Arizonan desert or down that Grand Canyon thing they had. Never mind, the bits I was going to see held out sufficient attraction. The Caribbean, Panama, the Pacific and Western Canada. We set sail with fair weather. The date the end of September in the year of ower Lord 1962.

The Captain was a goodly man by the name of Albert Gates. An untidy ship is a dirty ship. Something which he hates. The First mate we called 'Popeye', a wooden pipe he had for sucking. A delightful chap, big blue eyes and surprisingly good looking. The Boson was a Scotsman. With his 'Ocks' and his 'Ayes' and his 'Eey's. Big Bo we dubbed him so, but not a man to tease. The Chief Steward was fat and lazy and a Christian man I pray. We passed him on the windward side and called him 'Daisy May'. - - - - - And there were plenty of others. Some good some not so good but regardless we had but one mission. To deliver ower nations goods to ower contrary cousins across the blue water of the 'pond' and to 'tolerate' each other in the process. And so we pointed ower bows westwards and without more-a-do gently but surely left the festering dour 'greyness' of that 'brae' lowland Scottish city far far behind.

Daily life on board ship is not the easy romantic swashbuckling affair often depicted in the Hollywood cinema films. In fact it's often the reverse. 'Idle hands make the devil's work'. A maxim well known in the British Merchant Navy and avoided at all costs. We set to 'chipping' the decks the minute we left the harbour tugs behind. My day consisted of rising at 07-00 hours and preparing the seamen's mess for breakfasts. Unlike the M.V. St Merriel this time the 'mess' was housed athwart ship in the mid-section and consequently much nearer the 'galley'. Feeding my watch-crew's, those who had been on the first and second watches, was top priority for men who had spent most of the night bored out of their heads. Unless we had very bad weather the two late night watches could be mind-numbing even for the most brain-dead seafarer.

Then it was set to and clean the decks, bulkheads, tables, chairs and gangways in my section not to mention the ovens and tableware. At around 10-15 hours the lads on day work had to be 'watered' before the mess tables set again for dinner/lunch (depending on what region you hove from). After dinner and after another bout of dish-washing I had four hours off or overtime whichever was my fancy. It was time and a quarter for overtime, a whole four shilling and four-pence an hour (equates to approx: twenty-two pence an hour in modern terms). Gosh, I was going to be so 'rich' after this trip -! Another two hour stint to cover the teatime periods 17-00 – 19-00 hours and the rest of the day was mine.

All in all a twelve hour day, seven days a week, very similar to my butchering job and the pay was very similar also – meagre. But other than the 'bond' there was nothing with which to spend money on whilst the ship was at sea. A further five pounds per week was deducted by the company, in this case The Furness Withy Line, and sent home to my parents, whether I liked it or not. This seemed to stem from a nineteenth century practice of ensuring the seaman was not destitute when reaching his home port as most seamen tended to 'spend' everything they earned when in foreign ports. Understandable when you see what delights some foreign ports can offer. What was to stop the old lady from going out on the town with my fiver a week whilst I was on the other side of the world had somehow escaped the ken of these bureaucratic officials back in London. Still, that was the way it was.

I remember it was about three weeks out when the Big Bo collared me after dinner one day and gave me three cans of paint. Red, white and blue, the paint that was.

"You're on the for'ard hold. I want the whole thing covered. Here's some chalk -." he said handing me what looked like three blocks of yellow ochre donkey stone. "Ye will need a straight-edge. Ask the Chippy." I wondered what it was he required me to paint? I wasn't known for my portraits but my landscapes of Lancashire mountains had always looked pretty good. Well, I thought so anyway. But I would need some green and yellow and perhaps a smattering of brown paints to do the whole thing justice. At that moment I heard what I thought was a mechanical saw and it was getting louder by the second. As I looked up this bloody great bat like thing flashed by overhead not fifty feet above the masts.

"Bugger me -." I exclaimed thinking to pick myself up from the deck, only I didn't need to bother as this time there hadn't been time for me to fling myself down.

"Nay pegs." quipped Big Bo a grim sort of smile etched on his young features. "But yon chap might (he indicated the jet plane that had totally disappeared) if we don't get yon hatches painted afore the morning."

To those whose history lessons at school didn't include the 1960s it is October 1962 and we are sailing on the edge of the Caribbean Sea and a small island by the name of Cuba lies a few miles off ower port bow and not to put to fine a point on it the Americans and the Soviet Russians have decided to lob nuclear missiles at each other in and around ower present position without first asking us if we minded or not?

The painting on the hatch canvasses was of the Union Flag to distinguish ower vessel as a British ship and not Russian. As those Russian ships were known to be carrying nuclear missiles and warheads and we had only got whisky and whilst we were happy to tell the Americans we were British (due to their cowboy approach of shoot the bastards and ask questions later) we also didn't want the Russians to find out about ower cargo of Scotch. Russians and alcohol, especially whisky. We didn't want to give any excuse to either party to interrupt ower reverie. So I hitched up my jeans and made quickly for the prow of the ship.

We were 'buzzed' twice more that day and again three times the next. Each time by Phantom fighters or so I'm told, not being an expert on post war aviation. I could tell the difference between a Dornier and a Heinkel and even a Focke Wulfe and a Messerschmitt but these new fangled Cold War aircraft left me just that – cold. Whilst the whole world tottered on the brink of a Third World War and a consequent mutually assured destruction we of the 'Pacific Unity' sailed gaily on ower way circumventing the Gulf of Mexico and out into the Caribbean and on towards the Panama Canal ower brightly painted hatches looking to all intents and purposes the setting for some forthcoming jingoistic carnival, that or a venue for a seaborne rally for the British National Party. But we didn't care for in a few days we would reach ower first port of call and the drudgery of the daily ocean grind would cease and make way for some 'pleasures' of the flesh. But first I was to make two or three more minor mistakes. You know the kind of thing. Eighteen, curious, barmy. Normal adolescent behaviour. It happens. - - - - Well it does to me!

We were still four days out and 'Blondie' was feeling his age. That and a couple of other things I wager. I liked the Second steward. Unlike his boss 'Daisy May' who was the usual fat, overweight rolling barrel of a creature with an overt puncheon for young boys. Blondie was slim, blonde of course and still relatively good looking.

And he was helpful and courteous without being to obvious. I knew of course he being a steward it wasn't wise to make assumptions and when he asked me to play cards that night my first thought was to protect my rear end at all costs. My first thought should have been to say no, my rear end being my second thought. But I didn't and I paid the consequence. I suspect the two drinks I had were 'spiked,' for two drinks of vodka were unlikely to have put me in a frame of mind whereby I would say 'Yes' when he asked to perform oral sex on me. He did and I ended up upside down doing a handstand over the end of his bunk whilst he performed circus trapeze movements from every conceivable airborne position the target being my anus. He was a good shot I'll say that for him. I was sore for the next two days. A constant reminder and a lesson. Never trust a good looking blonde bloke when he offers you a glass and to put an olive in it for you. First and foremost an 'olive' might well be a euphemism for something else and if you do – make sure there's nothing that there shouldn't be inside it. To be fair I'm still not that sure I didn't just throw caution to the wind and make a bid for the experience. I could have 'wobbled' out of his cabin at any time during the night had I a mind to. And I have to say that 'liking' him didn't leave me with any feelings of regret either.

Lesson number two, take care when dealing with people's feelings. Or should I say, be aware of them if at all possible. I should have known. The last time I pushed an under-study too far I ended up with a steak knife through my arm.

Tinkerbell came at me screaming like a banshee, both hands clawing the air. He had no fingernails to speak of, he spent most of the day chewing them, a fact I had commented on when he kept on complaining he was 'pissed off' being treated like a lackey and cleaning up all the 'shit' after the deck crew had slobbered their way through his mess room. The mere fact that such was his 'job' seemed to have escaped his notice and I was in no mood to put up with his constant moaning. What I shouldn't have done was make the 'discussion' personal. "If yer'd stop farting about and chewing yer fingernails all day instead of moaning you might get somewhere you idle little bastard."

Again I suspect it was the 'idle little bastard' bit that upset him. Perhaps he was and perhaps his childhood had had unhappy consequences due to it?

Whatever, it made him a very angry unhappy bunny.

I went down like a sack of spuds. For a while I held my own trading blow for grunt. I was the one doing the grunting. He could certainly 'scrap'. There were fists coming from all directions. I kept looking for the swine who was helping him? There had to be more than one. Suddenly it went dark. We were in the gangway amidships so if the lights had gone out that could have accounted for it. However such wasn't the case. My sweater had been pulled back over my head. Now I wasn't 'just' a useless fighter I was a blind useless fighter as well. A crashing blow to the side of my head signalled a change in tactics. Discovering his fists were having no appreciable effect he began using his feet or to be more precise the boots he was wearing. CRACK – Oooo – that hurt, my right ear suddenly went dead. This was getting serious. Sensing rather than knowing I rolled and coiled myself around his ankles. I heard the words 'fucking bastard' and a sort of surprised wail and a hollow metallic thump. The struggling stopped and for a few seconds I held my grip around his lower legs thinking wisely it was better if he reverted back to his fists those having a lesser degree of pain to me. No blows came. I heard a moan. It wasn't one of mine. I could tell the difference. Mine had a lot of pain attached to them. This was somewhat different.

Relaxing my hold I sat up and yanked the sweater off over my head. Tinkerbell was lying alongside at a right-angle both arms raised cradling his head. Luckily – very luckily for me – with my grabbing his ankles he had over balanced and whacked himself hard with the back of his head against the steel bulkhead. Fortunately, for me, it was very hard. It had obviously put him out of the mood any more for killing me. Praise the Gods. We both sat in the centre of the gangway, him nursing the large lump slowly growing from the back of his skull and me trying to discover the remains of my right ear which although attached seemed somehow not part of me.

"Fair dinkum an' what's occurring 'ere then cobbers?" Ozzie an Australian member of the deck crew came by on a 'walkabout'. "Jeez. Ya two bin scrappin then?" I looked at Tinkerbell and gave a quick shake of my head. Not that I expected Ozzie to snitch to the Boson. Fighting was a punishable offence. But it was better if we practised the art of SNAFU. (Situation normal all fucked up).

"No." replied Tinkerbell. "I was showing him a few jujitsu moves that's all." Ozzie beamed his sunshine tanned face and mouthful of perfect white teeth.

"Fack-orf." he retorted and nodding his head moved on. I waited until he rounded the companionway. "Alright now then. Feel better do yer?" Tinkerbell scowled then must have thought better. "Fer your information I'm not a bastard, twat features." I nodded. "No. OK. Fine -."

We hauled ower battered carcasses off the deck, mine somewhat more battered than his. I replaced my sweater, making sure I stood a good distance away whilst doing so. I wasn't going to trust Tinkerbell within three feet of me in future. Noooo way.

"Do yer want I give you a lift?" I said smoothing out the bumps and bruises littering my lithe frame.

"Where to -?" he quipped, smiling now.

"Arsehole." I replied. Then, "I suppose arsehole's alright is it?" I asked.

"Yea. S'long as yer don't try an' get up mine." he grinned. And that was that. I gave him a 'lift' (a hand) to mop out his mess room and clear away the dinner things and for the rest of the voyage and because I considered him to be 'damaged goods', I henceforth handled Tinkerbell with 'kid gloves'.

Lesson number three began with my 'nicking' the 2nd Engineers illegal stash of Lemon Hart rum. Three-quarters of a bottle full. Not the best idea I ever had, all things considered.

I liberated the rum from inside an inspection cover on one of the engine room bulkheads. Why had I opened the cover in the first place? To see what was behind it of course. Why else? Why had no one else done likewise? Because they weren't a nosey bugger like me. Simple.

So -. I wasn't a rum drinker. In fact truth be known I wasn't a 'real' spirit drinker at all. But that amount of the 'amber' liquid couldn't possibly be left to its own devices now could it?

I couldn't trade it with a member of the crew for fear questions might be asked such as, 'Hey up Pegs and where did yer get that from out 'ere?. Not an easy question as spirits (other than the hoard of 'loose' whisky still lining half the sea-men's lockers) was absolutely forbidden whilst at sea. Save it for a rainy day? Possibly. But first a small libation secreted within the confines of a Coca-Cola bottle and a small celebratory 'party' for one on top of the 'poop deck' seemed a good idea at the time.

I settled down amongst one of the mooring rope coils and turned over to let the sun warm by back. I wore shorts and sweater and was careful to tie a towel around the back of my neck to ward off the burning rays of the sun which in the early afternoon could scorch in minutes. I had a few drinks and then I must have fallen asleep. The rest of the story is second hand because when I awoke sixteen hours later my head felt like someone had tried to flatten it in a vice, my legs hurt and I was tied hands and feet to the metal stanchions of my bunk by a stout hemp line.

And here I have to thank 'Blondie' and two of his cabin stewards for doing the right thing. It transpired I must have drunk more than I bargained for, an easy mistake to make when one is 'three sheets to the wind' to begin with, for it is 23-00 hrs and that blonde haired fair arsed Peggy, the one with the lithe body, is 'pissed out of his skull' and playing Superman on the fore-deck and doing a modern day impression on the ships rails of Leonardo DiCapprio going down with the 'Titanic'. On the instructions of the fore watchman I am carried bodily to my cabin and strapped in to secure my person from absconding over the side of the ship, involuntarily. I am now awake, I think, thanks to half a bucket of water. My bunk is 'wet' I am 'wet' and as for getting up and starting my 'watch' do me a favour! Tinkerbell covered for my morning absence and asked only for a sleeve of cigarettes in payment. I managed to get upright for the evening shift but walking was agony. The back of my legs had blistered from calf to groin. Large puffy seg-like structures that required treatment from the Chief Stewards medical kit. He enjoyed that. If he ran his fingers over my posterior once he did it a hundred times. Pervert! And the moral of lesson three. Wait for an opportune moment to divest the stolen property in a remunerative manner. Don't be so bloody greedy. Here endeth the lessons. Oh. And if you are going to get stoned out of your head. Do it on dry land. It's an awful lot safer.

'Cristobal'. A small town adjoining the city of Colon on an isthmus connecting Manzanillo Island to mainland Panama apparently built on sea-infill material. Considering the state of the place why am I not surprised at that? If Panama is to be considered a Third World Country, Cristobal should have been classed as Third Class Third World.

It really was an eye-opener, even for me who had come from the slums of North West England. At least we did have toilets, even if just the tub type. Most of these people seemed to use any convenient hole in the ground and some not even that.

We were awaiting our turn to enter the Panama Canal and an eight hour delay convinced some of the crew we should have a short foray into the town to see the 'sights'. The Captain wasn't so sure but relented under the proviso that no crew member should be allowed more than ten American dollars for the duration.

We shipped ashore in a harbour taxi. This proved to be a very leaky row-boat with a crew of one octogenarian rower. I fully expected to be left marooned amongst the 'pirate' boats that littered the bay when ower ancient mariner kept grabbing, with a pained expression, at his chest every time he coughed up half a bucket full of black flem which he then gobbed unceremoniously over the prow. Twenty minutes later we gratefully clunked the stone walls of the quayside and hurriedly made for the shore.

"I here when you come back senors. I bring ya to ship." wheezed the old man in between bouts of coughing. I looked at Ozzie whose eyebrows shot up in amazement.

"You sure about that mate. Gonna live that long are yer?"

We were six in number. Tinkerbell and yours truly, Ozzie, Big Scouse, Curly and one other Able Seaman. My first observation was the sprawling dereliction and rubbish that spread out from the stone buildings of the harbour and which immediately became tatty wooden shacks with rusting tin roofs and torn plastic or canvas sheets where doors and windows should have been. The pavements were wooden board-walks set up from the ground like the scene's from any self respecting 'ghost town' from a Hollywood film set only in this instance the town streets teemed with 'people' of every size, shape and colour. From thin, pasty pale white like me to the pygmy squat ebony black of the Amazonian head hunters.

Ower presence was immediate as every pimp, hawker, Indian tinker and wide-boy latched on to ower entourage. From little boys of five and six years old to grey-haired bearded coffin-dodgers they dogged ower passing with, "Hey Johnnie. You want white girl, brown girl, young black boy. Fuckie fuckie. Nice jerkie, suckie lovely."

Or at least that's what it sounded like. Well of course we did. Well I did anyway. But every time I looked around one of the group, with the exception of Tinkerbell, prodded me onward with,

"Don't stop. Keep walking. Don't look round. Keep movin' Pegs. Keep movin'."

After a time of this constant badgering one particular large brave 'black' señor elbowed his way to the rear of ower group with, "Hey man. I got some smooth white chicks for the fucking at the Union Jack Club. You want I fix you up?" Instantly and with the dumb confidence only an eighteen year old bright spark from ower town could do I replied,

"Yea sure. You payin' are yer?" The man's tone and features changed in an instant. With a snarl he replied.

"You fuckin' wid me white boy?" Oops! Not such a clever remark from yours truly after all. Big Scouse thumped me hard in the middle of the back. "Move yer ass and keep yer bloody trap shut. D' yer want to get us all killed?" he hissed. I shot forward a couple of extra feet and instantly clammed up. I had yet to realise this wasn't my town and these people not my buddies – unless of course they were taking money from me and then that was different. Fortunately Big Scouse's gesture that I was a bit short in the head satisfied the large 'black' man who grumbling moved away.

We walked on up the main street passing numerous 'bars' and 'brothels' interspersed with the odd grocery and hardware shops here and there until we came to what I thought was the front entrance to a 'fortified' concentration camp. It turned out to be the local 'Police Station'. Complete with watch towers, machine gun posts and triple barbed wire perimeter fence. Two of the local community policemen passed us by wearing large floppy sombreros and adorned neck to foot with ammunition bandoleers and each carrying a sub-machine gun. "Traffic cops", murmured Big Scouse upon seeing my mouth begin to open.

Needless to say I was catching on fast. I was the one in the centre of the ring and the locals were the sharks, circling.

We ended up in a bar, God knows where at the end of a warren of back alley's and straw huts that boasted upended beer barrels as seats and tables. But the beer was reasonable, the price that is, as for the quality I couldn't say. It was to be hoped it didn't contain too many foreign bugs but no one seemed to be worrying about that so I kept my 'trap' shut, as previously ordered.

"You wanna fuckie-fuckie Johnnie. I got young girl. Pussy smoke cigarette, ass smoke cigarette. You wanna see show?"

Now I don't know about you. But at aged eighteen I hadn't seen a 'pussy' smoking cigarettes! I mean ower mangy cat at home had on the odd occasion chewed one up but I'd never seen it pop one in its gob and smoke it. This I had to see.

"How much?" I ventured much to the amusement of some of the lads. "Five dollar." the old crone replied. Had I mentioned the 'lady' doing the offering was in her late sixties if a day. Then to be on the safe side, "Each." she added. I looked at Tinkerbell who gave me one of his 'what do I know' looks in return.

"Three dollars – each." I replied.
The old crone waved her head slowly from side to side then, "No. Eight dollar for two. Eight dollar for two. Show and fuckie, fuckie."

"Seven dollar for two. Both show, both fuckie, fuckie." The old lady beamed a smile from the remains of her aged dental decay and nodded her head. "Come." she said waving to the back of the bar-room. Tinkerbell looked at me wide-eyed. I don't think he expected my offer to be acceptable and he was most certainly not expecting anything of this nature although that is what we had both gone ashore for in the first place. Sex played a very big part in everything we did and was more often than not the main motivator for breathing.

"Shit-." he wheezed from between his teeth but couldn't stop his legs from pushing him up from the barrel and following the old lady as she pulled aside a plastic curtain leading off yet again into 'God knows where'. The lure of a 'bonk' was far too strong. She might as well have been offering a large tub full of money for nothing would have held either of us back save ower ship mates sitting on us and pinning ower sex-starved butts to the mud floor. And as they didn't I assumed all would be well – hopefully!
It was. And I can honestly say I had never seen anything like it in my life before. The 'pussy' and 'ass' she referred to wasn't of the feline or equine variety, both belonged and were part of her. Talk about wrinkled prunes and forest scrub. I nearly fell off my beer barrel laughing. And the veils, five in number, could have done with a bloody good wash. They were filthy – and come to think of it so was the 'show'. The music blaring from the old gramophone was of the 1920 variety and did nothing other than create an ambient atmosphere. I was on the point of cancelling the finale, the fuckie-fuckie part of the offer when a young girl of maybe thirteen or fourteen came into the room.

Grandma gave a bow and whipped the head of the gramophone off the scratchy record and closed the lid of the wooden cabinet with a reverent 'clunk'. It was the only piece of furniture in the room worth anything, the rest seemed to be strung together with ropes and badly sewn canvas patches.

"You pay four dollar now and after you pay three." she said indicating with a stretched out claw. I counted out the four dollars into the grasping palm. "You go together with Isla, together, not together. You be kind. No rough stuff eh?" I nodded. I mean what else was I supposed to do?

Tinkerbell didn't want to 'go together', which was just as well because neither did I. "You or me?" I asked. For all Tinkerbell's brashness I sensed from him this was 'foreign' territory. There was something lacking. A reticence to dive in head first and hope the water was deep enough. "You can go first if yer want." he replied. So I did. Isla stuck her rump up at me and indicated I climb on. So I did. It was over in a matter of a minute or less but not before I caught sight of Tinkerbell from below the corner of the bed viewing the whole proceedings from close quarters probably making sure he knew where to put his 'willie' when it was his turn. Either that or he was getting a kick from watching my groin beating a tattoo on the young girl's buttocks. I wasn't going to ask. At least I took my boots off. Tinkerbell didn't. He simply slid down his trousers and poked about a bit before giving a groan of immense pleasure as he crushed the poor girls face halfway through the raffia headboard. That was the second time I had a good laugh that day. At one and a half dollars it was the best value I've ever had – considering the girl was clear of any sexual deceases or tropical viruses. We were lucky. Very, very lucky to hear tell. Maybe she was new to the 'game'. Whatever this time I got 'away' with it. But it wouldn't always be so. That I could guarantee. It was just such an occasion as this that we had been 'warned off' about at the National Sea-Training School. Which just goes to show how a male teenager's brain works? If he wants some thing bad enough he's having it – regardless. - - - Q.E.D.

Minus any unwanted souvenirs we approached the Panama Canal Zone and proceeded to leap the land mass into the Pacific Ocean. Fortunately the 'Pacific Unity' was a more modern ship than the M.V. St Merriel and possessed an adequate 'reverse' gear for going backwards – when instructed -. This time we didn't lose any time or more importantly any lives in the process.

The Panama Canal is a series of twelve dual chambers which accommodated ower 'small' vessel in an almost motherly fashion, the motorised 'mules' (travelling winches) guiding us through with loving precision from one artificial lake to the next. In no time at all we were free from her claustrophobic restrictions and popped like the birthing of a new born camel into the vast blue horizons of the world's most beautiful ocean, the Pacific.

We turned north for Los Angeles and another meeting with my favourite people, the American Immigration Department.

"Why d' they want 'em again. I give them 'em last time in Duluth. That'll be two lots they've got. What they doing, checking I didn't con them the last time -. I thought this was supposed to be the land of the free? Bloody barmy if you ask me owt."
Nevertheless. It was finger printing time again and what's your mother's maiden name. "So how do you spell Theawdwitch -?" I corrected him but he had no sense of humour and so reluctantly I gave him the answer he was looking for.

"Butterworth – B.U.T.T.- ." The Immigration man scowled. "Yea. Alright buddy, I think I can spell that." He wasn't a happy bunny. I think he had a blood pressure problem. The veins on his head stood out like the sun baked coils of a mooring rope.

"So what did yer do with the last lot I gave yer. You haven't lost them have yer?" I wanted to know. I didn't want copies of my fingerprints fluttering around the world for all and sundry to see. I mean I might decide to do something nefarious and then they'd know it was me. Not my idea of 'fair play' at all.

"They go on file." Was all he would say. I warrant they are still on 'file' to this very day somewhere in the FBI archives in Washington and knowing the number of recent cock-ups that have transpired recently with mis-interpretation by so-called fingerprint experts, I could still be hauled back to the America's one day on some crappy duffed-up charges. Not what I called true democracy that wasn't. No way. And the blokes the Immigration Department employed left a lot to be desired. Miserable creatures. Welcome to the U.S.of A. Some welcome. I think not.

But I wasn't going to allow a few 'uniform besotted' officials to spoil the day nor my view of the American people. When we docked in Los Angeles there would be a few days shore leave.

I would then give my initial thoughts of this huge country based upon other more clinical observations as time went on. We still had a long way to go.

Disneyland. Nice but plastic and nobody was going to convince me those bloody big rabbits waving American flags were real.

Hollywood. Nice but pretentious. And why anyone would want to cram themselves into a bus load of old age pensioners just to be told where a load of snotty nosed Thespians lived was beyond me?

Downtown L.A. Big and full of concrete. Not my idea of fun at all. So did I like Los Angeles? Yes it was OK. A lot of big fat people wandering about with very little dress sense. Had nobody over here heard of colour co-ordination? Almost schizophrenic.

Plenty of money from the looks of it but after visiting one 'locals' house to be met with no carpets on the floor and the only items coveted and oozed over a cupboard full of guns of every description, I began to seriously wonder about the priorities of the average American male?

So on we sailed, ower destination this time San Francisco and the Golden gate Bridge – only it wasn't, 'Golden' that is. It was a dirty red colour and not a lot to write home about. And why spoil such a beautiful island rock structure in the middle of the bay with a huge concrete block-house is beyond me? Alcatraz. Still a prison in those days and not the best idea the American authorities have ever had.

Again San Francisco was concrete. Far more here than previously and many of the streets were as dirty as those I found in Glasgow, but by comparison Glasgow was a poor, old, neglected city and had hardly recovered from the bombings of the war. San Francisco was a new city, re-built from the ashes of the old at the beginning of the century and had suffered none of the trials and outrageous fortunes of a world war. There was no excuse for such a vibrant economy as America's to neglect its major cities so. It was a disappointment. The biggest one so far. So we sailed on - quickly.

Golden Gate Bridge as seen as we sailed beneath its red painted structure. How's that for a let-down. Wis got bigger railway viaducts in Ower Town.

'Alcatraz Island'. As we sailed past. What a waste of concrete. A 'blot' on the landscape.

The weather was glorious. October and the sun shone like an English Summer's day, that's one of those rare Summers' when we have one, a Summer, oh never mind it's too complicated. It was warm, not hot, a cooling breeze, not cold and milky white puffs, of a different nature than those I was sailing with, of cloud filtered through the pleasing afternoon hours as we moved north towards the distant coastline of the State of Oregon and the Columbian River. We were bound for Portland to take on ower first load of deck cargo, American Yellow pine.
I lazed by the stern rails. That morning I had done my dobbying (washing) and now the clothes needed my attention to dry in the warm Pacific breezes.

With one eye on the fluttering stone-washed, rip-torn Levi's and the other scanning the blueness of the rolling oceans waves I was suddenly aware of a regatta taking place not fifty yards off the starboard quarter. Porpoise, they must have numbered fifty or more. It wasn't that I hadn't seen these delightful creatures before, in two's and three's they would regularly race the ships bows quite often mile after mile like runners in a relay race that kept forgetting to drop out, but so many together was unusual. I just thought the young juveniles amongst them were getting boisterous for they leapt each and any way but in a straight line as was the normal practice. Then 'jaws' broke the surface! God what a monster! A killer whale. Ten or twelve times the size of the sleek grey missiles now milling around in total panic mode. I stared fascinated, all the while willing the small agile porpoise a swift get-away. What the end result was I couldn't tell. Quite often the killer whale goes hungry for he is not as stealthy a hunter as lies his looks. If he doesn't get lucky in the first few seconds there is often no second chance. Another amazing thing to a 'lad' from the 'Mount' happened on that same leg of the journey. Hey –hup. Flyin' fish! Tha' what? Flyin' fish! Fish that fly? Are you pullin' my ding-a-ling er what? Got bloody wings then 'ave they? Well – apparently the answer to that question was – Yes – but not wi' feathers. I was minding my own business, as you do, sunbathing, towel down, fully clothed with my hat pulled down over-hanging my eyes when, flap, flopity, flopity, flopity, flap, and I was staring into two huge bulbous eyes on the head of what looked like a miniature 'kimono dragon lizard'. It didn't have legs and feet but two large flappy webbed wings that seemed to keep it upright as I screamed -. Now I don't have a girlie type scream but as an ex- boy soprano I can belt one out when the mood takes me. The look of sheer annoyance in that fishes eyes as my treble cleft bounced off its spiky head spoke volumes. As if to say, "Did you have to do that – and so close to my blinkin' ears -." Always assuming a fish has ears. This one did and everything else as well and it wasn't small. The size of a young adult pike I would say – only I didn't notice it had any teeth. Not that I was hanging about to find out. With a leap ably assisted by every available muscle in my lithe frame I catapulted myself sideways leaving the 'fish' to contend with the steel decking.

"What's up Pegs?" Jacko, the Jamaican cook popped his head out from the 'galley'. "You alright?" I jabbed a finger in the direction of the 'monster' flapping around on the warm steel plating.

"Eh! Oh! Caught one 'ave you?" I looked at 'cookie' askance. I quickly smiled; I didn't have the heart to tell him the bloody thing caught me.
I had 'fish' for tea. Jacko grilled it for me. It was brilliant. Could have done with a load er batter around it and a bit more oily, but you mustn't tell the ships cook his food isn't anything but 'delicious'. Dear me no. When the Chief Steward had the temerity to complain about his bacon the first week out he had the 'runs' for a fortnight afterwards. And it was nothing to do with the bacon I can tell you.

I was on good terms with 'Jacko' for both 'Peggies' had a close association with the ships cook and the Chief Steward with regards the crews meals. I sharpened all 'cookies' knives the first week out and showed him the art of the 'downward' stroke as opposed to the 'backhand' so many chefs famously use. After nearly cutting his fingers off a dozen times or more he got the hang of it. I could always tell when he had been practising by the number of surgical plasters dotting the knuckles of his left hand. But he got there in the end.

We sailed passed Cape Despair in the late afternoon and sea-anchored to await the following morning and the river pilot for the sea hereabouts was full of shifting sandbars and many a cocky mariner has learned of it when it was too late. The coast north from San Francisco, when we neared it, was a mass of tall firs and here the Colombian River estuary was no exception with mile upon mile of dense forest almost down to the edge of the sand dunes and the stark grey stone cliffs. Breathtakingly beautiful. Which I suppose makes me a nature freak, wood as against concrete, no competition. I don't think it has anything to do with having lived all my life (so far) amongst decaying bricks and mortar, for I could find a kind of strange affinity with the slums of my mother town and still appreciated its familiar sounds and smells, a sort of 'hey-up pill-brain, you still alive then – 'ow come? But big cities, modern concrete, and so 'high'. Not my idea of fun really.

It was late the following day when we docked opposite 'Hayden Island'. Although we would be in Portland two days it was thought unwise to allow the deck crews ashore. So we went anyway.
It was here I got 'temporarily apprehended' for 'jay-walking'. I suppose I should explain that I didn't know what 'jay-walking' was.

Or that you could get arrested for it. Or that you should never put your hand to your inside pocket when an American policeman is stood facing you. Or that American policeman don't understand English or at least Lancashire dialect English. I was only walking across the street for 'Pete's sake'!

"Don't Move -. God-damn. - Don't move."

Yes Constable. Certainly Constable. Three bags full Constable and please will you take your twelve inch blunderbuss out of my anus there's a good chap, it's not use to such hard lengths.

It was ridiculous.

The police car had screeched to a halt alongside a good two minutes after I had mounted the pavement. So I ignored it. I was taking the view not to get involved with whatever was going on unless invited to do so and be back aboard ship before tea less the First Mate discover we had done a runner and we get two days pay docked.

Someone shouted. It sounded like, "Fuddy duddy." So I ignored it. It wasn't my name. The next one sounded like me. "Hey arsehole."

I turned. The man had on a light fawn uniform and one those pointy hats perched high on his head. He was big, about four times bigger than me, in both directions. I pointed surprisedly at my chest. Did he mean me? "Yea. You. Cock-sucker -. What's your game?" I was tempted to say, 'Rent-boy', which was what I assumed a cock-sucker would be involved in. Instead I replied with, "What yer on about? What game?" I think that upset him. Perhaps he was hoping for Baseball or Cricket or something, not that I know bugger-all about either.

"What's wrong with the crossing?" he scowled. Er -. Now he had me. I didn't know what might be wrong with the crossing, whatever that was and whatever it was I had nothing to do with it. It wasn't me, I wasn't there.

"Sorry -?" I replied, having nothing more to add.

"Soorrry -! Soorrry -! You and me both budddy." At this point I decided it was wise to fish my ID and Immigration slip from the inside of my jacket pocket as he would probably want to know who I was and what I had done to his 'crossing'. His reaction couldn't have been less dramatic had I gone to hit him with one of the paving stones. His gun appeared from his holster and sprang into his hands like a slow-motion scene from a John Wayne Western.

"Don't move. Don't you god-damn move. I'll blow your arse up around your hairline. Don't move." he shrieked beginning to crouch down and taking a bead in the centre of my hairline with the muzzle of the pistol.

"I was only - - ." I began to say.

"Against the wall. Against the wall. Turn around. Turn around. God-damn it I said turn around."

I did as the disturbed policeman asked. Well you do don't you when he's waving a bloody great cannon at your head. I was hoping he might have forgotten to take the safety catch off the gun, the way he was nervously twitching about. From my spread-eagled position against the wall of the building I tried to explain once more.

"My identification and immigration papers are in my inside pocket constable. I haven't got anything else." Meaning of course that I wasn't carrying any offensive weapons. Something must have struck a chord inside the man's head for he asked the question he should have asked at the beginning.

"You not from 'round here buddy?" "No constable."

"Where you from-?" "England. I'm English. A seaman."

"Shit -."

"Well – I wouldn't go as far as to say that. Some of us are quite normal." I replied hurtfully.

"Huh. God-damn Limey. OK. Turn around." I straightened up and turned.

"Papers." he said flicking the fingers of his left hand at me. I fished out my ID. He took them, glanced at the Immigration slip and slowly re-holstered his gun. "Name?" I told him. "Ship?" I told him. He grunted and handed the papers back. "Why did I stop you?" he asked. I frowned. That was a tough one. "Someone's bin messin' about wi' yer crossing?" It was the best I could do on the spur of the moment. How did I know?

"You were jay-walkin'." That one didn't register either. The policeman pointed down the road to where the intersection stood and a plethora of traffic lights and flashing beacons. "You are not supposed to cross the street other than at the designated crossings. You're breaking the law wandering about all over the god-dammed place."

"Really -!" I didn't actually need to feign surprise. I was surprised. I'd never heard of anything so silly in all my life. I was tempted to ask 'why' but didn't.

Instead I formulated an answer in my best grammatical English and -. "Good gracious me. Really? What a good idea. To stop accidents I suppose. Well I am impressed. Thank you very much for tellin' mi." I could feel the posh sliding away towards the end of the sentence, as I wasn't used to using it very often. The policeman drew himself up a shade and settled his shoulders back to the horizontal. "Ya. Well. Yea. As a 'visitor' you need ta know these things. Your first time here is it -?" I nodded. Then added. "Yes. Quite beautiful. Lovely town you have constable." That seemed to satisfy him for pulling down on his tunic and patting his large gut he began to turn away. "Stay on the sidewalk. Cross at the crossings. Stay safe. Hmm. Have a nice day." And with that he returned to his car and leaving half an inch of rubber and a cloud of pungent blue smoke he moseyed rapidly away.

I stood for a while watching his exhaust fumes disappear in the distance. If you could get shot for crossing the street, even when the street was devoid of all traffic, as it had been at the time, what happened if you murdered somebody? Drawing and quartering before the hanging? This was not a good start for my short stay in the State of Oregon.

The war had put paid to a full-scale deployment of television with the first seasons of the media from Alexander Palace being terminate for the 'duration'. It wasn't until '47' that the 'powers that be' decided to re-launch the transmissions and none of those reached ower neighbourhood until quite a few years later. It was the year 1957 when one of the wooden cabinet boxes with the built-in cathode-ray tube became ensconced in ower box-like sitting room. Three channels in the Queens English, with BBC relenting to thirty minutes a day to a Welsh language programme, and grainy black and white pictures on 325 lines (the number of lines it took to produce a 'full' picture) only ours seemed to bounce around between 100 and 300 lines willy-nilly as the mood took it.

The television set took four minutes to 'warm' up and ten minutes of fiddling with half a dozen knobs to get the picture to stand still. Talk about 'Muldoon's Picnic' wasn't in it! And what has this to do with the State of Oregon?

Well, we are now in Seattle which is just around the corner from Portland (in North American terms) and it's the 1962 World's Fair and yours truly is there watching a cartoon on a 'coloured' television set. And I don't mean like the one ower Uncle George had with the pieces of coloured cellophane over the screen. No Sir, this was for real. Broadcasting in 'colour'. Fascinating. I must have watched it for an hour or more. Three thousand dollars was the price but there was no point in buying it as coloured transmissions were restricted to a half square mile area somewhere around the city centre. But it was a portend of things to come.

Seattle was to my mind a beautiful city. Yes there were many new concrete constructions but here the architects and planners had the brains to restrict its use. Few buildings reached to the heavens and many had large areas enclosed by glass and other more conducive materials, more pleasing to the eye and the streets where considerably cleaner than those I had encountered before.

Again as in other places the legal drinking age was twenty one and therefore I shopped around for other forms of entertainment to while away my afternoons, there being no overtime to be had whilst docked in port. After a visit to the Seattle Space Needle and its Planetarium I opted for a visit to a local roller-skating rink that advertised a 'Sock Hop'. I hadn't heard of a 'sock-hop' but I assumed that if it was for teenagers it couldn't be anything too 'dodgy'. It wasn't. Fortunately I didn't have to remove my boots other than to don a pair of roller skates and wobble around a large spacious arena to the sounds of Elvis and Little Richard records. I suppose we were expected to take along a female partner but Tinkerbell was all I had available so he had to do. Here I encountered other people of my own age group, albeit of American lineage. I have to say straight away these young people seemed to have more about them than their older brethren and were without doubt less bombastic, loud or arrogant and they had a better dress-sense. That may have been from a reticence to appear knowledgeable or over-confident. It was however very refreshing to that which I had encountered previously and my attitude to ower American 'cousin' rose somewhat more sharply in my estimation. I was asked by one pimply spotted youth, 'did I want his lawyer's telephone number' in reply to my persistent questioning, to which the smart-mouthed lad got his girl friends handbag across the back of his head as a result -.

I pulled him to one side later in the proceedings and asked him did he seriously want to get involved with that 'bag-totting bird'.

I thought I was doing him a favour! He didn't appear to appreciate my efforts. Well you can't please everyone all the time can yer? Hey-ho, I skated away across the flow of traffic, which being American was coming from the right, felling a dozen or more 'dancers' in the process. It's all very well but you must realise I have spent all my life being told 'keep to the left- idiot, keep to the left- idiot'. It's a good job I wasn't driving around their streets at the time I can tell you, then there really would have been chaos.

Three days in Seattle then off once more, this time we were bound for New Westminster where we arrived just in time for my birthday, Vancouver and Victoria on Vancouver Island itself. British Colombia, the most picturesque and pleasant of my visits to the North American Continent. A delight in the summer and breathtaking in the winter, or so I'm told. It's summer now or at least if it's not it is certainly warm enough to be so. Late October and we are slowly but surely filling the whole of ower deck spaces with masses of 'standards' of timber which we chain-lash to the deck cleats for stability. I'm quite happy about this on the basis that if we sink, through one altercation or another, all this timber will serve to keep us floating that little while longer. On the basis of 'every little helps' it couldn't be a bad thing and it made an ideal 'hiding' place for contraband fags. The holds had been stacked with 'white' goods at Los Angeles and San Francisco but not before we unloaded ower seven thousand tons of whisky – less half a ton or so.

I have seen very large, muscular grown men cry. Not just weep and snuffle. Large heart rending guffaw like crying that would have embarrassed a Portsmouth whore.

"Here Pegs – hold this and write down what I tell you." The Second Mate, Little Willie, handed me a clip-board with pencil attached. Word had gone around that I spent some of my free time 'writing'. A book I said, and in truth a 'book' it was and so as like on this occasion when writing was required my abilities were not in question.

It's a good job no one ever asked Tinkerbell who in truth could just about spell his own name correctly and always messed up his home address.

"I will call out the batch number which you write down in the first column and the number of full cases which you write down in the second column – got it?" I nodded knowingly and hoped I looked intelligent.

"Right then -." The Second mate raised his hand and looked across to the crane driver on the quayside who immediately set in motion the raising of the cargo net which up until now had been resting in the hold. As the net came level with the hatch coaming the Second Mate signalled for a halt. Carefully he inspected the contents of the huge pallet. Six of the boxes had breaches in their cardboard coverings. The Second Mate removed the boxes and signalled for the lift to continue. The boxes should have each contained twelve bottles of whisky. Both had at least one bottle missing. What happened next was the reason Able Seaman Curly White had to be removed from the deck to sick-bay. The Second Mate proceeded to smash on the side of the ship every single last bottle in all six crates allowing contents and glass to sink to the bottom of the Pacific Ocean as only 'unbroken/sealed' boxes where allowed to be landed on the shore. Now I'm not reputed for my brilliance or my common-sense but if Little Willie had removed bottles from one crate and placed them in the other five crates to compensate for the loss and re-taped the cardboard coverings wouldn't this have lessened the wastage and thus the insurance claims? I know this comes from my upbringing – waste not want not – but surely this would have made more sense. Apparently not. A total of fifty four boxes or approximately six hundred bottles of good Scots whisky ended up at the bottom of Los Angeles harbour that day, Curly White was put on anti-depressants for the rest of the trip and I learned a valuable lesson in that people cared more about strict accounting than wasting the planets resources. Oh dear. That didn't bode well for the future either.

I measured the length of a sleeve of cigarettes then multiplied it by thirty then divided the length of two of the timbers by my first figure and set to work removing all of those particular lengths of timber but the remainder.

A complicated arrangement you might say? Not at all.

My thirty sleeves of Marlborough charcoal tipped are now safely resting in the middle of a huge block of deck timber and only I know which pieces of timber to remove to retrieve them, after the 'ferrets' (H.M.Customs) have been aboard of course. This I will do when safely back in Salford Docks and before the 'dockers' get around to unloading the ship's cargo. And so I give thanks to the Canadian lumber-jacks and sawmill workers for their sterling efforts and will make a small fortune when I return home selling them for half a dollar a pack, ten packs to the sleeve – that's a load er dosh sethay -!

"They let you do what! – On your own!" The old lady looked me over in astonishment. I have seen her quite taken aback on a few occasions in the past at some of my less than sensible antics but this one must have appalled her as her glasses dropped unceremoniously off the end of her nose. "Was everything alright?" The question came automatically as if there was nothing else in the English language one could use. I smiled. What else was there to do?

But this took place in a few weeks time when I was back ashore again. At the moment I have my eyes keenly peeled between the ships prow, which is relatively easy to distinguish in the darkness of the night by the folds of phosphorescence thrown up by the waves, and the feint greenish glow thrown on the needle on the ships compass as it wavers across the given bearing. The First mate wanders back and forth across my rear casting the odd glance in my direction. I know he's checking out the bearing to see just how far off course we are sailing. One degree in either direction is acceptable but more than that costs the shipping company a lot of money in extra fuel bills. Ozzie, ower antipodean ship-mate wanders across my line of vision moving from bridge wing to bridge wing binoculars slung from his neck. He watches for other vessels. Again we have no radar and thus have to do everything like in the old days when the ship would have had sails instead of a propeller. And why you might wonder have the shipping company entrusted their ten thousand tons of valuable merchandise to yours truly? Because they never asked to see my records before enlisting my services and the Second Mate thinks I'm lovely.
I have a yearning to take this throbbing vibrant mechanical beast with its miles of shuddering steel and minuscule futile humanity and bend it and them to my will. Before my vision stretches the vastness of the Pacific Ocean.

It's literally thousands of miles in all directions apart that is from the West coast of North America just off to starboard. I couldn't possibly hit anything out here – or so the First Mate thinks. It's as well he wasn't asking my old lady's opinion. She would have pushed out her chest, sucked back on her teeth and slowly shook her head with the words, "Well I wouldn't risk it mate." And if I'm being truthful she would have a point.

However. I need twenty hours 'steering' under my belt to qualify for my 'Steering Ticket'. With a steering ticket I can ship out on the next trip as an EDH (Efficient Deck Hand) and leave all this 'Peggy' routine behind. And so here I am. There's the Pacific Ocean and that small light twinkling off the starboard quarter is a 'Lightship' and I'm supposed to miss it.

I did. Miss it. By exactly the correct distance allocated on the shipping lane maps. The following afternoon Captain Gates took me into the chart room and showed me the line of ower passing on the daily chart. I hadn't realised until that moment the ship carried an AHG which drew an exact positioning line along the route the ship was taking. My 'driving' was there for all to see in china graph markings and duly copied inside the machine for the company to deliberate over should I have hit anything.

"I don't think I've seen a steadier course young Pegs. Well done." Oh dear! Compliments again. I can't do with compliments. I never know what to say. It comes from not receiving any great number of them throughout my childhood. Now criticisms. No problem. Any amount. Come on bring them on. Don't stop at 'cretin' or 'dip-stick'. Can't you do better than that?

"Er. Yes Sir. Er – Hmm. Yes Sir." And that was about all I managed.

But not to put too fine a point on it I always was very good when it came to 'handling' moving objects. Especially if my life depended on it. Ergo -.

"Don't let go." I looked to my rear. The old man grinned at me and made a point of indicating his hand was firmly holding the rear of the bicycles saddle. I trusted the old man. He never broke his word. If he said he was going to 'belt' us. He always did. And so I gaily peddled on. My new bike was a Christmas present for my seventh birthday and wasn't going to be much use to me if I couldn't ride it. Ergo -.

"You are allowed to move the handle bars if you want." he said after we had been travelling for about twenty minutes or so. "I've never seen anybody keep such a straight line. The wheel won't fall off if you move it about a bit." I wasn't going to move the wheel about. If I moved the wheel it would go in a different direction and then I would have to move my centre of gravity. Don't be ridiculous. Why mess about with things if they were going alright. Silly man.

It was a couple of miles further on when I realised both his hands were in his pockets. Even at seven years old I knew he hadn't got three hands. That's when I hit the Postman and his bicycle. Well – not exactly hit, more ran over. It was parked by the pavement and he was standing in the road and I and my bike needed to go there. He was not a happy bunny. The postman not my old man. My old man just shrugged his shoulders and walked on pretending I wasn't his. The compliments turned to criticisms as the postman limped off down the street desperately grabbing up all the letters and threatening all kinds of gory retribution should he ever discover my true identity.

And so I was awarded my steering ticket – for vessels not exceeding twenty thousand tons. They always put limits on things – just in case.

We made a point of dropping into San Francisco and Los Angeles again on the way back and San Jose before advancing to the Panama Canal. By now a routine had set in and we were almost through re-painting the superstructure and everything else that stood still. We were bound for a 'pick-up' at St Peter'sburgh in Florida where we arrived at the beginning of December during which time I saw my first 'real' sailing ship in the guise of the 'Bounty' of 'Mutiny on the Bounty' fame (as opposed to the schooner M.V. Vindicatrix which was steel clad) but which turned out to be just a 'replica' although I have to say a very good one. It turned out the original ship was 'torched' by the mutineers off the island of Pitcairn and this replica had been taken from the ships original drawings at the British Admiralty. Nevertheless I was impressed as it bore many similarities to life below decks on my first voyage on the St Merriel. (but minus the floggings).

'They call me the Wanderer, the Wanderer; I roam around, around, around, around, around. They call me the - - - - '. If I hear that bloody song one more time I will hurl myself from the topmast willingly -.

Ozzie had borrowed my record player, the one I 'acquired' that runs off batteries. The problem was he only had the one record and he 'liked' it, so much he played it, constantly, hour after hour after hour. It was like Chinese torture, my cabin being directly across from his. It was going to be demand my record player back, and he was a lot bigger than me, or suicide or wait until he was on watch and nick the blasted thing and dump it overboard, the record not my player. It was driving me mad. Not that any self respecting psychiatrist couldn't have told me that with me being here in the first place.

In a cold 30 degrees we set sail for England. In less than three weeks we should hit land, euphemistically speaking, Liverpool being ower first port and Manchester and home in time for Christmas. All being well and without meeting any hurricanes or Krakens on the way I was bound for the usual 'family' get-togethers so reminiscent of past years. Such joy!

"Boson's chairs two of. Ropes four of. See chippy." What? Boson's chairs? What's up? Is the Boson having a party? How many is he inviting then? Oh! Not that sort of a party. Shame. What are the chairs for?
     "Painting the ship's name out -?" What's occurring here then? Going 'pirate' are we? Hoist up the Jolly Roger is it?
     "He (the Captain) wants it in bigger letters -!"
We are to sling out a couple of boson's chairs over the prow, obliterate the name M.V. Pacific Unity and re-paint it in a larger font. This is a job for Ower Kid – only he's in Manchester Art College being 'abstract'.
     "Have yer got some large stencils Bo-?"
     "Yi what? Stencils! What fer ye want stencils? Just paint the beggars bigger."
     "Free-hand?"
     "Eh! Well if ye have got one oer them use it ta hang on wi. Naw get on wi it."
And with that Tinkerbell, Willie Bow the EDH and yours truly have ower orders.
Now it is true that part of ower training was in the use of boson's chairs, which is all very well on board a ship that is standing still. Ours wasn't. It wasn't going very fast, about 12 knots, but it was doing an awful lot of rocking about.

From side to side and up and down. An Atlantic wave on a pleasant day is between ten and twenty feet in height and ower paltry ten thousand tons or so isn't making a huge impression on it. Truth be told we're bobbing about like a cork on an Australian sheep shearer's hat. Thankfully 'chippy' had more brains than the Boson and insisted we sling under and make fast a cargo net before dropping down the rope ladders to the chairs. It was perhaps as well for Tinkerbell scored two downward plummets to my one whilst Willie Bow sat giggling himself silly and throwing fag ends down on us as we lay prostrate amongst the folds of the net below. Viewed close up the lettering was anything but decent but from the quayside or beyond it looked magnificent, even if I say so myself. And it was my 'freehand' and I warrant a dam sight better than Ower Kids if not quite as 'abstract'.

I purposely haven't mentioned 'Janice' or the fact that ower ship is classed as a pseudo-passenger vessel. The reason being some of the seamen are still a bit 'funny' regarding sailing with females aboard. Although this is the twentieth century 'jinxes' still run rampant amongst the sailing fraternity. We have two females Janice is the First Mates wife and doubles up as a nurse and table steward. The second is a Mrs Warburton who with her husband Henry came aboard in St Peter's burg, fortunately bound for Manchester. Neither come anywhere near arousing my interest as both are in their mid forties and would crush me like an over-ripe grape or as Ozzie put it, " I shouldn't bother yerself 'Pegs' it would be like throwing a chipolata into a fire bucket." I think I understood what he meant -?? But why I didn't get medical attention for my acute sunburn from 'Janice' instead of Daisy May still rankled. I might at least have been in with a chance –Hmm? Dreaming again – hey up never mind eh!

We made Salford Dock on the 24th December Christmas Eve day in a grey sombre mist. Snow lay dotted here and there amongst the detritus littering the banks of the ship canal and therefore would no doubt make this another 'White Christmas' to add to the many others. Not that the snow stayed white for very long, a few hours at most before the grime and the soot mantled it and slowly decimated its pristine appearance. I 'paid off' having decided I would stay at home over the Christmas period. Take a few weeks to renew old friendships before looking for another ship, possibly a South American trip or the Far East next time.

Tinkerbell stayed on. Something about his people being away for the Christmas period. I didn't believe a word of it but it was nothing to do with me and I don't think the old lady would have taken kindly to me bringing any 'strays' home. She was only just getting used to being free of me.

Two sleeves of fags!

"Haven't yer heard of inflation?" growled the Dock Yard gate keeper.

"Haven't you heard of daylight robbery?" I growled in return. But I said it with a smile on my face. That reduced my fags to five thousand six hundred. That represented a reduction of two pounds ten shillings to my coffers. I'll bet the guy made another week's wages on back-handers. Not a bad job at that rate. Some Father Christmas he turned out to be. Thieving swine. Still, it was better than six months prison – for smuggling.

M.V. 'Pacific Unity'. Somewhat more modern than my previous 'tub'.

At least she had all her 'gears' and wasn't prone to leaking.

'On the change again'.

"How many walls has yower house getten then?" The question seemed a little strange but 'Meffs and Pepp' was more than a little strange himself. I crouched on my haunches upwind of him.

"Er – oh quite a few. They's all round and wi' bits in-between. Half a dozen or so I should think – why?"

"Lucky little bastard then aren't yer. Got none 'round mine." 'Meffs' tilted the bottle to his lips and guzzled another mouthful of the pink liquid. He winched, a painful grimace showed the black gash of his teeth through the shed-load of white beard plastered around his lower face. He belched, long, drawn out and magnified under the low dome of the canal bridge. It seemed to ease the pained look on his face. "Don't want any either. Fuckin' busy-bodies. Everybody wants a bit er yer when you has walls. Wantin' this, wantin' that, wantin' t'other. Wantin' fuckin' if yer ask me owt. Nosey gets." I nodded and mumbled something positive. It seemed to satisfy the old bloke for he settled back against the grey stone wall and drew his knees up into a foetal-like pose clamping the bottle between his knees, his forearms and his belly. It would take four African bearers and an elephant gun to prise it off him in that position. Next news his breathing had turned to a low asthmatic puffing sound. He was asleep. Amazing! Well it would have been but for the amount of methylated spirits and peppermint he had undoubtedly consumed in the last couple of hours. Had it have been anyone else they would have been dead. His internal organs must have been made of armour-plated rubber.

Old 'Meffs' was a regular sight on the canal tow-path. He came through perhaps twice a month. Some years previously he totted around a small white haired terrier dog 'Pepp' which he kept close to him on a piece of string. As kids at first we taunted him, then he would threaten to let loose his vicious hound and we would do a 'runner'.

But as time went on and we became more used to his regular visits we came to trust him and his faithful companion who it turned out preferred to lick us to death rather than eat us.

It may have had something to do with the sweet biscuits we nicked from the old lady's 'fancy' tin and fed to them both.

Half for the dog, half for 'Meffs'. Today I'm giving him fags. Two packets. Well why not? He was always far more appreciative than those so called friends of mine down at the 'Medici'. Everybody loves a sailor, especially one who has just 'paid off'. I left old 'Meffs' to the elements and whatever else might choose to threaten his tenuous existence and 'jumped' a bus for town -.

I'm nineteen now and as such only half expected to take part in the family celebrations that must 'by tradition' take part over the Christmas period. That's Christmas dinner at home, the four of us and no messing! Tea, at about five in the afternoon at Grandma Butts and a walk across the common to say hello to t'other Grandma, the old man's mother, who is fast approaching ninety years old and beginning to smell a little (but nobody mentions it) and then tea again on Boxing Day at Aunty Eff's, after that 'tha can do as tha wants but stay out er trouble'.

Ower Kid is twenty one and getting a bit too interested, in my opinion, in one particular member of the opposite sex. Not that I was asked my opinion, nor was I about to give it. He still hasn't lost his tendencies for sticking 'one on one' (that's a poke in the eye) without thinking much about the consequences. It still surprises me coming from the left. 'Smack'. Bugger! 'Ow'. He is sometimes drawn up short if I threaten to remove his privileges. That's the two or three quid a week he manages to wheedle out of me for petrol to keep him mobile. He goes to 'college' in his mini van of 'many colours' and I suspect plays 'patsy' in the back with his 'models'. Things are beginning to 'even' out as the teenage years slip away -. But we are still as far apart as we have always been where brotherly love is concerned. I remember the day the 'chord' snapped. It was thirteen years previously -: The place: Billy Sidebottom's back yard on Entwistle Road. The date: October and bonfire day bearing down rapidly. The time: 18-45hrs and the sun has gone down and it's dusk. Present: Ower Kid, Yours truly, Billy Sidebottom, Patrick Meeghan, Martin Jones, Billy Drysdale and James Grandige. Scenario: Billy Drysdale, a member of ower gang, had in the presence of Ower Kid called Jimmy Grandige a dick-head and what's more that he was going to batter him the next time he saw him.

For reasons best known to himself young Drysdale then switched his allegiance to Jimmy Grandige's gang. I was miffed.

I called Drysdale 'out' in Billy Sidebottom's yard and told Jimmy Grandige what young Drysdale had said he would do to him. Young Drysdale denied saying it. I then turned to Ower Kid and asked him to confirm it. Ower Kid, already a member of Grandige's gang, to my absolute horror denied having heard anything and that I was a lying little snitch and that I should keep my 'trap' shut. I was stunned. One of the others lying or not wishing to get involved I could understand but this was my own brother doing the 'mouthing off'. I was so angry and frustrated I ended up in tears which I have to say was never one of my most favourite pastimes when amongst other people. It was at this moment I came to understand no matter what ones own belief even those closest to you can and do let you down. There must be something in Latin which says it better – something about 'Homo et lupus est homo tu'. Ower Kid would know – he took Latin but missed out on loyalty to the family – first! Never mind eh. It takes all kinds to make a world. There was one other important lesson I learned that day. Don't grass – unless it's vitally important to do so. It could come back and bite you in the ass! Life takes no prisoners, so let's move on.

Boxing night and Rene has arranged for an all night party in the 'Medici'. I 'jumped' the bus again opposite the coffee bar, the conductor was still upstairs taking fares so I saved myself two pence – well every little helps – and made my entrance.

"Hey-up. Hands off yer cocks and on wi yer socks. Guard yer backsides. Navy's present." Mike Carr flashed me a huge smile. Rene flashed an even bigger one as her eyes did a one armed bandit roll and registered pound note signs in place of her pupils. I was worth a fiver a day to the 'Medici' coffers and that was 'big' money in those days.

Chubby Checker and 'Let's twist again' had just bounced towards number one in the 'Hit Parade' and if there was one thing I was always good at it was 'dancin'. What gyrations I couldn't do with my 'spindle' like physic wasn't worth a mention. I think Maureen Williamson like my buttocks because over the next twelve hours she never took her eyes off them. She wasn't much of a dancer but then it wasn't her dancin' I was interested in. Adjacent the coffee bar area was a large room where the 'Carrs' kept some furniture and the stock for the bar. Next to this and only a door's width between was a small ante-room, possibly used as an office before the building's conversion, in which stood an old wooden desk and a filing cabinet.

I trundled the filing cabinet up against the knob of the door and showed Maureen my 'family jewels'. I had only just put my jewels away in her mouth for safe keeping when there was a thump on the door.

"Well dear me. I wonder who that can be at this time in the morning?" I said. Or words to that effect. Maureen thought she should answer it and gave me my jewels back rather hurriedly. To say I was a little consternated would be putting it mildly. It wasn't every day I got the opportunity to have my jewels polished so beautifully by someone other than myself. I could have killed the b******. I watched Maureen struggle to remove the filing cabinet. After all I wasn't in any mood to help her and it took some time to get my jewels out of the way so they wouldn't be noticeable.
Michael stuck his head around the stile of the door. Looked, grinned wickedly and said, "Just been on t' Wankalong at the Chinese Garden. He's happy to do us breakfasts. I need a lift." The Chinese Garden was the name of the Chinese Restaurant lower down the street owned by a Mr Wang Lon. It was all of fifty yards away and Mike could easily have got someone else to 'help' him. I suspected the little green man had been nibbling away at young Mr Carr's entrails as he wasn't with anyone at that particular point in his life and to see one of his 'helpers' helping themselves to the available female 'menu' must have been bugging him. It wouldn't be the last time young Michael would screw up my 'arrangements'.

I took on my usual Wednesday nights bar keeping for the usual five percent of the take. I had paid off the 'Pacific Unity' with one hundred and seventy five pounds and made a further twenty pounds or so on the cigarettes, those that were surplus to my own requirements, making near enough a 'couple of ton', certainly a small fortune by ower standards. The problem now was how having a wad full of notes might be influencing my body in the popularity stakes on the basis that 'every 'nice' girl loves a sailor'? But providing I was getting what I wanted I didn't see how that should be bothering me? Time would tell. Almost as soon as the money ran out no doubt. What I had expected would be just a short stay over the Christmas period turned into a marathon. I rang the 'Pool' (Merchant Navy Enlistment Office) once a week to ascertain available signings only to be told week after week that there were no immediate vacancies to be had.

A dearth of shipping from Salford and an increase in 'foreign' crews signing on British ships was creating shortages throughout the country and as I couldn't sign on at another port other than my home port – that was that. It all seemed a bit silly to me but common sense told me the shipping company's would employ 'foreign' crew members if they could be had at a cheaper rate. Market forces and all that.

"Hey-up and what does tha know about such things as 'market forces' then ey?" The old man was not impressed.

"Knowing too much can get yer killed – well – shipped off t' back er beyond at any rate. Market bloody forces? Sounds like sum fifth column t' me."

During my last trip to America the old man had at last taken the old lady's instructions – sorry – advice. He had terminated his employment for the local Direct Works Department and had set up a partnership with a fellow worker as 'Property repairers'. Proudly, together the old man and his partner Arthur Albert Drinkall and their trusty two wheeled bogey with double extension ladder posed for a photograph outside the back yard brick trowels pointing menacingly towards a neat pile of house-bricks left over from that time the house fell down. The local paper 'The Observer' had sent a roving reporter down to take notes and film the action that should have appeared the following Saturday under the caption 'Local lads take the bit between their teeth', until the old lady demanded to see a copy of the article for editing. "I know you bloody lot. Get it all back t' front and full of rubbish." Needless to say the 'copy' never arrived and neither did the article, so the 'launch' publicity was a cardboard sticker in the shop window in yellow and blue crayon instead.

Sixteen weeks went by before I finally got word from the 'Pool' to pick up 'articles' and sign on at Salford Docks.

But before I shipped out I decided to have one last fling, spend a bit of money as there would be little point taking any with me. I gave Wozzle a call on the telephone, ower telephone, now deemed essential as the 'family' were now truly in 'business' since dad was his own boss – well – in a new business anyway. I managed to prise Wozzle away from the apple of his eye for a night out in the big town, Manchester. Tonight we would go to the 'Bodega' (I think that's how it was spelt) on Deansgate, a jazz club of well renown.

We arrived in ower best clobber, suited and tied and with a bag full of money. The doormen, two gorillas in dinner suits with dickey bows, held the doors apart as we slunk between them feeling like condemned prisoners going to a hanging. I had never experienced anyone holding a door open for me. It fair worried me I can tell you. Inside the place was heaving, two thousand people or more and a tobacco fog that could have hid the whole of the attacking Japanese naval fleet at Pearl harbour. We cleaved a way through towards what we thought might be the direction of the bar. On stage and belting out what I suppose was a traditional jazz number a dozen sequinned striped trousers and jackets gyrated in jungle fashion instruments weaving and bobbing in every direction. The noise was horrendous. I didn't say I was a true lover of the jazz scene and I'm not. But it was the 'in' thing to do at around this time and it was better to have a 'knowledge' of the various scenes than to appear un-educated especially around some of Ower Kid's mates who displayed their individuality by scorning the popular music scene. Others took on the 'folk' scene otherwise known as the pauper of the genres and least liked of them all.

Wozzle ordered the usual two pints of mild beer and we tried to find a table. There wasn't one, not vacant anyway. So we stood amongst a thousand swaying jazz fans ranging in ages from sixteen to eighty six trying to sway in unison to the music whilst drinking ower beer. Not easy. In fact almost impossible. Most of mine went down the neck of a very irate woman who was so small she almost came up to my waist. Not being a beer drinker she wasn't pleased and told the large bloke next to her to 'destroy' me. Which had he room to turn around he would have. I melted into the mass of bodies merging my lithe frame with dozens of bodily appendages hanging around me. Wozzle went in the opposite direction to draw the bloke away, well that's what he said he was doing. We met on the opposite side of the room twenty minutes later.

Wozzle ordered two more pints from the bar on that side of the room and handed me mine. "Hang on a minute," he said. Just as I was about to take a drink. "There's no short-arsed women around at the moment. If yer wait a bit I'm sure one will come along. Hell of a way to get out of drinking it if yer ask me."

The truth was I wasn't a beer drinker but 'it' being the expected beverage amongst the 'boys' I tried to accommodate them especially when we were buying in 'rounds'.

A request for rum and pep or gin and orange, both of which I liked, would have been met with more laughter and derision than heard at an African hyena's committee meeting not to mention the fact such drinks were much dearer. Wozzle knew all this but insisted I have a 'man's' drink and so it was pints of foul tasting beer and get it down yer neck kiddo. The result was inebriation and lots of urination, with me it never seemed to linger long enough to get used for re-hydration purposes. The water went straight through and the alcohol topside, usually just over my eye line where it sloshed my brain about then plonked itself down like a lead weight.

To cut a long story short I got 'pissed'. I don't remember how we got home. I think Wozzle pushed me ahead of him on the walk back to the railway station most of the time pretending he wasn't with me. I don't think he liked my singing. I don't think anyone else did either considering the wide berth Wozzle said everyone gave me. I like to think they were standing back in admiration myself. Needless to say I wasn't any trouble to anyone, well not that I know of, and the old lady only thought fit to comment the following morning. Something about, "When was it you said you was leaving?" That was exactly the same question posed by the headmaster of my school a little while back. Am I missing something here - -?

This afternoon I'm due back at the 'Pool' and another voyage is in the offering. I wonder to where and into what more trouble I can get myself this time. It's not that I have ever wanted to mix with chaos – it somehow seems to find me no matter how careful I am. Still. I'm still here. For the moment -: See you again soon -:

'END'.

'DEDICATION'

'Ower Dawning' is dedicated to my great childhood friend Ian Turner ('Turnip'). A joy to have known and a loyal mate in every respect.
'Ian. 1944 - 2006. Who luv's ya baby!

Turnip 1961.   **Turnip 1954.**

This is really the end – but if you wish to know more see 'Ower Detinue' and 'Ower Dabbling' and the author (above) in the 1960s and 70s. Enjoy -.

Atlas D'four.

Born during the war-torn years of the nineteen forties in the North West of England to a working class family.
Nurtured within the then embryonic National Health Service and post-war education system whose attempts at creating a healthy, well-rounded, socialist child failed miserably. Schooled at a 'Boy's Technical School' (which thought itself akin to Harrow or some other rich self-serving establishment) it wasn't until after enrolment he was to discover only a large termination 'fee' would enable him to escape it's claustrophobic, torturous environs. (He still maintains the day he 'left' school was the best day of his life).
Following a spell of 'real' blood and gore in his native town he then embarked upon a life on the ocean waves only to be inexorably drawn back, in due course, to the comforting ways of his former life and a series of strange and sometimes dangerous enterprises the like of which were to eventually become his nemesis.
At forty years of age a leap into the unknown on a quest to find the new 'beginning' took him from his native soil and on to new horizons. Today he lives in another country. But he won't say which.

Other Books by Atlas D'four.

Published by UkUnpublished in 2010.
Re-published through CreateSpace 2015.

'SCRIPTS ON BLACK' Series. (WW2 non-fiction).
   (Chronological Order ref: date line).

Black Venge'nce   978-1-84944-044-8
Originally published by Blackie & Co.
ISBN 1-904986-10-2- now out of print.
Black Venge'nce 2015   13-9781517116255

Black Despair   978-1-84944-045-5
Black Despair 2015   13-9781517367589
Black Hors' d' oeuvres 978-1-84944-046-2
Black Hors d' " 2015   13-9781517233266
Black Dawn   978-1-84944-047-9
Black Dawn 2015   13-9781516927432
Black Masquerade   978-1-84944-048-6
Black Masquerade 2015 13-9781517429409
Black Princes   978-1-84944-049-3
Black Princes 2015   13-9781516957835
Black Shark   978-1-84944-050-9
Black Shark 2015   13-9781517010997
Black Dove   978-1-84944-051-6
Black Dove 2015   13-9781517339555
Black Dust   978-1-84944-052-3
Black Dust 2015   13-9781517325188
BlackJack   978-1-84944-053-0
BlackJack 2015   13-9781516886500

'OWER KID' Series.   (Bildungs-sach-bucher).
(Autobiographical). (Chronological order).
Ower Darkling   978-1-84944-041-7
Originally published by Able & Co 1999
(Titled as Slugs and Snails). Now out of print.
(Re-issued with changes. UkUnpublished 2010).
Ower Darkling 2015   13-9781517141509

Ower Dawning   978-1-84944-054-7

Ower Dawning 2015   13-9781517477295
Ower Detinue   978-1-84944-055-4
Ower Dabbling   978-1-84944-056-1

Printed in Great Britain
by Amazon

85152814R00132